ReLeasing
CReativity

JOHN WHATMORE

RELEASING CREATIVITY

how leaders develop creative potential in their teams

FOREWORD BY JOHN ADAIR

KOGAN PAGE

To Anne with love and thanks for so much.

First published in 1999

Kogan Page Limited
120 Pentonville Road
London
N1 9JN
UK

Kogan Page Limited
163 Central Avenue, Suite 4
Dover
NH 03820
USA

British Library Cataloguing in Publication Data

A CIP record for this book is available from the British Library.

ISBN 0 7494 3010 9

Typeset by Kogan Page Limited
Printed and bound by Biddles Ltd, Guildford and King's Lynn

contents

foreword

JOHN ADAiR

I am delighted to welcome John Whatmore's *Releasing Creativity* and I commend it most warmly to you. It represents a real contribution to our understanding of both leadership and creativity, two subjects which have engaged my interest over a long period of time. Here I offer you a few reflections on them, mainly to whet your appetite for the more substantial food in John's thought-provoking and informative chapters that follow hard on the heels of this foreword.

The three-circle model – task, team and individual – continues to be at the core of my own thinking about leadership. It is the interactions – positive or negative – between these three overlapping areas that to my mind constitute the dynamics of small working groups and their large counterparts, organizations. Together, they define the role of the leader, both in terms of the functions required and some of the key personal qualities needed, too. In a way John poses the question: 'What happens to this model if the individual circle is occupied, so to speak, by individuals who are highly creative by nature?'

The answer which stems from John's research is, in a nutshell, that such a situation calls for leadership of a high order. Now we are witnessing a general transformation of management into business leadership, a process far too slow in most industries and in most nations for the needs of the times. John's important message is that in organizations which look for and depend upon innovation (and who does not?), the neglect of such good leadership is a seriously limiting factor.

Why leadership and not management? Partly because creative groups are working in situations of change and uncertainty, of mapping the unknown, precisely the kind that we know merit leaders rather than managers. Managers, in contrast, are more suited for situations where continuity is central and where only incremental changes are needed, not significant steps forwards. Partly, too, because creative people tend to be individualistic, intelligent and (sometimes) difficult to get on with. To enable gifted individuals to work together in harmony and – as if in an orchestra – to produce great music, calls for leaders like those conductors who are not only supremely musical themselves but also have the talent for leading others. Leadership is a rare aptitude at this level but it can be fostered, encouraged and developed.

I tend to make a rough but useful distinction between creativity, having ideas, and innovation, bringing new products or services to the market place successfully. Whereas the seeds of new ideas are always produced by individuals – often highly creative ones – it is teams that make innovation possible. Now creativity, in this wider sense of being able to contribute to building or developing new ideas with receptivity and enthusiasm, of being able to work in those innovation team networks, is actually much more widespread than managers often assume. Most people, for some of the time at least, are quite capable of innovation, if properly and wisely led.

In other words, do not make the assumption that *Releasing Creativity* applies only to industries which are self-evidently creative, like advertising agencies or pharmaceutical research laboratories. The principles and ideas in this excellent book apply to all industries, including yours. For the wealth of nations lies in the creative potential of all its people. As John Buchan once said, 'The task of leadership is not to put the greatness into people, but to elicit it, for the greatness is there already.'

acknowledgements

As this book brings together my own research and other recent work on the subject, I would like to put on record my thanks to the late Mike Cox in the Department of Trade and Industry's Innovation Unit, for espousing my research, to Roffey Park Management Institute for housing it, and in particular to Jo Howard for being a masterful supervisor. I would like to thank all those who worked with me, particularly Christina Evans, all those who in various organizations helped us to make it happen, and all those who gave up precious time to enable us to meet and talk to them. There have also been many supporters, whose encouragement, sometimes in droplets, sometimes in waves, I could not have done without. I would like to thank Richard Adeney for being a willing and expert reader of drafts, and other experts in the publishing world for helping me to turn my scribblings into something that I hope you will find a good and useful read.

PART I

MANAGING CREATIVITY AS SOMETHING DIFFERENT

1

releasing creativity

AN OVERViEW

In these times of rapid change, leaders in all kinds of organizations have to generate creativity, innovation and change. This book aims to answer the question: if you want people who work with you to have good ideas, what do you do?

It uses the evidence from various creative worlds to show how leaders support and encourage the development of ideas. As such, it is directly relevant to those who manage teams in science and research, art or architecture, sport, the media, and in advertising and design; but it may also be as important to those who are involved in industries and organizations where there is rapid innovation and change.

People are working increasingly together in groups; not only in science and technology, and in art and design, but also in many fields where innovation and change are increasingly pressing. Some groups produce a singular creative performance (Crick and Watson in science), others produce them regularly (3M, Microsoft), others try but fail. It was reported recently that when the DTI asked 100 bosses if their companies were creative, most said yes, but a closer look revealed that only 15 actually were. So what are the problems?

A great deal of research has gone into the question of what makes people and even groups creative, but far less has gone into investigating the contribution which managers or leaders play in such groups.

The fact that many people regard creative folk as 'difficult to manage' suggests that the task of managing creativity does require different (and less widely understood) approaches, yet some people have a special talent for getting the best out of creative people. If we understood more about that talent, we might be better able to select and develop managers for all organizations where innovation and change are becoming increasingly important.

My work has used the ways in which creative people see their tasks, their problems and their success to develop frameworks within which others can place their own thinking and their own projects by way of comparison.

ARE CREATIVE TASKS AND CREATIVE PEOPLE DIFFERENT FROM OTHERS?

While most problems require some creativity but to different degrees, the kind of problems with which more creative groups are dealing are characterized by uncertainty. The creative 'process' addresses persistent paradoxes, controversies and ambiguities, especially those which appear tough, which unlock other problems or have big pay-offs. Creative problems tend to be more conceptual and less task-oriented and it is their very persistence that invites the search for new ways of looking at them (see Chapter 3).

Similarly, most people are creative but to different degrees, and those who are more so have different values, objectives, approaches and styles, from those who are involved in other kinds of projects (see Chapter 2).

LEADERS OF CREATIVE GROUPS AS HORSES ON THEIR HOME COURSE

... with experience of the field (see Chapter 4)

It takes someone who has experience of the field to be able to formulate questions which are timely and appropriate in their field, as well as being ripe for solution. For this reason, effective leaders of creative groups tend to be technical experts: they become leaders in their own fields and they come with their own questions to answer.

... personalities to work with their team (see Chapter 4)

Successful leaders of creative groups are empathetic, understanding and sensitive to 'process' in their groups. They are warm and approachable, passionate and enthusiastic and generous of spirit. And they are very fluid in their contributions to their groups.

... *choosing their teams (see Chapter 11)*

Effective leaders take a great deal of trouble in the selection of their teams. They match the needs of a project not merely to the skills and abilities of prospective team members, but also to their aspirations. They look for team members who are open and trusting, who will get to know one another very quickly and very well, and who will use each other's different perspectives. (They often recruit as new members those with whom team members have worked in the past.)

Moreover, the most creative teams see themselves as 'all developing on a life journey together' and thus as participating in a project that has a birth, a life and a death.

The creative world is also inhabited by 'big egos', people who dare to take risks which others might not (knowingly) take, but leaders also speak of how the extra support they might need can detract from the way the rest of the team works together.

... *playing the right team-roles (see Chapter 11)*

Most often, leaders of the more successful and more creative groups are Visionaries, Ideas Generators or Ideas Prompters. They are Team-builders, as well as Shielders of their teams from organizational pressures. They are also adept as Entrepreneurs and as Politicians – they have an ability to handle paradox, to see and to present the same facts in different lights in different circumstances. In very unusual circumstances they are Autocrats, sometimes they are Manipulators when they are trying to coach or elicit specific performances, but more often they are 'democratic' in the way they lead their groups: members choose the projects they want to work on and decisions are taken by the group as a whole.

... *constraints and freedoms as turn-ons (see Chapters 5 and 6)*

Effective leaders have an ability to use the constraints and at the same time to give people freedom. They do this by shaping tasks so that they are appropriate challenges to the individuals undertaking them, by providing individuals with the kinds of freedom that each finds liberating and an enticement to experiment, and by using culture and climate to set the organizational constraints in ways which are seen as less obstructive or disabling.

... stimulating (see Chapter 8)

Effective leaders are always looking for opportunities that will help the members of their team to get a different perspective, to see the problem differently, and thus to stimulate new ideas about how it might be solved. They understand the way their minds work and they act to generate the kind of process that helps their particular ways of coming up with ideas.

... encouraging team-work (see Chapter 12)

Effective leaders also spend a lot of their efforts in encouraging team-work. In creative groups, different tasks and different stages of each task require different patterns of team-role types. Effective leaders play various roles, even different ones at different times, and leadership in creative groups 'hops from shoulder to shoulder'.

... discreetly orchestrating the performance (see Chapter 13)

Having selected a good team, the leader orchestrates the interactions between its members, and consciously finds opportunities for them to get to know one another in all sorts of different circumstances (frequently including taking food and wine together), so that they develop an intuitive understanding of each other and of how they can help or support one another.

Effective leaders encourage divergent thinking, by putting people in new circumstances and with new people, by putting 'dither' and contradiction into thinking, and by encouraging members of the group to build on each other's ideas.

... giving support to people taking risks (see Chapter 9)

Creative people often feel insecure, exposed, even 'naked'. They are frequently very sensitive especially because their skills and talents are the very essence of their lives. Moreover, pain and difficulty, problems and paradox cause tensions, and act as challenges which in turn generate creativity.

Effective leaders are highly supportive: they provide (or they ensure that someone provides) both emotional and cognitive support. They affirm successes: they help people bounce back from set-backs; they stimulate; they encourage the development of ideas and they protect those ideas in their early stages. They ensure that ideas are rigorously examined at the right time ('a constant interplay of creativity and criticism') and they provide feedback on how they felt it went. They provide physical support (money, people, space, tea and flip charts) and they ensure that the 'client' also provides the right support.

... protecting the atmosphere from unhelpful influences (see Chapters 14 and 15)

Organizational environments can provide awkward settings for creative output. Where they are very client- or task-oriented, where they are felt to exercise power and control, where they are hierarchical and/or compartmentalized, and where standards and policies are dominant, their cultures are the antithesis of the freedom, of the acceptance of risk, of the experimentation and the urge to try something different, all of which characterize creative groups.

Effective leaders act as their group's shield. As such, they are usually people who have earned the trust of the rest of the organization, have big networks and are skilled at telling about those aspects of the group's work which will reassure the rest of the organization that its objectives and policies will not be subverted by the creative group.

Then they create a 'cell membrane' round their group so that within it the members can have 'time' and 'space' to work closely together, to discuss and debate, to build on each other's ideas, to 'act crazy', to experiment, and to try out ways of 'doing it differently', in an open and trusting atmosphere without terrifying the rest of the organization!

The overwhelming interest of creative people is in using and developing their talents and to those ends they are highly self-motivated. Groups that are less successful are those that do not take account of this and of the fact that they, their organization and their members might therefore all have widely different objectives.

Other groups which are less successful include those without the right ambience (work spaces not inviting interaction), without the right atmosphere (mutual understanding, openness and trust) or without the right attitudes (of encouragement and support).

... and just lending a hand where they can!

Being sensitive and self-motivated, people in creative groups respond to climates and cultures more than to policies and plans, and effective leaders exert their influence in their groups not so much by what they say as by what they pay attention to, what they do, and how they do it.

Yet they live in a world whose essence is ambiguity. They contribute very fluidly to all sorts of aspects of the work: 'just lending a hand where I can', and they influence others as much through their values and beliefs as through the various things they do: 'being a chameleon with integrity!'

How do they develop their skills as leaders? (see Chapter 16)

Some of them see their parents as having inspired their interests and their attitudes, some talk about how schools and universities have shaped their thoughts and ideas (often they have been captains of sports or involved in the performing arts) and some are propelled by the way they had been treated at some stage in their lives as having had a traumatic impact upon their outlook, leaving them with a passionate determination to help or support others in a particular way. Many dismiss the usefulness of courses as inappropriate in various ways. Most recall bosses they had experienced as among the most powerful influences on the development of the way in which they manage others, often including a 'bad boss'. Many talk about their guiding principle as aiming to manage others in the way they would like to have been managed themselves. They learn, they say, mainly by doing and by private reflection about their personal experiences.

This book offers frameworks for understanding the ways in which leadership is seen by people who lead different kinds of creative groups and by those who work with them. It is based on profiles of the very people and situations from which they say they learn (see Figure 1.1). It therefore offers the material and the opportunity for helping to develop the skills of managing creativity in organizations.

Figure 1.1 *Developing frameworks for the subject*

WHAT AND WHERE

Part II examines what distinguishes projects as creative and what distinguishes them from one another, and relates leadership skills to these distinctions. Part III analyses the main factors in the effective leadership of creative groups and explores in what circumstances some seem more relevant than others, while Part IV discusses how leaders seem to develop their strengths. Finally, Part V discusses 'enablers' and 'disablers': what makes the difference and what causes failures.

While there is a number of characteristics which are essential if you are to be the leader of a successful creative group, such as, for example, the ability to give people the freedoms they want ('a light rein', see Chapter 6); to provide just the right kind of support when and where it is needed (Chapter 9); and to champion personal development (Chapter 10); there are others which are important only in certain circumstances, such as the ability to be an entrepreneur (Chapter 4); and the ability to shield the group (Chapter 15). Together, these characteristics constitute elements from which job descriptions can be built up for selecting leaders for particular projects.

In Chapter 11 I discuss the criteria leaders use in the selection of their groups, including the importance they attach to team-role skills, to the ways in which the members get on with one another, and how they use constraints as challenges (Chapter 5). I also discuss how they nurture their groups into teams, getting members to become very close to one another, among other ways, by eating and drinking together! (Chapter 12.)

Organizational cultures often have characteristics which make them awkward settings for creative groups. In Chapter 14, I discuss these constraints, such as lack of support for their leaders and badly designed work spaces. Effective leaders often have to shield their groups from these pressures (Chapter 15).

In Chapter 16, I discuss how leaders 'give messages' through the things they attend to and the way they behave, making and using 'situations' in which metaphors and tensions are stimulating, and acting as Facilitator or Coach as the need indicates, creating and influencing the culture, almost like actors playing different roles and politicians championing different causes from moment to moment. And sometimes leaders fail to create the ambience, the atmosphere or the attitudes in which creativity flourishes (Chapter 17).

Part IV discusses formative influences in the development of leaders and of their skills and talents as leaders. Often bosses they have experienced, including frequently a 'bad' boss, and powerful early experiences formed their approaches to life.

Finally, Part VI reviews the key factors involved in managing/leading creative groups.

2

leading adventurers through the fog

'Managing creativity is becoming like flying ever faster through the clouds.'

MANAGING CREATIVITY AS A NEW ROLE

Pressures in business to innovate continue to increase, with the result that the management (or the leadership) of creative groups is continually increasing in importance in organizations of all kinds. Managing creativity is important not only for organizations whose explicit mission is to devise things that are new and valuable (drugs, machines, advertising), but also for every organization that has to deal with the practical consequences of change.

Scientific and technological developments have had increasingly dramatic effects upon the ways we work and live. To mention but a few, medical research continues to enhance and prolong life; telecommunications shorten time and distance; and the Information Technology revolution influences every aspect of work. Nobody expects the speed of scientific change to do anything other than to accelerate, and organizations are increasingly aware that scientific and technological change and the increasing speed of change are key elements in their continued existence.

Creative solutions are demanded at higher speed. They are called for faster than previously and they are required to be delivered on time. Several organizations can be looking simultaneously for the same scientific and technological breakthroughs, and developments in one field can quickly make products and services in another become out of date. The concept of timeliness and the idea of 'windows of opportunity' have become increasingly important elements in management thinking. Research and Development (and innovation) used to be seen as leisurely and opportunistic activities, but they are now time-driven and purposive.

Creative solutions are also required to be of higher quality. Solutions are called for which will gain more than a temporary advantage over competitors. Organizations (at least in the West) often see their new products in terms of quantum change. 3M, well known for its creativity and innovation, expresses it in terms of developing new products that 'redefine what is expected by the customer and that leapfrog the competition'; they are required to 'redefine the industry'. [1]

At the same time, science and technology have become more complex and more specialized. The knowledge and skills of those working in any one field have become more sophisticated and it has become increasingly difficult for someone working in one field to understand someone working in another field.

> **Creativity is something that is carried on in groups – in which leadership just happens**

Whereas science and Research and Development used to be conducted by individuals working by themselves in back rooms, they are now usually carried out in inter-disciplinary and/or in multi-functional groups, and are often seen as the key functions of a business (one science-based company recently moved its Head Office to the site of its R&D Division).

Quicker and better creative solutions are demanded from people working together in groups in ways that have never happened before and those factors focus attention on the relatively new task, that of leading creative groups.

THE UNITED KINGDOM AS SUCCESSFUL IN CERTAIN CREATIVE FIELDS

The Japanese Ministry of Industry and Technology reported several years ago that 51 per cent of the most significant concept breakthroughs of the 20th century had come from the United Kingdom, whereas only 21 per cent came from the United States where Research and Development expenditure was five times higher. We are seen in the United Kingdom as inventive and successful in a number of creative fields (the wealth-creating fields documented in the Foresight Panels' recent report), notably in certain fields of research, such as biotechnology (five UK scientists have won Nobel Prizes in the biosciences compared to none from the United States), aerospace technology and custom engineering; and in the graphic and the performing arts, including advertising and design, film and theatre (among them, for instance, pop music and fashion design). However repeated studies by the Department of Trade & Industry and others indicate that we are not nearly so successful at innovating, at getting these ideas into practice.

The statistics on research and development expenditure indicate that we are well behind most major countries (in what the DTI calls R&D intensity, the proportion of their resources which companies devote to R&D), and that although the overall UK figures have been improving marginally (in some industries more so than in others), the UK current R&D intensity is less than half the global average and continues to lag behind the aggregate R&D intensities of the other G5 countries.

> ## The UK is seen as creative but not innovative

It is surely worrying that some companies seem to have built cash mountains rather than spend their profits on new ventures. By their actions they seem to be saying that they do not have the confidence in their ability to create/innovate successfully.

In science, and in Research and Development, a great deal of effort is devoted to deciding what to do, but much less to questions about how to do it. Organizations devote care and attention to determining fields of research activity, and into evaluating (through peer review) what projects are worth supporting. And while there has been a great deal of interest in creativity and in what fosters and encourages it, in stark contrast, there has been very little work done on how to *manage* creativity.

If we are indeed successful in certain creative fields, might there be lessons to be learned from those who are successful leaders in these fields, lessons which could be applied in other fields which also demand creativity, including especially those which call for us to be better at innovation and change?

MANAGING CREATIVITY AS A DIFFERENT KIND OF MANAGING

Some people argue that creative people are no different from anyone else and therefore that there is no reason why the management or leadership of a creative group should be any different from that of any other kind of group. But leaders of creative groups will tell you otherwise; they will tell you that creative people are at least as interested in the development of their own talents as in the pursuit of organizational objectives. For example dancers or scientists are often seen as sensitive and temperamental, even as 'more neurotic'. Their approach is experimental and intuitive; they are 'more open to experience, and... more extrovert'; they can be arrogant; and they can appear undisciplined and unpresentable (ie working all hours of the night and wearing 'odd' clothes).

Creative people are often regarded as difficult or impossible to manage; some are often seen as 'big egos' and as 'prima donnas'. Yet some managers – Maria Callas had only one Director with whom she said she could work well – have a gift for getting the best out of talented people, and even of getting more out of them than they thought they had in them to give.

Managing creative people is like herding cats

The skills and talents of people who manage or lead creative groups appear to be distinctively different from those required to lead other types of group; more to do with developing individuals and their talents, and creating or sustaining culture and climate than with achieving specific objectives.

There is also concern that large organizations have certain characteristics which are inimical to creativity, factors which managers/leaders of creative groups have to be able to handle effectively if they are to be successful.

Current wisdom has it that scientists and engineers tend to be promoted to first-line management positions more because they are experts in their subject than because they might make good managers. When they get there, they need to make significant changes in the focus of their interest: to people rather than facts, to action rather than theory, to enterprise rather than ambiguity, and towards achieving responsibility rather than scientific credit.

It is clear that first-line managers/leaders of creative groups in all sorts of creative fields have had little or no training for their new job, and they have to learn the new skills required very rapidly. The Foresight Panels identified some of the management issues in those fields in which they saw this country as being an important participant in the future, and described them in terms of 'action on the diffusion throughout industry of best practice in relation to business processes; continuing education and training in process/teamwork skills; improved market knowledge and vision; improved networking with customers, partners and suppliers', adding that 'significant changes will be required in the organization of management training and management careers if these shortcomings are to be redressed'.

LITTLE TRAINING FOR MANAGERS OF CREATIVITY

Research Councils spend very little on management training and what they do spend is a very small proportion of the amount spent on such training by large institutions in all the major countries of the world. The Medical Research Council, for instance, whilst acknowledging the need for more management training, especially at the level of first-line management, found it difficult to determine how to attack the problem because of the wide diversity of cultures in its various units. Interest in management was also expressed by the Wellcome Trust because their first cohort of prize-winning scientists had commented about the performance of their own (first-line) supervisors.

Scientists sometimes talk as though management is like a field of knowledge, something which is mastered by being read up and understood. In doing so they neglect the skills and the art involved, and they misunderstand that many of the skills are learned experientially.

Nor is scientific research the only creative field in which there is little management training; the same is true in the performing arts and in the graphic arts. And commercial organizations have a very different attitude to these issues compared with scientific and academic organizations; the contrast between the abundant interest in management development shown by the Wellcome Foundation and the negligible interest shown by the Medical Research Council was striking.

LITTLE IS ARTICULATED ABOUT THIS KIND OF MANAGEMENT

Despite the evidence for the rapidly emerging need for skills in the management of creativity, very little work has been done to identify what it is that makes people successful managers/leaders of creative groups, to help the leaders of such groups to become better leaders, or to enhance leadership in such groups in general.

Some research work has been carried out within individual creative disciplines: in a limited way in the performing arts,[2] and in a practical way in sport;[3] and a number of studies have been undertaken in science and in research and development: in addition to studies within individual laboratories, units or organizations,[4] there are the wider studies that have been based on managers in a number of institutional scientific or R&D laboratories.[5] Studies have developed frameworks for understanding the factors which influence success in scientific and R&D laboratories and other creative settings. There are also many studies on related subjects, such as leadership and 'creative leadership',[6] 'problem-solving groups', 'innovation', organizational creativity, and groups, including highly effective groups. And, of course, there is a body of work about how leaders learn their skills and develop their talents.

Helping to make sense of understandings about management in different creative domains

---

Most of the work on this subject has three main difficulties: the first, epitomized by the large-scale UNESCO study (of 1,222 laboratories)[7] and by studies in ICI, is that the focus is either too general or too specific. The UNESCO studies encompass so many types of laboratory, project etc that the research demands to be disaggregated if it is to provide us with useful messages. The ICI work[4] is both focused on one laboratory, and unfocused in that Gratton's study is unspecific as to level of management. The second difficulty is that many, though not all, of the studies use categories, concepts and assessments which are potentially misleading because they were derived from other fields and other contexts rather than from the context itself. And the third difficulty is that those studies which have been of the greatest potential interest (ie those which compare different kinds of creative units) have been quantitative as opposed to qualitative studies, and have thus failed to unearth the richness and flexibility of human endeavours; and while a correlation of 0.6 between two factors may be of considerable academic interest, it is of little practical value.

While some people express the view that being a successful leader of a creative group is an innate talent, something which is born not made, and while examples are frequently given of how training courses are unhelpful, bringing the wrong people together and in the wrong ways, there are initiatives in hand which endorse the view that such talent is developed and enhanced by appropriate experiences, and that the conscious shaping of those experiences is itself a task worthy of study. Despite Jonathan Miller's view that, 'You don't teach it – you just know that some people have got it and some people haven't', which is why I think that on the whole schools of directing are a complete waste of time', the Calouste Gulbenkian Foundation's 1989 report *A Better Direction*,[2] has resulted in a number of new programmes for the training of directors in the performing arts.

NOTES

1. Coyne, Dr W E, Senior Vice President Research and Development (1996) *Building a tradition of innovation*, the UK Innovation Lecture, 3M, Department of Trade & Industry, London, 1996.

2. Rea, K (1989) *A Better Direction: A national enquiry into the training of directors for theatre, film and television*, Calouste Gulbenkian Foundation, London.
3. Whitmore, J (1992) *Coaching for performance: a practical guide to growing your own performance*, Nicholas Brealey Publishing, London.
4. Gratton, L (1987) *How can we predict management potential in research scientists?*, *R&D Management* **17**(2), pp 87–97.
5. *Stimulating creativity and innovation*, Report of European Industrial Research Management Association Workshop IV, European Industrial Research Management Association, Paris, 1993.
6. Isaksen, S G (1992) *Facilitating creative problem-solving groups*, *Readings in Innovation*, ed S S Gryskiewicz and D A Hills, Center for Creative Leadership, Greensboro.
7. Andrews, F M (1979) *Scientific Productivity: The effectiveness of research groups in six countries*, Cambridge University Press/UNESCO, Cambridge.

Dr Julius Axelrod: a Nobel Prize winner in action

Julius Axelrod won a Nobel Prize for Medicine in 1970, for his work on the metabolism of noradrenaline, which he carried out while working for the National Institute of Mental Health (NIMH) at the laboratories of the National Institutes of Health (NIH) at Bethesda, Maryland. This extract from Robert Kanigel's book *Apprentice to Genius: The Making of a Scientific Dynasty* [1] depicts him at work. The book's thesis is that successful science is frequently carried out by 'genealogies' of scientists, each acting as mentor to the next generation. The extract illustrates Axelrod's excitement and enthusiasm, his support (especially in giving juniors success and confidence), his try-it-and-see approach, his intuition, and his skill in selecting issues to tackle.

Something important to tell Julie. That's what his students lived for, competing with one another to supply it.

When Axelrod got excited about something it was like the sky had lit up. His enthusiasm for intriguing data and his encouragement of those furnishing it were legendary. 'Axelrod's special gift,' a student once said, 'was that he could always convince you that whatever you were doing was earthshakingly important.' Another veteran of the lab, now himself a lab director, observes that a young scientist needs, most of all, 'somebody to tell you you're good. Encouragement is very reinforcing, very important in training young people.' In Axelrod's lab he got gobs of it.

'There was "an informal hierarchy" around the lab,' says Michael Brownstein, who later went on to head his own lab at NIMH, 'your place in it varying from day to day depending on how Julie viewed your work. If he wandered by two or three times a day, your status rose; you knew he was interested. He'd go over the data with you, get excited, and soon be telling you all the great experiments you could be doing two months from then, firing off one idea after another.'

Sometimes, he could get on your nerves that way. 'Julie can be kind of a noodge,' says Brownstein, using the Yiddish word for nag or pest. 'You might scarcely have set up your experiment and there he was, all hepped up, breathing down your neck for the data.'

Far worse, though, was when he wasn't interested at all. His encouragement carried weight, needless to say, only because it was not dispensed lightly. 'If you hear enough, "Oh, this is really interesting," but there's no content to it, it has no value as coin anymore,' says Brownstein.

Axelrod felt uncomfortable when he first took on his own students; he'd been in their boots too long himself. Hans Thoenen, a tall German of Lincolnesque gauntness who worked with him in the late 1960s, credits Axelrod with 'profound tolerance. He took us with our weak points, considered us as established, competent, and equal partners', no doubt, suggests Michael Brownstein, because 'Julie realized the damage that the massa-boy relationship can have.'

Axelrod tried to give his students problems at which they were apt to do well, yet not so transparent as to be trivial or dull, a tricky balance to achieve. 'Your first project,' says Brownstein, 'was something at which you might succeed in a month or two, where you'd be able to land on your feet, running, and get lots of strokes from Julie. In the meantime you could think about what to do next.'

Axelrod showed them [his young colleagues], says Jacques de Champlain, now at Université de Montréal, that science 'can be a creative act, discovery a source of joy'. Says Lincoln Potter, 'It was that sense of wonder, magic, discovery, and delight that we had when we were kids that Julie brings to science.'

'Just follow your nose,' Axelrod would say. Research, as he approached it, was no grand, elaborately structured affair where you thought out everything beforehand and did everything with meticulous care. No, it was trying this, trying that, going where the muses moved you, guided as much by intuition as by logic.

Faced with choosing between a fresh, important problem and a minor one that's been picked to death, many scientists will go for the stale, the trivial, and the small. Perhaps because it's safer, the route better marked, the results more certain. Axelrod, with what to his peers seemed unerring instinct, picked the good problems, the meaty ones, and picked them when they were still largely untouched by others. 'You have to ask the important question at the right time,' he says. 'Ask a year later and it's obvious. You've got to ask before it becomes obvious.'

All you needed were good ideas and the willingness to try them. What you didn't need, and didn't want, was too exhaustive a knowledge of the existing literature, because, as one former student puts it, 'all it can do is tell you what you can't do'. As in so many areas of his scientific style, it was as if Steve Brodie[2] were speaking across the generations, or at least down from the seventh floor of Building 10.

'You don't learn anything by thinking about what to do,' Axelrod would say, 'just by going into the lab and doing them.' The experiment doesn't support your idea? Too bad. Try something else. You always have to be ready to drop a cherished theory, no matter how long you've worked at it. You can't get too emotionally involved.

Axelrod never proved anything, not really, but rather was content to confirm an inference by various approaches and let it go at that. Which usually meant going onto the next problem without being absolutely sure of what he had. For those not so confident of their scientific intuition, nor so ready to rush ahead to the next step, it could be unnerving, like stepping along an icy sidewalk, the pavement forever threatening to slip out from beneath your feet. Scary? 'Damn right,' says Martin Zatz, who first joined Axelrod's lab as a research associate in the mid-1970s and now works in Michael Brownstein's Laboratory of Cell Biology at NIMH. 'Can I work the way Julie works?' he'd sometimes wonder. 'And I'll think, "I want to, but I can't."'

'Julie plays with ideas the way a kid plays with toys,' says Brownstein. 'He doesn't bowl you over with intelligence; he never would be first in his class at

Bronx High School of Science. But he has a gift for following up important things.' His peculiar specialty was, as Brownstein says, 'quick and dirty experiments based on his own special insights'. And there lay the danger for anyone wishing to ape his scientific style; 'that your insights won't be as good as his, that you'll miss things'.

Roland D Ciarnello, now at Stanford, tells how he can never see the *New York Times* without thinking of his mentor. They'd sit at Axelrod's desk going over the data and the moment Ciarnello got them bogged down in useless detail, Axelrod's attention would drift. 'When you got to the differential equations, his eyes would wander to the *New York Times* on his desk. At that point I knew I had to simplify further.'

'I don't like to do complex experiments. I'm not a complicated person,' says Axelrod, as evenly as you could imagine, mildly, as a statement of neutral fact. But another time, extolling the virtues of simplicity in science, some of the modesty falls away. 'Picasso,' he says, 'makes a single line – but it takes a lot of time and thought.'

His experimental strategy was loose, flexible. 'He put it together every afternoon.'

NOTES

1. Kanigel, R (1986 and 1993) *Apprentice to Genius: The Making of a Scientific Dynasty* (pp 120–26).
2. Dr Bernard S Brodie, 'the father of drug metabolism', was widely felt to be a candidate to share the Nobel Prize with Axelrod. He had been second-in-command at the Laboratory of Chemical Pharmacology at NIH, and Axelrod had at one time been his laboratory technician.

Professor JP: leader of a multi-media training project

Professor JP was the leader of a project to devise a multi-media package for enabling Fire Service Fire Controllers to learn how to control fires. Entrepreneur, Motivator and Team Builder, (and failing all else, a Controller) he carefully selected the team and facilitated the development of potential and talent in all its members in a mutually supportive way, consciously supporting and shielding them through its life cycle, on a project which gave them all great satisfaction, enjoyment and learning, as well as a sense of achievement. The eventual product was both very successful and very creative, winning national and international awards.

He regarded the selection of the group as of great importance and as his personal responsibility. 'I demand to be able to select... you then begged, borrowed, stole, lied or bullied the establishment in order to keep certain people.' He chose a small team with different skills, high capability but not necessarily qualified, easily communicated knowledge and high potential.

After their technical skills, he sought in his team a good spread of 'process' type skills (eg team-roles); and next he sought the fullest 'engagement' by all involved with the project – that the life-journey of individual team members should coincide with each development stage of the project – that what they sought to achieve in and for themselves at that moment in their lives should also be key contributions for the project. And he saw this group as having a life-cycle of its own: a birth, a growth and a death; and this piece of research as the wake of the particular project. He felt that all the members of the group were 'engaged' in the project in this way, and that they were so relaxed in each other's company that trivial, funny, even silly ideas were allowed to have some time.

He also felt it was critical to select team members who would get on with you; who would have a particular high level of trust, who would be able to bond quickly, have a 'reciprocity of perspectives', and quickly become familiar with each other's approaches.

'A team of complementary weakness was its strength.' 'They were lost, but I could see that they had tremendous potential.' 'You must have a real challenge for the group and a context for that to be revealed; everyone must grow; a long project entails supporting each other in different ways at different times; and we must know each other so well that the ability to know how another member feels about something changes the conversation in the group.' 'He tried to build on strengths and control weaknesses to release members' potential.' 'He recognized that those who were involved were best helped by having a worthwhile work success.' 'Putting people into a context where they can shine together is important.' 'I see crisis and recovery as a good mythology.' 'Group success built a mountain of confidence in the group.'

He created an environment for freedom of expression and encouraged it from individuals. 'He is very good at making you feel significant.' He provided 'space'; and trusted individuals to come up with the goods through using their particular skills. He treated it as an adventure: 'let's try something new!' 'Trust,' he said, 'is not a traditional leadership function;' but '... given trust and scope, you have the opportunity to go as far as you can.'

He was open, smiling and welcoming; 'he "persuaded" almost by good healthy spirit'; he 'exercised his leadership through friendship, laughter and socialization.' He was a great believer in breaking bread (and wine) together. The group speak of his animation, his excitement, his enthusiasm, his encouragement and his positive criticism.

'He acknowledged individual members' styles, and deferred to them.' 'He encouraged the team to solve their own technical problems and to work together to establish priorities with respect to quality, and to assess quality' for themselves. 'He encouraged mutual counselling where his own was not appropriate.' 'He held formal and informal meetings to develop shared understanding.' 'His leadership was democratic, fluid, not dictatorial.' 'It was a partnership, in which we did things together: decisions were based on context not on status.'

'He cared for the person and the project, but the person came first.' 'He was as concerned with the social environment (and home) as the task.' 'He worked hard to prepare members for life after the project.'

Lack of theory, lack of funds, the on/off attitude of a trade body of the fire officers, and a feeling in the school that it was irrelevant and/or impossible were turned into a challenge which stimulated the group's commitment, enthusiasm and desire for quality and success.

He was the entrepreneur of the group; 'he addressed people outside the group, looking for openings;' 'made presentations to funders, and had to take final decisions.' 'You are the leader, the money-getter and the spokesperson'; 'fronting, funding and presentation'.

'He provided the context for freedom – a protected vacuum, "I am holding back the normal pressures to give you this space" – a womb.' The group could be seen as a cell, and he as the membrane round it; he allowed it to become neither overblown nor degenerative in relation to its environment.

He was a Shielder: 'He was honest, but would put a positive gloss on team performance.' 'When things were going wrong, he portrayed success to the system, to keep it happy.' 'He tried to maximize salaries and support the team.'

'The leader needs to be a "process" scientist.' For instance, 'it is important to understand when the team is in a development role. If it is, let it go!' 'He would engineer important occasions which seemed to others to turn out by chance.' 'A visit to Amsterdam kept us going in enthusiasm for eighteen months,' commented one member of the team. 'The kit we had been developing, and which we had intended to present, broke down; and we created a presentation in which each one of us simply represented a part of the kit; as a result, as well as coming up with a new product, we understood the project better – and we got a standing ovation for it!' 'I was listening and finding out what people can and can't do. When we were there, I knew what we could do and needed to push us; and match things up,' said JP.

'It was a team with a responsibility to generate ideas.' As one person said, 'there were times when JP was just another person taking another perspective.' For instance, 'when as a group we went off together, it is hard to say where the ideas came from, often out of conflict in the group. Even though someone verbalized an idea first, it was a group thing; and difficult to locate in one person.' 'I have become conscious of the fact that we link ideas and attribute them to others in the group.' 'Someone articulates a half-baked idea, then someone fully bakes it; something flashes round in the group, which motivates everyone.' Everyone in the group was very good at acting as a supporter; 'we each help each other in different ways'.

JP saw team-work as a highly sensitive and dynamic interaction between its members, 'telepathy told you when it was and wasn't working; people just knew how to fill the gap, if there was one, and touches were very gentle; about behaviour as expressing attitudes.' 'Sharing attitudes, notions, feelings.' 'All of us were engaged on a happy conjunction which defined our lives, a group of individuals developing together.'

'He was full of ideas (and needing to sort out the good ones). The team knew how to get the best out of him.' 'He knew his faults: "Well, you know I'm not good at this!"' 'I am not a project deliverer.' And, 'I am a poor critic.'

Even though there were certain things that fell to JP to do, 'when we were working together, "leadership" was a concept that was alien to us,' 'there was no leader involved in much of what we are talking about'. 'We adopted whatever roles were necessary. In a way, we were on each other's shoulders, helping each other in different ways.'

Peter Brook: a theatre director reflects

Peter Brook is probably among the greatest theatre directors in the world today. He has been described as a 'pathfinder' and as a 'Pied Piper pursued by an audience who knew that he would take them somewhere they had never been before'. [1] In his long career, he has never ceased to question, to look for new answers, to experiment and to try the new. In 1970 he founded the Centre for International Theatre Research, where he has since worked with his own international company in Paris, making forays into uncharted territories, to explore the very foundations of the theatrical process.

In this edited extract from an interview with him,[2] he considers some of the aspects of a company coming to work together on a piece, including the heightening of sensitivities in the group and how that may provide actors and audience alike with a taste of finer feelings, clearer perceptions and deeper understandings. And he responds to questions, about how he approaches the first day of rehearsals – with speeches, by fondling one another, with lunch and vodka, and with exercises to help keep out the cold!

When a group is meeting for the first time, they certainly are not sensitive to one another in the whole of their body. I was very recently in Germany and I asked actors in the big German theatres, 'Do you do any exercises?'. Either they said, 'No, never', or they said 'Oh yes, once or twice a week we have gymnastic classes and we work on our bodies.'

But the interesting thing is that such classes help no-one except the individual, because the real exercise with a group of actors is not for the person by himself. It isn't to make him cleverer or a better actor, or a better athlete or dancer. It's to make a group more sensitive to itself. Something quite different. When one does exercises, it isn't to make people more powerfully skilful, it's to make everybody from the start quite simply more sensitive. Once a group becomes more sensitive, each person feels the reward. He begins to find (as does the director, especially if he does exercises with the actors) that as you study the work you're doing, you are actually seeing this work better, more fully, than when you sat at home trying to do it all by yourself. Step by step, through exercise, through preparation, one begins to see that everything that matters in the theatre is a collective process. Then you come to the point where a group who have had time to prepare something meets a group like yourselves, who have come from all different corners and are sitting in seats. Then you see that the most rewarding aspect of all theatre is when, in an extraordinary way, the audience also becomes more sensitive than it has been when it's in the foyer or the street. That is what, to me, the whole of the theatre process is about. In big buildings, in small buildings, in the open air, in cellars – no matter where – with plays, without plays, with a script, with improvisation, no matter – it is about giving everyone who is together at the moment when there's a performance a taste of being finer in their feelings, clearer in their way of seeing things, deeper in their understanding, than in their everyday isolation and solitude.

[Audience question]
When you get a group of actors together for a new production, on the first day, could you tell us briefly what happens?

PB: I used, for years and years, to start by lining them up, showing them a model, and making a speech. Then one day, I noticed that not one of them was taking any notice of what I was saying. So after about twenty years I thought, 'That's not the way to start.' After that we tried many methods. In the sixties, with the international group, we did something which worked then, but everything must change according to its time. The international group came from all parts of the world to this space, and they'd no idea what was awaiting them or who they were going to work with. As they came through the door, I said, 'Close your eyes.' I then led them into the space with their eyes closed and put them together in couples. Then I said, 'Feel the other person', so everybody did that and after about five minutes I said, 'Open your eyes.' When you have fondled somebody for five minutes with your eyes closed, you can be sure that a lot of ice has been broken. At other times we've had a big meal. In Paris we started a production of *The Cherry Orchard* with a big lunch and a lot of vodka. A marvellous technique for getting going. The best occasion was when we were doing *The Cherry Orchard* in New York. We had actors of all ages and I thought, I must start by doing exercises, but I know that 50% of them are not going to want to do it. If I say now, 'Right, we all start doing an exercise', there will either be a very bad feeling or they'll do it so badly that it isn't worth doing. How can one lead people who don't want to do exercises and have never done them, into it? Especially when you have a range from young actors who are bursting to do it, to old ones who have never done anything like this in their lives and think this is a very suspicious new-fangled thing. How can one go about it? I came to the rehearsal room with no solution at all. It was freezing cold, in the middle of winter, and New York was frozen. As I came into the rehearsal room, the stage manager said, 'A dreadful thing has happened, the heating is broken.' The actors were standing there, ready for the first rehearsal in their coats. Thank God, that gave the solution. I said to them, before we start, let's do this [hugging and slapping yourself to keep warm]. Everyone began. Then I said, 'A little faster', then, 'Stamping with your feet', then 'Let's imagine there's snow on the ground, make snowballs and start throwing them.' Before they knew what had happened, everyone was doing the fullest physical exercise for an hour and felt terrific. After which the idea of starting with movement was completely sold and we never had another problem.

NOTES

1. Irving Wardle's Foreword to *Peter Brook: A Theatrical Casebook*, compiled by David Williams, Methuen, London, 1988.
2. Peter Brook gave this address at a Platform at the Royal National Theatre on 5 November 1993 in the Olivier Theatre. The transcript was printed as part of Platform Papers: 6, published by the Royal National Theatre, London, 1994, and is reproduced with their permission.

PART II

IDENTIFYING THE TASK

3   *analysing the magic*

WHAT KiND OF CREATiViTY DO YOU NEED?

'His experimental strategy was loose, flexible; he put it together every after-noon.'

(Said of Nobel Prize winner, Dr Julius Axelrod)

One of the greatest sustained creative feats ever must be the development of the computer, from the moment in 1945 when Vannevar Bush published a dramatically vivid and visionary article in *Atlantic Monthly*, depicting the 'memex', something very like the computer we have today, more than 50 years later. Since then, people have contributed to its development from all sorts of fields, and in all sorts of ways.

The behavioural psychologist Howard Gardner[1] has suggested that there are at least five kinds of creative performances: producing permanent works (or, to put it more all-embracingly, exceptional works) in a genre (Mozart writing a symphony); executing stylized performances (a ballet); solving recognized problems (determining the structure of the human genome); formulating a general framework or theory (the Theory of Relativity); and performances of high stakes (a Cup Final).

A further level of analysis is suggested by Tim Gallwey in one of his books about the 'inner' side of games,[2] who has depicted how, to take the second of these, executing stylized performances, different conductors may take different approaches to making music: Max Rudolf, disciplinarian and scholar, who explains the historical reasons why he wants it played that way; Gunther Schiller as encouraging his musicians to respond spontaneously, leaving room for mistakes and magic; James Levine as instilling trust through sheer love of music, by describing the sound qualities and the emotional expression he is looking for; Leonard Bernstein – a dynamic and energetic conductor – an overpowering personality, who *becomes* the energy of the music he conducts.

So what is the essence that makes us call something creative? Creativity is somehow mercurial, but it may be usefully defined as 'coming up with something which is distinctively new and potentially valuable'. The term is used not simply of progress, but where progress has taken place in a 'leap', and this is more likely on some types of task and in some situations than in others.

WHAT MAKES A PROJECT A CREATIVE ONE?

It is at the moment fashionable to want to be 'creative': it has become a universal objective, accolade and panacea. There are always some topics which are seen as more interesting to work on or as 'sexier' than others, and so give more kudos. Sexy areas for 'creativity' currently include, in medical research, the biochemical mechanisms associated with heart disease, in the performing arts, 'performance' theatre, and in the graphic arts the use of computer imagery and computer-driven graphics. Not only do domains and fields of activity have areas which are at any one time more exciting and more attractive than others, but so also do organizations. One Research and Development project, whose objective was to develop a new product in collaboration with a Japanese client, attracted strong interest from the scientists who worked on it because of the kudos involved.

> **Creative projects are about problems, paradoxes, controversies and ambiguities that are persistent**

What distinguishes creative projects is that they address questions which have resisted solutions. Problems, paradoxes, controversies and ambiguities that are persistent, especially where they may have widespread impact, may unlock other issues and are of public interest. Issues that persist can only be cracked by being looked at in creative ways. Thus, to see them from another point of view, they are those issues whose resolution could be very beneficial, in which new ways of looking at them have not so far borne fruit, and therefore where another more radical (more 'creative') way of looking at them may do so.

Moreover, creative people are attracted when new approaches in a subject are likely to generate progress which is either large in relation to the previous history of the work, and therefore seen as a difficult leap to make, or which may have a wider and deeper impact on related issues, issues which are currently felt to be of importance, and therefore seen as potentially particularly beneficial.

> **Three concepts are closely linked with that of creativity: opportunity, perceived difficulty and potential benefits**

In their report, the Technology Foresight Panels[3] used very similar concepts in order to rank various fields of scientific endeavour. Those rankings were based on 'feasibility', defined as the likelihood of an advance in the technology and the strength of the UK science and technology base to achieve this advance, and on 'attractiveness', defined as the likely economic and social benefits, and the ability for the UK to capture these benefits.

The purpose of that exercise was to identify areas of scientific endeavour which should be regarded as priority areas for government support and funding, and it therefore involved making comparisons across all of the sciences. Comparisons of creativity in science with creativity in the arts or sport are less commonly made, and while the elements which make us call something creative (opportunity, difficulty and benefits) are essentially the same, there are also, of course, some differences.

People often draw a distinction, for instance, between creativity in science and creativity in the arts. Science is felt to be about 'universal' laws, a field in which there is something inevitable about progress as one discovery builds on previous work. And because several scientists often come up with the same solution at about the same time, science is more anonymous. By contrast art is more about the verities of the spirit, some of which may be more widely shared than others. It is also felt that art is more about change, that it deals with the communication of particulars which can be shared by others, and is only 'universal' in that sense, and is associated more with given individuals.

> **Whereas science is about 'universal' laws, literature is about truths of universal interest**

There are certainly contrasts between the meaning of 'truth' in these fields: in science, it is an explanation of events which satisfies and enables most people to work with it for the time being; whereas in art, Aaron Copland, the composer, has written: 'And just as the individual creator discovers himself though his creation, so the world at large knows itself through its artists, discovers the very nature of its Being through the creations of its artists.'[4]

Science is therefore seen as creative in terms of the task of finding ways of explaining things, ways which will be widely accepted, whereas in the arts, the task is one of finding ways of expressing things so as to enable others to see, feel or understand them in a certain way.

The Nobel Prizes for science are awarded simply for 'the most important discovery or invention' in given fields, without any qualification as to how important a discovery, or how extensive a leap forward it shall be for the prize to be awarded (adding, incidentally, that 'when a scientific work by a team is proposed, it has been said that there is always a "master mind" that should be found and selected', although in recent years an increasing proportion of Nobel Prize winning work is collaborative work). Compare this, for instance, with the remarkable frequency with which we found that successful leaders of creative groups were 'Visionaries', 'Ideas generators' or 'Ideas prompters' (see Chapter 4).

The criteria used by those who have had the task of selecting the Nobel Laureates for Literature have indeed shifted with time, according to who was on the awarding committee, their objectives and their perceptions. Nonetheless there are several clear themes which are remarkably parallel to those used in other creative fields. These include idealism/humanity, as furthering knowledge of man and the human condition, and endeavouring to enrich and improve human life; artistic style, as the way the work presents itself, 'great', masterful, graceful, immediately accessible; of universal interest, as speaking to a wider general public; and 'pioneering', as innovative, experimentalist, pathfinding, of radical significance.

> **If there is a characteristic that distinguishes creativity in sport from creativity in science or in the arts, it is perhaps its fleeting and ephemeral nature in the former field**

What makes the comparison of 'creativity' between different fields so tricky is that a project in one field which may be more difficult could also be less potentially beneficial than a comparable project in another field. (And for that matter how does one compare different kinds of difficulty and different kinds of benefit?) Ultimately, of course, 'creativity' is a social label not a scientific category.

Creativity as a characteristic of people

'Creative' is also used as a characteristic of people. Individuals are seen as more creative or as less creative, though it is possible to 'enhance' one's creativity, and many are the techniques, programmes and courses for doing so (see for instance the many 'self-help' books and audio-tapes on the subject, especially in the United States). Creativity improves with practice. And creative people – artists, inventors, designers – find that they are more creative at some moments than at others.

Another commonly drawn distinction is that between 'personal' and 'global' (or absolute) creativity. Writing one's first sonnet or cooking one's first soufflé may be examples of personal creativity, whereas producing an artificial eye, a new drug for treating snoring, or a new way of making milk would be regarded as inventions, as 'world firsts', and as such would in all probability be patentable (where one's first soufflé might not be!).

Moreover, there are different kinds of creative talents. Howard Gardner also draws a distinction in his studies of exceptional people, between masters (Mozart, George Eliot or Rembrandt), makers (Freud, Jackson Pollock, Charles Darwin, Charlie Chaplin, John Lennon), introspectors (Virginia Woolf, Marcel Proust, James Joyce, Anaïs Nin) and influencers (Gandhi, Karl Marx, Machiavelli).

Creativity as a process or an activity

And there is the third use of the term 'creativity' – as about the act (or activity) of creating. Sir Peter Medawar, the Nobel Prize winner, scientist and writer, in a 1985 essay about 'Creativity – especially in Science', defines creativity as 'the faculty of mind or spirit that empowers us to bring into existence, ostensibly out of nothing, something of beauty, order or significance'. Moreover he adds: 'I believe that there is no qualitative difference between creativity in science and in its many other contexts.'

The processes and activities of creative problem solving have themselves been extensively studied, developed and documented, and the Synectics Corporation was a pioneering exponent of them. Moreover, they are regarded as equally applicable in every field of endeavour.

The fact is that everyone has some creativity in them, some more, some less; all tasks require some creativity, some more and some less; and creativity is indeed an activity, one that individuals can and do perform, but also one that is increasingly performed by groups.

CREATIVITY IN RELATION TO INERTIA

How much of a leap forward it has to be for us to call it a creative leap is to a degree a function inertia. It is harder to change something which has been done for a long time in the same way (one programme in a long-running radio series), or by the same group of people (who have worked together over a long period), or in an organization with long-defined objectives (people who work in a chemical company do not look for solutions that involve electronics). As one leader put it, 'when you look at something long enough, you see it like everyone else does.'

CREATIVITY AND RISK

Closely parallel to this distinction is another, about degrees of exposure and risk, and the likelihood of failure. In a recent research project of mine,[5] an IT development project was seen as risky in that it was breaking new ground; broadcasters and designers said that they felt 'naked' before large and/or critical audiences; and scientists and artists felt 'exposed', their reputations on the line. The greater the risk involved, the more creative is the outcome likely to be.

Risk is related to the nature of the criteria against which a project is assessed: the larger the number of criteria, or the more varied, uncertain or fickle they are (criteria change with time – tastes and views change; people give different weight to different things, and see things differently), the more open the leader and the group may feel to risk.

The UNESCO studies of scientific laboratories in 1974 settled on seven criteria of effectiveness: the general contribution of the unit to science and technology; the recognition accorded to the unit; its social effectiveness (the value and usefulness of its work); its training effectiveness; its administrative effectiveness (in meeting schedules and budgets); its R&D effectiveness (the productiveness and effectiveness of its research); and the effectiveness of the application of its results, including the use made of development activities.

> **In many creative fields, criteria for success are intuitive and visceral**

However, in contrast to all this analysis of how success or effectiveness is or can be assessed, in many creative fields the criteria for success are intuitive and visceral, often expressed in the simple phrase, 'Does it work?' Does it succeed in expressing how we think or feel about it, or achieving something we want?

Creative projects are almost never seen as having only one objective, and they may be seen as more creative in some ways but less so in others. There are objectives at different levels associated with individuals, with groups and with organizations; in different fields: computers, tax, engineering and chemistry; and concerning different aspects: selling, learning, staffing, designing etc.

Moreover, whether something is regarded as creative may depend upon whose point of view you have in mind. From the recipient's point of view, something may be well received in the way that is appropriate in the field, as entertaining, efficacious or influential, and thus as successful, yet from the point of view of the expert in his/her field, it may address less interesting questions, demand less skill, or be less rewarding; it may be 'less difficult' or 'less potentially beneficial', and thus be seen as less creative.

CREATIVITY AND LEARNING/PERSONAL DEVELOPMENT

There is of course a very close relationship between learning and creativity; they are seen as very similar if not as the same thing. Creativity in the absolute sense (as producing a new drug, devising a new theory or producing a new product ie over which one might have patents or copyrights) necessarily entails learning and creativity at the personal level. However, while personal learning may indeed produce outcomes that are creative in personal terms, those outcomes will not necessarily be creative in the absolute sense: someone else may have got there first! Learning is therefore a necessary condition for global creativity, but not a sufficient one.

The degree of focus on personal development varies, both in the leader, in the project group, and in the organization, but the more creative a successful project is, the greater the focus is likely to be on personal development.

CREATIVITY AND STAGES OF PROJECTS

The greatest scope for creativity may lie in one stage of one project and in another stage of a another project, and different stages may demand different kinds of creative skills (see Figure 3.1). These stages can be described in terms of:

1. Information.
2. Objectives.
3. Plans.
4. Actions.
5. Review.

or in terms of scientific method as:

1. Reviewing existing knowledge (literature) and determining what issues to address.
2. Setting objectives eg to find how a particular mechanism works.
3. Devising a theory or hypothesis.

4. Determining how to test it; and testing it.
5. Reviewing results.

(Frequently projects require repetitions of this cycle, often many times.)

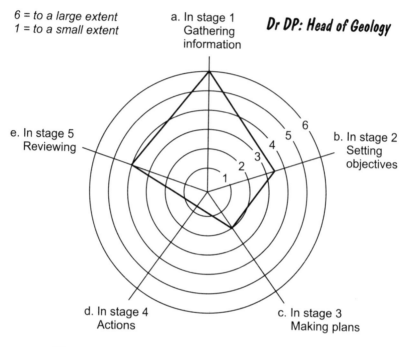

6 = *to a large extent*
1 = *to a small extent*

a. In stage 1
Gathering
information

Dr DP: Head of Geology

e. In stage 5
Reviewing

b. In stage 2
Setting
objectives

d. In stage 4
Actions

c. In stage 3
Making plans

Figure 3.1   *Scope for creativity at each stage of project*

In some circumstances the greatest scope for creativity may lie in formulating the question(s), in others it may lie in conceiving solutions, and in others in trying them out.

In a research project in geological sciences, the group paid tribute to their leader's skill in formulating questions in relation to the strategic opportunities in the subject as well to his ability to 'speculate readily'. In a Research and Development project in a chemical company, the essence of the project lay in the next stage, in the conception of possible solutions. And in a production of an opera, the scope for creativity lay (in practice) in the performance itself.

> **Different stages of a project may demand different types of creative skill**

While each of these stages may entail creativity, they may also demand different types of creative skill. Identifying rich questions requires a deep knowledge of the domain and the field as well as of the subject, and leaders need to have a nose for how their questions may be ripe for solutions. The second stage, the conception of solutions, requires a deep understanding of the subject together with the ability to envisage possible approaches (to 'see how it will look', 'hear how it will sound' or in research, to imagine how it might work); and the third stage requires experience of and an ability for *mise en scène*, for translating concepts or precepts into experiments or events.

More poetically, some projects[5] were also seen by their participants as having a birth, a life and a death. There was sometimes seen to be an 'engagement' between the life-journey of individual team members with that of the project – when whatever they sought to achieve in and for themselves at that moment in their lives should also be key contributions for the project. 'All of us were engaged on a happy conjunction which defined our lives, a group of individuals developing together.'

SOME TASK-ORIENTED TYPES OF PROJECTS

Some projects do not so much address persistent questions as require something to be done, or (what may be a minor variant) done differently. Projects vary according to the extent to which there is a task which the group has to achieve – an output or a tangible outcome which relates to people outside the group – clients, peers, fellow practitioners or audiences: an activity relocated, patients walking out of the hospital door, a programme on the air, an advert on TV etc. At the other end of this continuum are tasks whose main objective is simply to devise something new and potentially useful, such as a new drug, a new theory, or a new widget (a new method, understanding, or product). And in the middle of this continuum are projects which perhaps have equal emphasis on the task and on the creativity (as in the production of an opera).

Some projects are of the kind to which project management techniques apply, especially those whose activities are pre-plannable, and those whose outputs are pre-definable. In some projects, the emphasis is upon ensuring that each of the tasks necessary to achieve a defined end-product is achieved in time and/or to budget, and to an adequate standard. I would epitomize these projects as 'what to...' projects, because achieving a successful outcome depends mostly upon deciding what to do.

The relocation of a hospital and the carrying out of an audit can be characterized as task-oriented projects, more of the 'what to...' type. Many projects simply entail carrying out a set of readily identifiable steps, where the members of the group have done similar things before, and in circumstances that are similar. All that is need is to get on and do it, simply to give it a bit of 'sheer bloody hard work'! Applying a project management style of leadership in a 'what to…' type of project is likely to be successful without also necessarily being creative.

Projects of the 'what to…' type may also have wide scope for creativity, and they may still produce creative outcomes even though they are led in a project management style, for as a psychiatrist put it: 'out of structure [comes] spontaneity' (see Figure 3.2). The main contribution of the coach to an Olympic sailing crew at a particular regatta had been to help the team to set objectives, in terms of tasks which had to be achieved, such as a sail improvement programme, and to provide emotional support. It was seen as the application of meticulous preparation in a sport to which such rigour was less often applied. Yet, for its ultimate success, his team needed an element of creativity and they were unsure about whether they had that in them. They did not rate their performance as creative, but they did rate it as fairly successful and in the end they achieved the Silver Medal.

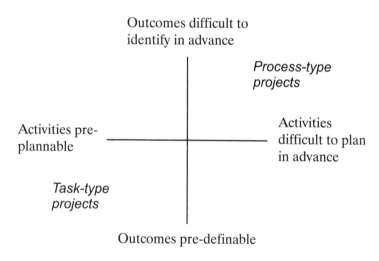

Figure 3.2 *Process-type and task-type projects*

In the production of an opera the conductor, while being regarded as a good planner, organizer and communicator, was also respected as a coach, supporter and developer of his talented students, and as regards the production, as an enabler. It was a group of highly creative participants whose talents, almost inevitably, produced a creative outcome out of the tight constraints of the production (though not without complaints!). The production itself, well reviewed in *The Times*, was rated as fairly creative and very successful.

SOME TASKS AS 'PROCESS-ORIENTED' TYPES OF PROJECTS

These task-oriented projects contrasted with others in which the end-product was hard to define, either because the objective was abstract, or because there was a variety of ways in which the project might be brought to effect. I would epitomize these projects as 'how to...' projects because achieving a successful outcome depended more upon deciding how to achieve it.

Moreover, in many 'how to...' projects, the way forward could not be planned because each next stage depended upon how the previous stage had developed. Each project was, in that sense, 'evolutionary' or 'iterative', and some more so, and more rapidly so than others.

Some 'how to...' projects are more radical than others and as such entail more sharply divergent, more dramatically radical thinking. For example, producing a new range of coloured printing inks with enhanced qualities by using chemical compounds is a less radical task than exploring new technologies in order to achieve the same effects.

As with projects of the 'what to...' type, projects of the 'how to...' type can also be extremely successful without necessarily being creative: another rendering of Beethoven's Fifth, a me-too drug or a copycat advertisement provide examples. One creative project, in broadcasting, had as its main objective to do it differently, to involve audiences more, and to do so by running a series of the programme out on the road as opposed to in the studio. The outcome was not rated as very creative, but it was rated as very successful, as satisfying, as well received and as breaking new ground.

To summarize this section, I have suggested that 'creative' is a social award given to those who succeed in making a leap forward in unlocking a persistent problem where difficulty, opportunity and potential benefits coincide. Such problems are often dogged by inertia and/or fraught with risk because of their difficulty or because the criteria for success are various, and are often unlocked, enabling us to see them in a new and fruitful way. This may entail gathering a group of people who will develop together and that the creative 'process':

- may be more relevant to one stage of the project more than to others;
- may include 'task-orientation' or 'process-orientation';
- entails using aspects of the environment to offer different perspectives on the problem.

NOTES

1. Gardner, H (1997) *Extraordinary Minds,* Weidenfeld and Nicholson, London.
2. Green, B and Gallwey, W T (1986) *The Inner Game of Music*, Pan Books, London.
3. Report of the Technical Foresight Panels, Office of Science and Technology, May 1995.
4. Copland, A (1952) *Music and Imagination*, Harvard University Press, Cambridge, MA.
5. Whatmore, J (1996) *Managing Creative Groups: what makes people good at it,* a study of project group leaders in science, research & development, sport, the performing arts and the graphic arts, Roffey Park Management Institute, Sussex.

Figure 3.3

Reproduced by permission of Neil Bennett and *The Times*

4 *the right kind of 'fixer'*

CHOOSiNG THE RiGHT LEADER

Analyses of leadership illustrate the close relationship between the effectiveness of leaders and the sociology of the times in which they live. Montgomery would have been as unsuccessful in Alexander the Great's time as the generals of World War I would have been today.

The idea that we are moving from 'command and control' leadership towards 'collaboration and co-operation' mirrors sociological changes that have been taking place over the last 50 years. The roles that leaders play, their skills, their styles of leadership and their personalities will, if they are to be effective as leaders, reflect these changes. The speed of change is one of the distinctive characteristics of our own time, and it seems likely that the skills of those who are effective leaders of creative groups may be relevant not only for leadership in many of the leading fields of today, but also for everyone who is involved in innovation and change.

WHAT IS LEADERSHIP?

Until recently, our thinking about leadership has been dominated by models from the Services. Field Marshal Slim defined leadership as 'that mixture of example, persuasion and compulsion which makes men do what you want them to do.' The Leadership Trust defines leadership as 'winning the hearts and minds of others to achieve a common purpose'. More recently, Howard Gardner,[1] the Harvard academic, defined leaders more simply, as individuals who significantly affect the thoughts, feelings and/or behaviours of a significant number of other individuals. A children's book summed it up by describing leaders as people who have ideas that make a difference.

People find themselves together in groups for all sorts of reasons, just as there are many reasons why people follow one another. While troops may indeed follow a man with courage who has to lead an attack out of the trenches, they are more likely to follow a man who can read the map if they are out on patrol in the jungle. One newly commissioned officer's personal report simply commented that, 'some soldiers will follow this officer – if only out of curiosity!' John Keegan, the military historian, has pointed out that leadership is a function of context, demonstrating for example how the concept of heroism has changed in its significance over the centuries by contrasting the times and the leadership styles of Alexander, Wellington, Grant and Hitler.[2]

> **In creative fields, leadership is a quality needed of different people at different moments**

A more commonly applicable model of leadership in creative fields is that it is a quality needed of different people at different moments. At any one moment, a group can be profitably led by the person who is in possession of a vital piece of technical knowledge, or who has a vital contact, or a vital understanding about what the group should do now, eg stop for a coffee break. Leadership consists in making your particular contribution an influential one for the group in its particular situation, a less heroic but perhaps more subtle role.

In the recent past, leadership has come to be seen as a dominating authoritarianism, but the second half of this century has placed a higher value upon democracy and self-determination. Leadership is seen today to have its place even in democratic and self-determined groups. Flatter organization structures and an increasing emphasis on personal development have made leadership into something that happens in organizations wherever it happens, and as such, a vital quality in every organization. Leadership therefore needs to be examined in relation to the circumstances in which it is exercised, in relation to the task, the team and the organization.

THE EVOLUTION OF THE 'LEADER' IN CREATIVE GROUPS

In many of the fields in which creativity is of the essence, work is increasingly taking place in groups, and groups always need leadership. To take an historical perspective for a moment, in science and technology the concept of the working group is continuously finding increasing application, but it is a relatively recent one, dating back perhaps to the first part of this century. In the performing arts it is infinitely older, yet the rise of the formal leader – the conductor or the director – only dates back to the early 1800s. It was between the wars that the role of the theatre director first began to take shape: his job was to interpret the text and therefore to elicit specific performances from the players. About the same period in the orchestra and rather earlier in opera, the growing complexity and organizational requirements of music demanded a more charismatic and dominant figure, who also came to be the interpreter of the composer's work.

In science and engineering, until recently, research was conducted by boffins, mainly working away by themselves in their laboratories. It is only in the last 30 to 50 years that we have seen the rise of the Project Leader. The same development can also be seen in architecture, where major projects are now handled by teams of architects with a senior architect as their leader.

TV and films, advertising and design are more modern arenas in which such leaders have shown that they have a distinctive part to play. Poetry has been written co-operatively – Dylan Thomas wrote over two hundred poems with a friend called Daniel Jones, each writing every alternate line! And plays and TV scripts are increasingly written and developed in an evolutionary and collaborative way.

The rise of the coach and more recently the team manager has shown pervasive growth in sport. Professor Szymanski, in a study at Imperial College, estimates that Alex Ferguson could be worth as much as £17 million as the Manager of Manchester United and Kenny Dalglish as much as £29 million to his club, which has to be compared to an average turnover of about £30 million a year for a first division football club.

> **Could we be witnessing the rise of the superstar leader in science, engineering and technology?**

At the time when we have been witnessing the rise of the superstar leader in sport and the arts – the Fergusons, the Dalglishes, the Von Karajans and the Peter Halls – could we also be witnessing the rise of the superstar project leader in science, engineering and technology? Perhaps that is why it has seemed right at this time to be asking what it is that makes people effective leaders of creative groups.

WHAT'S IN A TITLE?

The focus here is on 'first-line leaders', those who, when you move up the line of authority, are the very first people someone would report to; they are the most numerous group of managers and arguably the most influential. Such leaders go by many and various titles, and these titles often given indications about the nature of the leader's task in that situation. In practice, the more creative the group, the more the role does a disappearing trick! Susan Letzler Cole has described the theatre director who is 'creating in company' as the 'Invisible Director'. [3]

'Managers' are found in more traditional, hierarchical and authoritarian groups, especially those where he or she is appointed, and where organizing, planning and getting something done are important elements of the job. Some titles describe their functions more than others do, they are in a sense specific or technical. An Olympic coach is a coach, Head of Opera in the Guildhall School of Music and Drama is the Head of the Opera Department, and a Brand Manager is responsible for managing his or her brands.

Another common title is 'Head of...'. Those who run specialized groups in the National Health Service or research projects in medical schools are often called 'Head of...', a title which implies a certain prominence, as well as the 'taking of the lead', together with the responsibility for the service or the project.

'Co-ordinator' is another common title. The head of a group in the National Health Service commented, 'I am a co-ordinator, not a leader: the name is a sensitive issue. There are degrees of neutrality, and co-ordinator is the most neutral. Yet as a manager, I have to represent this group in a traditional hierarchy.'

In the arts and in sport, the manager is often seen as the person who makes the arrangements and in that sense, this is a more limited role than that of the manager/leader in many other fields.

Leadership as authority and responsibility without domination or control

---

The title most commonly accorded to leaders of successful creative groups is that of 'Leader'. Senior management in the research division of the Wellcome Foundation was very specific in focusing on 'leadership' as the title that reflected the desired form of management in research groups, and as what was rewarded with more power and influence.

In creative groups, leadership often means taking the lead when you have the most appropriate contribution, whether that contribution is technical, 'process', the making of contacts, the finding of resources, supporting someone else, or whatever, and as 'authority and responsibility but without domination or control'.

However, whatever there may be in a title, as one leader said of his role in his group, 'When we were working together, leadership was a concept that was alien to us; there was no leader involved in much of what we are talking about. We adopted whatever roles were necessary. In a way, we were on each other's shoulders – helping each other in different ways.' And as the leader of workshops in musical improvisation commented, 'The role of leader and participant are of equal importance. It is important to be both sometimes, within the same activity'.

DIFFERENT CONCEPTS OF LEADERSHIP

Three concepts of leadership can be clearly distinguished in creative fields. There is the Group Head, who is appointed to lead a group of people on a given project. The group – whose life will be the life of the project – will probably include widely different people and their main *raison d'être* is to be creative.

Then there is the 'moment-to-moment' leader – the person who takes the lead in the group at any one moment – often described as the person who 'has the ball', who contributes something which takes the group along in a particular direction.

And third, there is the coach. Because creativity is closely associated with the development of skills and talents, leaders help to produce creative outcomes by coaching people in the development of those skills and talents.

Not only is the name a sensitive issue, but so also is the role. 'I had thought that one might fade into the background as a manager,' said one project leader, 'like wallpaper.' 'My aim is to provide the setting within which scientists can feel self-determined, yet whatever they choose to work on will be relevant to the organization's needs,' said another. 'I'd rather you didn't call me a manager: I find it unhelpful.' 'If X thought he had arrived at a particular solution for his group by himself, when I [his boss] had spent a great deal of time discussing it with him, so much the better.'

There are several reasons why the title and the role of leadership in creative groups could be a such sensitive issue. People have written about management (in science) as being a dishonest profession, in which those who practise it abandon their subject and their interests in favour of the objectives of the department and the organization. Second, managers are thought of as doing boring, uninteresting and perhaps demeaning work, such as budgets, reports, appraisals, pay reviews, disciplinary matters and so on. Third, managers are seen as being in authority, whereas successful creative groups are characterized by mutuality of contribution and support.

> Some people feel that if you try and articulate the
> creative process, the magic might just fly away

Some people also feel that if you try and articulate what managing creativity is, the magic might just depart. The Head of Drama at the Guildhall School of Music and Drama suggested that the roles of ambiguity and the unconscious are more important than trying to articulate what good management is. Aaron Copland, the composer, in his series of lectures at Harvard underlined the risk involved in too close inspection of the subject: 'The inspired moment may sometimes be described as a kind of hallucinatory state of mind: one half of the personality emotes and dictates while the other half listens and notates. The half that listens had better look the other way, had better simulate a half attention only, for the half that dictates is easily disgruntled and avenges itself for too close inspection by fading entirely away.'

The distinction between 'management' and leadership' has been well chewed over, and all that I will add is that in the context of creative fields, whereas 'management' is seen as the sustaining of a group and its function in the context of an organization, 'leadership' is more about a group of people on a journey of discovery.

Leadership can be described in various terms, which may help to elucidate what it takes to be a leader of a creative group in different circumstances. In Chapter 3, I discussed types of tasks that call for creativity; I discuss next the roles leaders play in their groups in different circumstances, and how that varies with different tasks, teams and environments, their styles of leadership and their personalities, and in Chapter 13 I discuss how they do these things.

ROLES THAT LEADERS PLAY IN CREATIVE GROUPS

The team-roles that members of creative groups play are different from those that are required for other kinds of tasks. Not only are they different, but different sets of team-roles are necessary for different kinds of creative tasks (see Chapter 11). There are, however, certain team-roles that leaders of creative groups play more frequently; certain roles are more common in certain situations, as are other roles in other situations. (Some of these correspond to those which Belbin[5] found in his seminal work on team-roles: others will be seen to relate more specifically to activities which are required in 'being creative'.)

6 = *leader made a major contribution in this role*
1 = *leader made an insignificant contribution in this role*

Professor JP (See p 20)

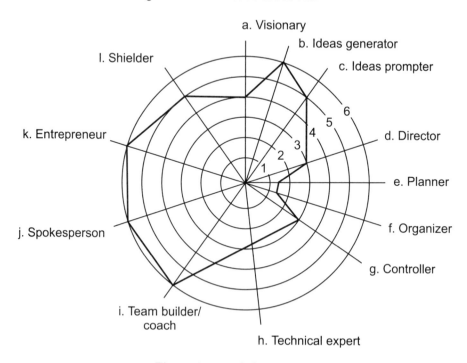

Figure 4.1 *Role leaders play*

Effective leaders as Visionaries, Ideas Generators or Prompters or as Directors, Planners, Organizers and Controllers

In the previous chapter, I drew out a distinction between those creative projects which are of the 'what to...' type and those which are of the 'how to...' type, and I suggested that in several respects they were distinctively different kinds of projects. Where the question is of the 'how to...' type, project groups tend to be led by people who are Visionaries, Ideas Generators or Ideas Prompters; and it is they who make the most significant contribution in generating and shaping ideas. Where the question is of the 'what to...' type, which is less common, project groups tend to be led by people who are Directors, Planners, Organizers and Controllers.

> **Leaders have a certain powerful yet shadowy intuition...**

Visionaries have a clear vision either about how it should be or about how to get there, what the theatre director Peter Brook has called a 'formless hunch... a certain powerful yet shadowy intuition that indicates the basic shape, the source from which the play is calling him as director'. Visionaries are recognized as such because their visions frequently turn out to be useful, and since people work best with their own rather than others' ideas (the-not-invented-here syndrome), Visionaries tend to be given responsibility and authority for leading creative groups, with the objective of making those visions a reality.

The leader of a medical research team was seen as a Visionary, as having played a major conceptual role in the project, and as having the ability to address the practical aspects of a visionary idea (he 'conceives the future'). The director of a TV series was regarded as a Visionary, as being able to control what happened because she knew exactly what she wanted, but she was going to use what people did best to achieve it. 'As well as working with my vision, I would like them to think that the vision grows organically and becomes better than the initial idea,' she said.

In Chapter 8, I discuss where ideas may come from, the ways in which Visionaries work, namely, what kinds of stimuli they find productive. Certain sources of stimuli are more prevalent in some creative fields than in others and individuals may also have preferences for particular kinds of stimuli.

Peter Brook has written about how the theatre director needs most of all to develop in his work a sense of listening:

> Day after day, as he intervenes, makes mistakes or watches what is happening on the surface, inside he must be listening, listening to the secret movements of the hidden process. It is in the name of this listening that he will be constantly dissatisfied, will continue to accept and reject until suddenly his ear hears the secret sound it is expecting and his eye sees the inner form that has been waiting to appear. A director works and listens. He helps actors to work and listen.[6]

Some creative groups achieve their creativity 'in the act'. 'Performance theatre', jazz and chamber music groups (and on some occasions, other/larger groups) come to shape their performance in the process of the act of discussing, rehearsing or performing; and in this process, the vision seems to be shaped and shared in the act. In such groups, the team members often seem to have a similar depth of experience though from different disciplines; they toss ideas around the group continuously and develop their vision for themselves as they progress. In such groups, leaders tend to be Ideas Generators or Ideas Prompters and in the rare case where the leader is not a technical expert in the subject, he or she is likely to be the latter, an Ideas Prompter.

One leader commented:

From my point of view, being the Ideas Generator is not the most important thing, I would have thought it important for all the Producers of programmes... If I spent all my time generating ideas, I would just love all my ideas so much (which is what all Producers do)... I think that the people who are feeding the engine, that is their role...it is not that I shouldn't have ideas, but I think it would be bad if I was the source of it.

By contrast, in the less common 'what to...' groups, leaders tend to be Directors, taking charge, leading and taking decisions; Planners, determining what will be done, when and how; Organizers, assigning people to jobs and co-ordinating their activities; and Controllers, monitoring and checking what has taken place and adjusting plans accordingly. They tend to exercise what could be characterized as 'project management skills', making a complicated pattern of events happen in a co-ordinated and effective way.

In groups whose task is more of the 'what to...' type, leaders tend to play roles with more specific content, such as Completer/Finisher, Evaluator, Quality Controller, Decision-maker and External Spokesperson, roles that have the flavour of a different style of management, of delegation and Command-and-control.

However, there can also be situations in which talented and creative people simply need the discipline associated with the 'command-and-control' style so as to ensure that all the pieces necessary for a creative performance are in position, leaving that little bit of extra space in which people can show their virtuosity in the performance. And that was the role in which the Head of Opera at the Guildhall School of Music and Drama saw himself as the Producer and the Conductor of a Mozart opera. He carefully communicated the objectives of the work and planned and organized it, but he was also a skilful coach, encourager and provider of feedback.

Effective leaders of creative groups tend to be what might be called 'Inspirators', people who are either Visionaries, Ideas Generators or Ideas Prompters; or else, but less commonly, they tend to be Managers: Directors, Planners, Organizers and Controllers.

Effective leaders as technical experts

Effective leaders are experts in their field, and they continue to contribute in that field, as scientists, producers, engineers etc. It is thus that they remain up to date, credible, and able to carry out projects in their field. As such, they play a significant role in their groups as a Technical Expert. They have what Amabile calls 'domain-relevant skills' and they have them in abundance.

> **Without being experts in their subject, they are
> not in a position to know whether an issue
> is a good one to explore**

Concern has been expressed, at least in the field of scientific research, that those who are promoted to be leaders of project groups tend to be those who are particularly successful in that field of work, placing a question mark over whether they have the necessary skills and talents for being effective leaders in such groups. On the other hand, without being experts in their subject they are not in a position to know whether an issue or a question is a good one to explore, whether its resolution may have widespread impact, may unlock other issues, or is of public interest, and whether it is ripe for solution.

Of the (archetypal) leader of one academic research team, an expert in his field, it was said that his 'main role was looking strategically at where opportunities for useful research might lie'; and 'setting out the strategic role and getting the team together'. He 'has a great deal of knowledge about a wide range of subjects; and his grasp of the subject is such that he can speculate quite readily'. He 'understood the methodological developments that were desirable,' and he 'had experience of all the jobs needed in the team'.

> **While not all experts in their field will necessarily
> make effective managers/leaders, you are unlikely
> to do so unless you are an expert in your field**

Effective leaders as Coaches and/or Team Builders

Effective leaders of creative groups need to be able to help develop the skills and talents of individuals in their teams, as well as to build their groups into effective teams. Groups that look to interaction between members to generate their ideas, and to develop those ideas, need to have team members with a variety of skills and perspectives; and those members also need to know, respect and use each other's strengths.

Effective leaders of creative groups are skilful Team Builders (see also Chapter 12). The Team Builder has to build team spirit, to encourage team togetherness and to get the team to work towards a common goal, by encouraging openness and communication within the team.

> **Helping people to develop their potential as an unpredictable virtuous spiral in which some unexpected advance in one person acts as a trigger for another**

In acting as Team Builders, leaders make opportunities for team members to get to know each other well, and more than just their work persona; to meet, discuss and contribute to each other's work, both formally via meetings and presentations and informally over tea, coffee and toast, and wine and food, and both on-site and off-site.

Groups which look to individuals more than to the group (as a group) are likely to need a coach more than a Team Builder (see also Chapter 10). As Coaches, leaders pass on knowledge and experience, give advice and support, and help individuals and teams to identify and develop their talents and skills, especially where they have undeveloped potential.

Helping people to develop their potential may perhaps be one of the greatest sources of creative output, since it can lead to an entirely unpredictable virtuous spiral in which some unexpected development in one person acts as a trigger for another. ('All of us were engaged on a happy conjunction which defined our lives, a group of individuals developing together.')

One such leader was described as 'helping people to develop their values, and their potential into better performances'; another as 'caring for the person and the project, but the person came first'. In creative worlds an important part of both coaching, and of team building is the 'support' (see below and Chapter 9) which leaders provide to members of their groups.

Effective leaders as spokespersons

Effective leaders of creative groups need to be able to represent their groups to the rest of the organization and indeed to the outside world. They need to present the group's work, but they also need to be the medium through which to influence and be influenced by those outside. This role consists in acting as the Spokesperson for the group to users, to customers and potential customers (whether inside the organization or outside it), and to collaborators.

Among other things, the Spokesperson voices the views of the team and finds resources – people and equipment etc – for the project. One such leader was seen as 'addressing people outside the group, looking for openings', and as dealing with 'fronting, funding and presentation'. Another was seen as 'the gate-keeper to the rest of the organization'. 'I need to know that he can explain [to others what I am doing]'. 'He was particularly effective when he was deploying his knowledge in support of his belief in the work' and 'in developing a good relationship with collaborators'; 'giving the project a high profile, talking about it a lot, both internally and externally'.

People who have recently made the transition into management often feel that they need to become better at the 'politics'. They have moved out of a world in which they were shielded by their manager and they feel like novices in a new world. They feel they need to be better at selling themselves and their projects; to know more about other departments and their managers; about the larger issues of policy and strategy; and about the broader scene, the characteristics of and the forces for change in the whole field in which they are operating. They see themselves as communicators between their group and the rest of the organization, and they wish to understand and be understood by, and to influence and be by influenced by the world outside.

Effective leaders as entrepreneurs

Effective leaders of creative groups often need to act as Entrepreneurs especially where their projects are more remote from sponsors' missions and objectives. While the rationale for a project may be that it will produce something that directly meets the organization's mission and objectives, in creative fields other rationales are likely to be prominent: the project may simply be of special interest to the leader or to the group; it may help to develop the group's knowledge or skills; or it may develop a platform for work which will (later) be of more direct benefit.

In one case, a project was somewhat remote from the mainstream activities of the academic department, in another it was recognized by management as a skunk works activity (ie as something which goes on in spare time and spare space and without the formal consent of management)! In yet another case, in its early stages, the project had been continued entirely without the support of the organization (because promises of commercial returns had been made too often which had turned out to be unachievable).

Some domains and some organizations call for entrepreneurship more than others. In medical schools, for instance, the funding of research is often provided by drug companies or medical research charities on the basis of peer recommendations, and this requires an entrepreneurial attitude on the part of the project leader.

Effective leaders as Shielders (see also Chapter 15)

Effective leaders of creative groups commonly need to act as Shielders of their groups. Creative groups often have special characteristics, styles and atmospheres which contrast with and are threatened by the world around them; they often find themselves part of an organization which has an alien or even hostile culture. Effective leaders act to protect the members of their groups from the disabling influences of the organization or of the outside world.

'Shielding' consists in acting in one way towards the members of the group – supporting, encouraging and helping in the development of its members – and in another to the organization – responding to its systems and processes as though the group was just like any other part of the organization ('fielding the bureaucracy').

The members of one project group felt that what united them was their weaknesses, and their success was to a considerable extent the result of the confidence and inspiration their leader gave them. While the project was not central to the mainstream activities of his department, the group needed time and space for its creativity, and the leader provided what the group described as a womb within which they could develop their solutions to a unique problem.

Another group, whose interest and skills were in psychodrama, was shielded by its leader from his fellow partners in this large accountancy firm, a field in which they saw his activities as risky and threatening to their main business (which was 'risk averse'), and they saw it as an ill-suited bed-fellow. He had to shield the group so that they could focus their energies on their particular skills and task, which was to change the understandings in an IT group in a large Far Eastern Bank, and help its members to make what was perceived to be a more significant contribution to their company.

SOME SKILLS OF EFFECTIVE LEADERS

Leaders as empathetic, understanding and as 'process' aware

Effective leaders of creative groups have a feeling for and understand the thoughts and feelings of the members of their group. They need to accept differences of opinion and of feeling, and they need to be sensitive to 'process' and to group dynamics (see Figure 4.2).

They are generally very sensitive people – empathetic and very aware of the thoughts and feelings of the members of their teams – epitomized in a recent description of one opera director, as someone who has 'an eerie instinct for what's going on in the private lives of his singers, and can turn that to dramatic advantage. He doesn't delve; it's almost a sixth sense', just as the members of their groups often have a sixth sense. For instance, the members of Furtwangler's orchestra were said to be aware, though they might be elsewhere in the building, the moment he had arrived in it.

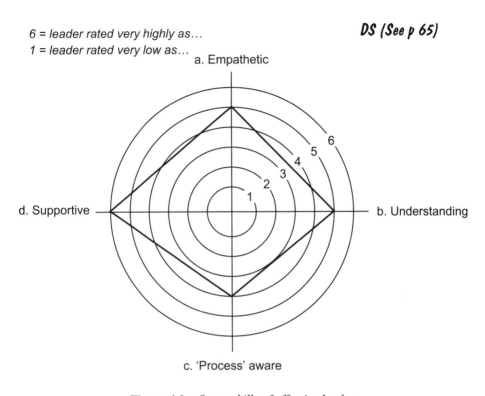

6 = leader rated very highly as…
1 = leader rated very low as…

DS (See p 65)

Figure 4.2   *Some skills of effective leaders*

Many of the leaders of creative groups, as mentioned above, are 'technical experts' in their own subject and they often draw a distinction between their interest in their subject (or in things) and their interest in people.

They need this empathy and understanding:

- in selecting their team and in using a variety of parameters in doing so (Chapter 11);
- in using the constraints of a project as the very challenges which would help team members in the development of their own talents (Chapter 5);
- in providing the freedoms which team members seek and which they find as an encouragement to experiment (Chapter 6);
- in using milestones and other opportunities for setting up tensions which might lead to creative breakthroughs (Chapter 7);
- in making themselves available as constant 'supporters' of the members of their teams (see below and Chapter 9);
- and in 'shielding' them when necessary (Chapter 15).

Effective leaders also have a strong awareness of and interest in 'process'. One commented that 'after a time momentum in teams becomes unstoppable, but it takes time and hard work: the 'process' side needs working at.' 'The leader needs to be a 'process' scientist' (see Figure 4.3).

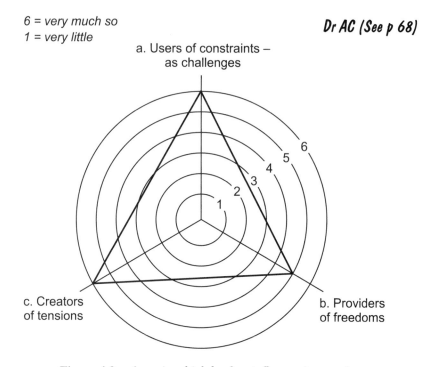

Figure 4.3 *Areas in which leaders influence 'process'*

In environments in which there is often a strong emphasis upon personal development, individuals change; just as in environments which are marked by high levels of interaction, and of discussion and debate, perceptions change; and as the stages of projects evolve, groups develop and change. A number of elements of 'process' in creative groups are dynamic, and the interactions between them unpredictable and therefore potentially creative.

Effective leaders as supportive (see also Chapter 9)

Effective leaders of creative groups are 'Supporters': they help people to achieve their objectives and they encourage an atmosphere of mutual support in their teams.

In a later section, I discuss how 'appropriate' support is related to the needs of individuals and of projects. Three themes run through that section. Creative people are often described as feeling insecure because they live for their talents, and because they feel that their reputation is only as good as that of their last project.

Emotional support is the most significant kind of support and consists in providing opportunities for achievements ('opportunities to shine'/ 'hitting the ground running'). It also consists in according recognition – as generating confidence – by means of affirmation when people have had success or of reminding them of their talents when they have had a failure. Emotional support is vital in situations which are especially risky or exposing, or which involve high failure rates as it is where individuals lack confidence or recent success.

Emotional support can be contrasted with cognitive support – helping people to develop creative ideas; to build on, to sift through and to shape them; and supporting that interaction between people who make use of each other's different perspectives, which plays a significant part in the development of concepts and ideas.

STYLES OF LEADERSHIP; DEMOCRATS, MANIPULATORS OR AUTOCRATS

While a democratic style of leadership is more appropriate for most creative project groups, there are some projects for which a manipulative style and some for which an autocratic style is appropriate.[7]

Many leaders of creative groups perform their functions (as Visionaries, Supporters, Team Builders, Coaches etc) because it is in their nature, though it must be added that to be effective it is certainly easier if one's natural style is consonant with the culture of the organization as a whole!

Some are democratic – they are facilitators of a democratic process in the team, though they also act as its boss in relation to the outside world – as its Spokesperson or Entrepreneur. There are others who use different styles of influence in order to achieve specific performances, who risk being denigrated as manipulative for their own ends. One described himself in terms of a 'latent controller' and another saw her job in terms of being a 'Manipulator'. And then there are others who are 'Autocrats'.

Most but not all successful creative project groups are led in a democratic style in which people exercise choice about the projects on which they are interested to work, and decisions are made in a democratic way (see Figure 4.4).

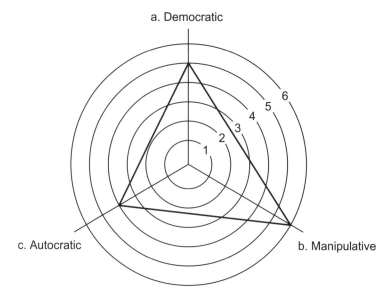

6 = *leader's style was highly...*
1 = *leader's style was not at all...*

JS (See p 70)

Figure 4.4   *Styles of leadership*

Democratic leaders

Effective leaders of creative groups adopt a democratic approach over decisions about what to do and usually they require unanimous decisions. One
leader expected not only to share the work with his colleagues but also to share
the leadership: he sought to encourage 'autonomy and responsibility without
domination and control'. Of another, one member commented: 'It was more
like collective working and I too was part of the decision-making process.' 'We
worked things out as a team and if there were any disagreements then the manager acted as arbitrator.' (All of these were multi-disciplinary teams, either
working sequentially on different phases of projects, or in one case, all contributing skills from their different disciplines to the many different projects which
each person undertook.)

Manipulative leaders

There are, however, situations in which the skills of a manipulator are key to
the success of a team. One film director, who saw herself as a 'Manipulator',
had put the team of actors, who were to play a team of police officers in a
'back-up' police van, through a team building course before they started

rehearsals together, so that they would be able 'to swear at one another within a day or so of being on set, just as the members of such a group might do in practice'. She had then sought to structure the situations in that course so as to mould the way individuals in the group might be seen by other members of the group, and thus help them to relate to one another in ways which the script called for.

She had a vivid visual imagination, and a clear picture in her mind of how she wanted the various scenes in the film to be shot, and she saw her task with actors and actresses as one of eliciting performances from them which would portray on the monitor her interpretation of the script and its plot.

One leader of an exceptionally creative and successful group was a latent 'Controller'. Seen by his group as giving them freedom and trust, he was a motivator and encourager who adopted a democratic, informal and flexible style at the same time as providing support and care. He commented however that, 'Management does give one a desire to control; ...by nature, I am a controller; if someone upsets me, I will revert to "controlling" my way out of the problem.'

Leonard Bernstein, the conductor, illustrates this approach when he says:

> The great conductor must not only make his orchestra play, he must make them want to play. He must exalt them, lift them, start their adrenalin pouring, either through cajoling or demanding or raging. But however he does it, he must make the orchestra love the music as he loves it. It is not so much imposing his will on them like a dictator; it is more like projecting his feelings around him so that they reach the last man in the second violin section. And when this happens – when one hundred men share his feelings, exactly, simultaneously, responding as one to each rise and fall of the music, to each point of arrival and departure, to each little inner pulse – then there is a human identity of feeling that has no equal elsewhere.[8]

Manipulators are adept at setting up situations in ways that will enable members of the group, whether consciously or unconsciously, to produce appropriate performances.

Autocratic leaders

And sometimes there are occasions and situations in which autocratic leaders produce outstanding creative performances from their groups. Three of the leaders in a recent study of mine[9] were described as 'autocrats', two of them doctors and the third a former male nurse, now a manager in the NHS. Of their projects one was a very task-oriented project which the leader, as an Organizer and Controller, ran – to its considerable success. The second, run by a psychiatrist, was successful but not very creative; and the third, again run by a psychiatrist, was rated neither successful nor creative.

We also worked with at least two 'dominant' leaders – one, a psychiatrist, was described as a 'star'! They were dominant in the sense that they were very strong influences over the direction of the project; they commanded great respect in their groups; they played a large number of team-roles in the team, and all of the key ones; and whilst their influence, through taking charge of situations, was immanent, in practice they allowed others room to express themselves. They were not described as Autocrats, rather they were more like virtuosi leaders and their projects were both successful and creative.

There is a story of a composer who came to the Guildhall School of Music and Drama to conduct a piece which he had written, and which he did by using the orchestra as a collection of test tubes, to get them to play the piece in such a way that it would have precisely the effect that he wished it to do. There was no question of the orchestra being a contributor to the conception of the piece or of their being a part of the creative process; that had already taken place in the head of the composer. There is also a story of a drug hunter in Bart's Medical School who for a number of years ran a highly autocratic but highly successful small research team on a very focused area of research.

Both of these leaders could be regarded as Visionaries, whose control over their groups enabled them to test their visions as quickly and as efficiently as possible, but not at the same time to enable those involved to learn and develop their own skills in the processes of creativity.

Autocrats will be most successful on task-oriented projects which have agreed criteria for success, where they play the roles of Organizer and/or Controller. They need also to be Visionaries, working on projects which enable them to test out their visions as quickly and as efficiently as possible, and where the development of those with whom they are working is, for some reason, less important.

THE PERSONALITY OF EFFECTIVE LEADERS

Effective leaders as warm and approachable, passionate and enthusiastic

Effective leaders of creative groups are generally warm, approachable, relaxed, easy-going, amiable and social (see Figure 4.5). Among the leaders in this same study were two Sisters, respectively leaders on an Accident and Emergency and on an Admissions Ward, the first of whom was described as 'receptive and approaching', and the second mused that her even temperament perhaps contributed to the fact that her staff did not first have to work out what sort of a mood she was in! (Both were also very empathetic.)

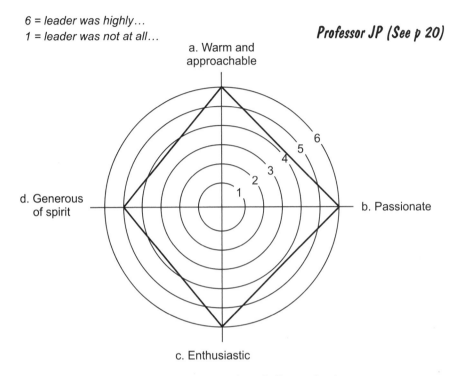

Figure 4.5 *The personality of effective leaders*

Warm and approachable people will find it easier to get to know members of their group, and in non-work situations they may well 'see' skills and talents they had not noticed at work. Their ability to get close to individuals may help them to be providers of (cognitive and emotional) support. And they may also find it easier to move into that 'non-leader' role described above.

Most such leaders are also passionate and enthusiastic, passionate about their people, their work or their subject, and enthusiastic for success (as well as able to share the enthusiasms of others), characteristics which spill over from the fact that they are themselves experts in their subject, and continue to practise in it. As Visionaries their lives are, of course, very much bound up in the projects which they have been instrumental in conceiving, organizing and running.

> **Passions traceable back to events
> in the early parts of their lives**

In this same study, several of them vividly traced their passionate attitudes about the way they managed back to events in the early parts of their lives which to this day were felt to be powerful influences upon what they did and the way they did it. A good listener, now an athletics manager, had to listen every day to his barrister father deploying to his sons at the breakfast table the arguments which he intended to use in court that day. A champion of the victimized and a fighter against the unchallenged tyranny of authority, now the leader of a consultancy group specializing in psychodrama, had been bullied at school without the authorities or his parents intervening or even being aware. A supporter of the right of talent to be able to express itself, now the leader of a multi-disciplinary R&D group, had suffered under the disdain and disinterest of layabout and arrogant Oxbridge graduates in their laboratory.

Effective leaders as generous of spirit

Effective leaders of creative groups are happy to help others to achieve success, and content to achieve their own successes through others. They do not need acclamations for the achievements which they may have been instrumental in bringing about.

They are usually natural facilitators, who tend to enable others to achieve their performances by arranging things or allowing things to happen in ways that are appropriate for the performers to achieve their best.

The leader of the Guildhall School of Music and Drama's Workshops in Musical Improvisation was highly sensitive to the atmosphere he was creating, and to how this would reduce participants' inhibitions and help them to take risks. The leader of a drug research project was delighted to act as an 'encourager, a persuader, and cajoler', 'to nudge' and 'inspire' another member of the team. An Olympic track and field manager saw facilitation as his main role as Team Manager (if the javelin event took place downwind, his man had a better chance of being inspired to throw well).

Effective leaders as very fluid in their contributions

Belbin has suggested that fluid role players are not normally successful team players, yet many leaders of more successful and creative groups are very fluid in the roles they play and in their overall contributions.

They have to be able to live with ambiguity, and if creative problems are defined as persistent problems, paradoxes, controversies or ambiguities, then the lives of leaders of such projects are continually about unresolved issues, about 'persistent problems'. And in making use of analogies, similes and metaphors, they are also creators as well as users of ambiguities.

Not only leaders but also team members play different roles at different stages and at different moments of a project. For example, the leader of a medical research project moved from playing the role of Visionary in the earliest stage, into the role of Empowerer, and in later stages into that of Evaluator. And if members of the group felt that there were gaps – roles not being played by individual team members – someone would move into them. Effective leaders need to be able to slip between roles to suit the needs of the group and of the moment.

There are also dichotomies in the roles played by leaders of creative groups. First, almost all of them choose to continue with some of the work in which their team is involved; and they have to move between being 'implementers', when they are doing their own work, and 'enablers', when they are leading others. In particular they must be sure to reserve their role as an Ideas Generator for their own work, and adopt the role of Ideas Prompter in other projects in which they have leadership responsibilities.

Second, they have a role as the appointed leader of their group, with responsibilities for all of its administrative support; yet when the group is in 'conception mode' – when it is tossing ideas around so that they can be built upon as they move round – that same leader must be a non-leader; he or she must be just like any other contributor in the group; in a situation in which you take the leadership if at any one moment you have something which you think can move the problem forward ('you take the ball and run with it').

And, third, those who are effective as Shielders often have two sides to their nature: one personality for being a leader in their team ('democratic', 'revolutionaries', 'protectors of the victimized'); and another personality for being a manager in the organization ('trusted', 'having the same values and objectives as the rest of us', 'won't rock the boat').

Leaders of creative groups have to deal with a number of paradoxes: for example, they have simultaneously to set challenges yet help people to achieve them; to provide rigorous feedback yet give support against feelings of insecurity; and to think in process terms despite the fact that the language of discourse is often very much in task terms. The effective leader needs to be able to pursue contrasting objectives simultaneously, and from one moment to another to argue to different ends from the same facts, a problem described by the head of a research laboratory as being able to be a 'chameleon – but with integrity'.

It is therefore perhaps unsurprising that one view of the effective leader of a creative group is that he or she simply fits in and provides whatever is necessary wherever it is necessary: he or she is a 'fixer', whose main role is to be or to provide whatever is needed, or as one job description (deceptively succinct) put it: 'Just give a hand where you can!'

Effective leaders of creative groups are like 'fixers:

- they are experts in their own fields;
- they are discreet and self-effacing;
- they are conspicuous as Visionaries and Ideas Generators;
- they are Team Builders and/or Coaches who support those who work with them and shield them when necessary;
- they often act as an Entrepreneur and as the Spokesperson for the group;
- they are warm and approachable, passionate and enthusiastic;
- they are usually democratic, though sometimes also manipulators;
- they are generous of spirit;
- they are very fluid in the way they work as leaders.

NOTES

1. Gardner, H (1996) *Leading Minds: An anatomy of leadership*, HarperCollins, London.
2. Keegan, J (1987) *The Mask of Command*, Viking Penguin, New York.
3. Cole, SL (1992)*Directors in Rehearsal*, Routledge, London.
4. Copeland, A (1952) *Music and Imagination*, Harvard University Press, Cambridge, Mass.
5. Belbin, R M (1981) *Management Teams: Why they succeed or fail*, Butterworth-Heinemann, London.
6. Brook, P (1993) *There Are No Secrets*, Methuen Drama, London.
7. Tannenbaum, R and Schmidt, W H (1958) *How to choose a leadership pattern*, *Harvard Business Review*, March–April.
8. Burton, H (1994) *Leonard Bernstein*, Faber and Faber, London.
9. Whatmore, J (1996) *Managing Creative Groups: what makes people good at it*, Roffey Park Management Institute, Sussex.

DS: Project group leader in a telecommunications company

DS, as Sales Manager, led a team in the systems division of a major telecommunications company in a successful and creative bid against other major suppliers for a large and complex project to link all NHS sites electronically, using existing (and widely diverse) hardware on each site, thus removing the dependency on large amounts of paperwork. A generator and shaper of ideas, and an arch sales-person, he inspired confidence through his technical competence; and he was a pioneer.

DS felt it essential to get the team to think creatively about every single activity on the project and to continually ask themselves 'How will what we are offering be different to that of the competition?' and 'Why will we win the bid?'

The team seemed to be split into two: the 'core team' (in which DS was much more interested), the people who were involved in the creative thinking and in identifying the strategic direction and tactics for winning the bid; and a 'secondary team', whose work was more procedural eg getting the necessary paperwork signed off and 'taking the dross away', who provided the 'core team' with the space for creative thinking.

One of DS's strengths was his willingness to pioneer, to 'work the system', a leadership style which those in the 'core team' found a refreshing and stimulating change, though the 'secondary team' found it slightly threatening.

DS established clear goals and responsibilities for the project and then let individuals get on with the details. He recalled that there was an unrealistic optimism about the bid, 'an expectation that the company would win the bid without much effort,' so he got the team regularly to revisit the questions: 'Why are we different?' and 'Why will we win?'

One of the initial challenges for DS was to win the team over to his way of working and to make use of his previous experience. He aimed to allocate lots of time at the outset for 'brainstorming, discussing and debating what the bid strategy needed to be,' and about what the customer might consider to be 'best value for money'. These planning meetings, DS recalled, were self-selecting: people joined who 'added value to the process', mainly from the 'core team', other members feeling a trifle bitter at being excluded. These and DS's style of management facilitated a shared appreciation of individual strengths, a strong commitment not to let others down, and a sense of involvement and of feeling valued.

DS pointed out that one of the tactics was to steer the customer 'to focus on the right things that were price sensitive', not only the initial hardware costs but also the on-costs of providing a full electronic messaging service. They developed a modelling programme which showed off their bid to advantage by demonstrating 'value for money'.

The team encouraged other suppliers to collaborate with them rather than compete against them, thus narrowing down the field of competition. They presented themselves to other suppliers as an extremely professional team, by demonstrating that they were on top of the IT and were confident in their ability to win the bid. They developed some simple but very creative means for achieving this. One was a consolidated contact list on laminated Filofax size card, instead of having to hand out a fist full of business cards. 'It looked very impressive but in fact was very simple and cheap to produce.'

In presentations to the customer, they aimed to 'draw attention to the salient facts' and to present information in a way which was noticeably different to other suppliers; by drawing upon image processing techniques and other pictorial aids, rather than using standard text slides.

DS provided a source of inspiration to the team, enabling and facilitating the development of ideas. He 'provided opportunities to get away from the workplace to talk about issues and scenarios,' and 'was not prescriptive and was willing to take ideas and contributions from others in the team.'

He aimed to get them to free themselves from the restrictions imposed by organizational practices by constantly challenging methods and techniques. The leader is so inspirational that you were naturally drawn to him to help shape ideas. Sometimes though you found yourself wanting to go and discuss every little idea with him; there were times when I had to stop myself doing that ... DS though was very good at making time for you, even if he was locked away somewhere, you could still search him out and talk to him.

Just as the team were drawn to DS to help them shape their ideas, DS was equally drawn to the team to help shape his own ideas, he was a willing sharer of embryonic ideas. However, he recognized his weakness of getting bored with ideas before they have been shaped into something which is tangible.

It was through his driving of the process and the task that DS provided his leadership, even after a Bid Manager was assigned to the project. He described the team-roles thus: 'Person x, he was Mr Researcher and Mr Questioner, and Person y, he was Mr Process.' Once responsibilities had been defined, then the 'core team' was very much left to get on with the details themselves, but each acted as a sounding board to the others, though DS did get more involved in detail with the 'secondary team'. '[DS] achieved things through persuading and influencing people as to what needed to be done'... 'by informing rather than telling'.

He inspired confidence amongst the team, customers and suppliers by demonstrating his ability to grasp complex and technical issues quickly, and through his ability to spot gaps or flaws in arguments. However, in doing so, the goal posts could get shifted, which some colleagues (especially in the secondary team) could then find difficult to keep up with, and hence threatening.

He believes that most people don't present arguments in a logical way because, although we all use the same words, we frequently ascribe different meanings to them, and this can prevent a common understanding. He uses several techniques to overcome this, including breaking each argument down to arrive at the underlying premise, presenting information in pictorial form, and making extensive use of analogies.

The team agreed that the key roles were those of Ideas Generator, as this was the raw material from which they were able to out-think the competition; Salesperson, as this was essential for building the rapport with the customer, to the extent that the customer was so confident and comfortable with us that they 'wanted us to win'; Technical Expert, as it was important to be seen as 'wheeling out the technical expert', particularly when dealing with customers and suppliers, and finally, Pioneer, individuals who were prepared to 'work the system'. 'We didn't have a set way of doing things... we threw the book out at the start, but filled it out later. We were all mavericks, a bid project needs mavericks... this caused conflict with others who saw the process as an end in itself.' And DS was a key player of all of these roles.

Dr AC: Head of a family-oriented mental health service

Dr AC headed a small unit in an NHS Mental Health Trust, which focused on families and on the individual in the context of his or her intimate and other relationships. An Ideas Generator, dominant, part author, designer and star, and a multi-role player, iconoclast and dialectician, with his main interest that of trying to make sense of madness, he led a group which welcomed ambiguity and was in constant perturbation, and which encouraged learning and self-development, a successful and creative group, of which he was the initiator, shielder, protector and preserver.

His influence was achieved through his interactions with other members of the staff, and he dominated meetings, imposing structure and an awareness of time management. He led his weekly staff meeting from his central chair which swivelled and allowed for him to act as a conductor, turning his attention to the speaker and taking the others with him, effectively giving people the floor.

He encouraged open debate which is managed constructively, so that different voices up and down the hierarchy could be heard and different perspectives seen. He quickly cut short avenues of enquiry which he saw as being non-productive. He challenged the assumptions on which ideas are based, with the intention of strengthening their foundations. He accepted and followed ideas through, turning ideas into actions. He encouraged creativity through open debate, openness to ideas, focusing on dilemmas and encouraging people to think outside the specified problem, and by the application of new techniques.

One member of the group commented that 'the culture [here] is one of keeping things in perturbation – fluid and creative'; of simultaneously providing order and chaos, for instance of 'sticking rigidly to the agenda and more subtle chairing skills'. 'A culture of contradictions.' 'A tight structure allows more views to be heard. Structure creates the opportunity for spontaneity.' And 'when [clients] feel unsafe, it is irritating, more tiring'; 'you have to contain the stress'; 'and when it becomes too tiring, [we] sleep'.

'But that is what gives you respect for the work and helps you to keep stretching and developing; or else you are not challenged. You don't realize how much you value [this atmosphere] till you go for for another job; it is then that you appreciate it and the openness that makes it all possible.'

He encouraged individuals to use their full potential. He encouraged freedom at work, freedom to speak openly and freedom in work practices.

He was 'dogged bloody-minded': he used 'directing, persuading, nagging and chasing up' as significant elements of his style.

'There is always "jolly conflict" here,' he observed, 'and from time to time, quite high levels of conflict, which though painful, are positive and creative.' 'The person in the team who acts as the mediator of anxiety depends upon the context and the issue.' The unit felt that it had been under siege for 20 years in its NHS

Trust. 'Our model of treatment arose like a phoenix out of a maverick group – which ultimately closed down. It survived because of its specific approach, which was at variance with the then thinking in mental health; but now there are needs for more of this type of unit.' 'But our fantasy is much more realized now,' said Dr C, 'because we have been given a respected place within the Trust.'

The atmosphere was described as frank and open, encouraging and supportive; but it was also tense and pressurized. The culture was one of providing a structure within which uncertainty, paradox and controversy, allied with support, challenge and constructive debate, made it all possible, very worthwhile and satisfying.

The place seemed to breed people with the kind of process skills that supported its particular culture. In one group there were at least two and sometimes more people who played each of the key team roles almost equally well, as Ideas Developer ('crystallizes thoughts, builds on ideas'); Constructive Critic ('challenges assumptions; perceptive, evaluates'); Wrestler/grappler ('right at the heart of the project, tackling big issues, dynamic'); and Team Builder ('builds team spirit, encourages openness'). Dr C was seen as making the most important contribution on all the most important roles (along with his appointed successor), indeed on most of the team roles except that of Shielder ('shields team from politics and bureaucracy'), where he did the job alone.

JS: Film director – directing a television series

In directing three programmes in a *Police* series for BBC TV, JS was a helper of those who could help her to present her (clear) vision 'of the world in which it is believable that these people live', and always a seeker after challenges, both technical and process, which would help to express that vision. An Organizer and Planner, creating an atmosphere which felt controlled yet open to spontaneity, she was also sensitive and shy. Enthusiastic and demanding, she was a conscious manipulator of people. The group rated the productions creative and successful, and the programmes had received very good viewer ratings.

She 'had a very clear idea of how she wanted to shoot the material'. 'Yes, I have a very good visual imagination and memory – no other memory!' 'JS knew what she wanted but was going to use what people did best to achieve it.' 'I am conscious,' said JS, 'of structuring early work in order to convey my vision. The "vision" is the world in which it is believable that these people live; and that vision evolves over time – from all sorts of conversations, discussions and meetings.' One person commented that, 'Some directors won't disclose anything – but they have a right to keep it secret;' to which she responded: 'I think that to keep secrets like that is patronizing and manipulative. To share enables the relationships to develop.' 'As well as working with my vision, I would like them to think that the vision grows organically, and becomes better than the initial idea.'

Always interested in challenges, she had sought to find a way of hanging the camera inside the police van so that she could capture what was happening there while it was on its way; and she had arranged for the actors, who were to be in the van, to participate, before shooting started, in a team building course to enable them to get to know each other well enough to be able to swear at one another without offence, and she felt that this had saved a least a fortnight of rehearsal time.

She pays great attention to detail (organizing meetings, sketches, drawings, etc) and is a thorough planner. Her plans are operationalized through precise instructions and demanding goals. 'The feeling that the Director has researched everything, puts you on your mettle.'

She is open and collaborative, with team members feeling they can make suggestions in all areas. There was 'no anger around, no need to hide true feelings because they didn't threaten others'. She was 'approachable, friendly and understanding'; 'provided the goals are clear, to contribute to achieving them does not threaten, and pays tribute to their skills'. Not extravagantly social, she also felt that she related best by doing.

She is sensitive to the needs of team members and to the problems they might experience. She is 'very aware of how the creative process works with actors and how to make it work'. She 'knew her strengths' and was 'good at choosing people to work with, and didn't try and control something she didn't know about'. She 'finds (with the conscious consent of the actor) images of what excites actors', and 'helps them find themselves in their characters'. She 'deals with people's insecurities in the context of the work in hand'.

While maintaining tight control over direction, she also understands the importance of spontaneity and remaining flexible, and has a sense of when to let things develop 'out of the moment'. She 'gave you a complete interpretation, so through organic movement, you could end up somewhere you had not considered at all – an unartificial, unpresented performance. She is 'very in-the-moment; comments, references, similes all relate to what is happening now'. 'The freedom of it is in how we all respond to it in the moment.'

She is a 'Director of integrity – she is unwilling to give people special treatment (whether or not they have special talents).' 'The Director was the creative source in the film, interpreting the material.' She 'uses other people legitimately to produce performances'. She was 'very upfront with what she wanted'.

She is 'an enthuser and congratulator'; and her style was one of calm, and of gentle but firm suggestion.

She sets demanding goals to which people respond. She was 'very sure in what she was doing; ... inspiring and demanding high standards.' She was 'good at giving actors the colour, and getting them to come up with their contribution'. She 'extracted challenging demands for us from the story (for technicians)'.

She herself was well supported by her producer. 'I couldn't have been the leader I was without the Producer backing me at every turn, and without the freedom she gave me. It is rare to find such honesty and trust – combined with absence of ego. Most producers are concerned with monitoring what you are doing and changing the goalposts.'

A former art and then drama teacher, she was 'always interested in what makes people the people they are; and that interest is my lifelong vision;... and my interest is in what damages people and turns them into failures'.

She created an atmosphere that was enjoyable and exciting, at times, comfortable and relaxed, at others challenging and intense, but always under control, and conducive to high quality work and fine craftsmanship.

PART III

LEADERSHIP IN ACTIONS

5 *the leader as designer of obstacle courses*

USiNG THE CONSTRAiNTS

'The more constraints one imposes, the more one frees one's self of the claims that shackle the spirit.'

(Igor Stravinsky)

The best creative work is often done against the greatest constraints; the most difficult deadlines, the tightest briefs, the meanest budgets. The painting of the ceiling of the Sistine Chapel was carried out by an artist lying on his back for several years! Creative projects seem not to founder on constraints as much as succeed because of them.

CONSTRAINT AS A FEELING

Constraint, like freedom, is a feeling. One person's constraint may be another's freedom: if you have been in prison for ten years, to be stuck in a long check-out queue may be of the essence of freedom.

CONSTRAINTS USED AS CHALLENGES BY LEADERS

Persistent problems are inherently challenging just as they are inherently risky, and successful leaders of creative groups accept constraints by seeing them as challenges, where others see them in negative terms, as rendering the problem difficult or impossible. As one put it: 'I applied for this job because I wanted the challenge.'

Leaders are challenged by particular projects for various reasons: sometimes because of a deeply-held conviction or purpose, sometimes because an aspect of the project coincides with a current interest, or with an objective in relation to their own development, sometimes because it is an objective of the organization's, and of course for combinations of reasons.

The interest of one project leader was inspired by his profound dislike of 'the establishment' and its insensitivity to what actually happens; and of people's unwillingness to challenge accepted approaches – attitudes which stemmed from his early life. He was attracted by opportunities to challenge those situations, and by projects in which others would be empowered to do the same.

> ## I applied for this job because
> ## I wanted the challenge

Another in the Department of Engineering in a university, whose interests had evolved over various fields in the course of his career, was now especially inter-ested in teams and how they work, and saw in a particular project an opportu-nity to explore the significance of 'events', and their impact on the way teams change and develop. He was also attracted by the fact that people saw the pro-ject as difficult, by the lack of theory, the lack of funds and the attitudes of sponsors – they did not see it as so very interesting. All of these problems and difficulties he saw as challenges, though he also had an obduracy and a desire to challenge authority! Denial and refusal by others are often seen as increasing the difficulty and so increasing the challenge.

The leader of workshops in musical improvisation was inspired by 'the vari-ety, the unpredictability, and the independence. I like being creative, flexible, interactive, collaborative,' he said, 'being a facilitator has me on a wave.' Another leader of a project group in a division of British Telecom, was inspired by his desire not to travel a 'well-worn path', but instead to seek out opportuni-ties to work in non-conventional ways. For another, in an NHS Trust, it was change that provided his challenge.

THE CHALLENGES OF PERSONAL DEVELOPMENT

Leaders often see projects in terms of challenges in relation to their personal development: a film director saw her challenge in terms of being a better coach, and of getting others to buy into her vision; another, the leader of a tax team, saw her task as a personal test for her and her management and as an opportu-nity for her to work more with people (to understand their problems and relate to them), and to be more confident, and more creative in problem-solving.

Another saw his project as an opportunity for personal development, to learn to handle frustration and to deal better with people. The Head of Opera at the Guildhall School of Music and Drama said simply: 'My job is to develop talent: it's all psychology, not music!'

Leaders also see challenges in relation to their organization and/or their career. The leader of a new product development group in a chemical company was stimulated by the fact that this was a high profile area in which to work in the company, as fast-growing and key for the company; and he was stimulated by having a highly motivated and skilled team who really enjoyed the work and wanted it to succeed, as he was by the commitment and recognition that key people in the company accorded it. The head of a tax group in a large accountancy firm was inspired by the objective of being the first woman to have achieved that level in the organization.

One leader, the head of a department in a university, saw himself as nearing a crossroads, at which he would have to decide whether he was going to continue a research career in his own field of science, or move into one in the management of science; and he felt that in his department at this moment, he was falling short of his aspirations in both respects.

Not only do effective leaders see constraints as challenges, but they seem to match up constraints to the needs of individuals, so that they become challenges which those individuals use for the development of their own talents and skills ('setting hurdles at the right height'; 'change seen as challenge').

WHAT KINDS OF CONSTRAINTS?

Constraints can thus be seen in the context of:
- mission, aims and objectives ('clear goals, direction, focus'; 'a clear and concise brief'; 'matching objectives to situations');
- output (eg 'a uniform service'; 'a programme to do x');
- resources (time, money and people);
- process (structure and time management);
- medium (graphics, music etc).

These constraints can be in relation to individuals, to the team, the organization, or to the customer or client; or to abstract principles of various levels of generality (as in the story of the three stone-masons, the first of whom described his task as 'building a wall', the second as 'working on the contract to build the cathedral' and the third as 'building God's Kingdom on earth').

LEADERS SETTING CLEAR GOALS

Most leaders of creative and successful groups have among their strengths the ability to set clear goals, aims, objectives and responsibilities. As the leader of a research group in a medical school commented (whose group was seen as being one in which members had clearly defined roles and tasks), 'Some people need more clearly defined goals than others.'

CONSTRAINTS AS THE PROBLEM OF THE HOUR

There are also constraints which are the problems of the moment. I mention elsewhere how one team arrived at its destination to find that the kit which it was to demonstrate was inoperable. The challenge of the situation produced a solution which not only helped them to develop a new product but also 'kept them going for months'. A scene in Orson Welles' film *Othello* is said to have been shot in a Turkish baths because the costumes had not arrived!

Out of structure, spontaneity

And there are constraints which are the problems of the second. Structure provides opportunity for spontaneity and creativity, and security a solid base which makes people feel able to 'do the craziest of things'. The leader of workshops in musical improvisation commented that: 'Sessions do need leadership, to channel and focus ideas.' 'The parameters... had to be clear to everyone, so that they could be comfortable to come up with ideas'... 'giving an impression of security and safety'. A director of a film for BBC Television commented that: 'Only when you have got it all organized can you show your artistry – in the established performance.' 'You need to leave 5 per cent for inspiration of the moment.' 'I am too heavy-handed, yet people can get lost with too much freedom.' And in a mental health unit in the NHS, a participant added: 'The culture [here] is one of... simultaneously providing order and chaos... a culture of contradictions.' 'Structure creates the opportunity for spontaneity.'

SKUNK WORKS AS FREEDOMS IN EXCHANGE FOR IMPLICIT CONSTRAINTS

Perhaps what Tom Peters[1] has called skunk works (where small groups in organizations work away by themselves, unknown to the rest of the organization, on problems which are of special interest to them) are in essence groups which obtain a freedom by virtue of being hidden from the constraints imposed on the rest of the organization, but whose constraint is that they will, at best, lose that freedom if they do not ultimately deliver something of value to the organization.

LEADERS USING PARADOX AS A BARGAIN

So one of the effective leader's skills is being able to use constraints as challenges and then to give people the freedom to pursue them in their own way. It is one of the paradoxes of the job: you have to be able to argue one thing one moment, and its opposite the next, rather like being a good politician!

One leader hinted that creative people accept what Howard Gardner[2] has suggested is a Faustian bargain: they accept the freedoms they seek in return for the constraints which their organization or their domain of enterprise imposes. What matters to them is that the constraints they accept do not run counter to their 'intrinsic motivations', in 'pursuing their own life adventure' or in 'developing their talents'.[3]

To summarize, effective leaders of creative groups:

- see constraints as challenges as opposed to problems;
- accept this often in relation to their own development and the development of their talents;
- set clear goals and objectives;
- realize, however, that constraints can also be the problems of the moment or of the hour.

If those who work with creativity are seen as accepting a Faustian bargain – freedoms in exchange for constraints – it is unsurprising that those who manage or lead them have to be experts in the handling of paradox.

NOTES

1. Peters, T (1987) *Thriving on Chaos*, Macmillan, London.
2. Gardner, H (1993) *Creating Minds*, Basic Books, New York.
3. Lexington, MA and Heath, DC (1980) *The Psychology of Self-determination*, Lexington Books.

6 _freedom like weightlessness_

'Freedom as "boldness of conception".'

(Concise Oxford English Dictionary)

'It is nothing short of a miracle that the modern methods of instruction', wrote Albert Einstein, 'have not yet entirely strangled the holy curiosity of enquiry; for this delicate little plant, aside from stimulation, stands mainly in need of freedom; without this, it goes to wreck and ruin without fail.'

Problems, paradoxes, ambiguities or controversies that are persistent demand to be looked at in new and different ways because so far they have not yielded to the new approaches that have been tried. Experimentation and play are common ways in which people look for new approaches that may be fruitful, and they often find one that 'looks promising', and which they will then develop.

Freedom from the constraints under which people have so far looked at the issue, and freedom to look at it in totally new ways are vital elements in the climate necessary for creativity. 'A generous level of freedom, in terms of time and resources, can encourage people to play constructively at work, to combine ideas in new ways that might not seem immediately useful in generating products or solutions.'[1]

THE ABILITY TO GIVE FREEDOM

One of the skills of effective leaders of creative groups is the ability to enable people to have freedom.[2] To quote from the members of one group in drug research:

'I had all the freedom.' 'I never felt I had a manager, we just exchanged opinions.' 'It was a responsible team who could be left to get on with the minimum of supervision (within their frame-work).' 'We have freedom as long as we get on and meet our objectives.' 'If it is going well, no management is needed.'[4]

And the same is true in basic science, in development, and in research and development, just as it is in healthcare, in training, in marketing, in music, in consultancy, in film making, and in radio and TV: in all creative worlds.

FREEDOM FROM... AND FREEDOM TO...

The psychologist Eric Fromm asked: 'Is Freedom a psychological problem?'[3] He compared the psychological growth of the individual away from its mother with the story of the Garden of Eden; and he draws the distinction between 'freedom from...' and 'freedom to...'. In the former case, the individual attempts to free him or herself from dependency, but the pain, suffering and isolation can be so great as to see individuals seeking new forms of dependency. By contrast, 'freedom to....' or positive freedom, he sees as consisting in the spontaneous activity of the total, integrated personality, most often seen in the artist, certain philosophers and scientists (in so far as they are successful, he adds!) and also in small children. It is, says Fromm, 'the one way in which man can overcome the terror of aloneness without sacrificing the integrity of his self.'

> **People cannot discover new oceans until they have the courage to lose sight of the shore**

Those who work in more creative fields speak about freedom from restrictions and constraints, as they do about freedom to experiment. The crew of a ship leaving port for the high seas feel freedom, freedom from all the constraints of being in port, and the freedom to go anywhere, and only at the behest of the wind and tide. So what is freedom, and why is it so important for creative groups?

FREEDOM AS A FEELING AND FREEDOM AS RELATIVE

Two important aspects of freedom are, first, that it is a feeling; and, second, that it is relative. Because it is a feeling, two people in identical circumstances may feel entirely differently about their freedom. For instance, a chemist used to the drudgery of laboratory analysis may find the task of devising compounds which might have useful therapeutic effects an interesting task, the freedom as a release; whereas a scientist accustomed to exploring the mechanisms of hypertension might find the same task a limiting one, as curtailing his or her freedom. It depends where you come from.

> **One man's freedom may be another man's prison**

And people who may feel equally free may find their freedom in different ways: one in freedom from close accountability, another in freedom to work whatever hours suit him or her.

Second, freedom is relative. One client's advertisement may have the freedom of being able to be designed in colour: another may have to be in black and white. An actor typecast for years in a soap opera may find his or her freedom in a Shakespearian role. Chains, as they say, cannot bind the mind; but they may do so!

CREATIVITY AND FREEDOM

Creativity seems to be closely associated with freedom: freedom to... experiment, to try something new, as an essential stimulant to creative output; to break the bounds, the habits, the limits, the rules, or more simply to do it differently. It is a truism of course that if someone thinks, feels or does something differently, he or she will make new connections (which of course may or may not turn out to be productive in creative terms).

As a feeling, its value seems to lie in being a metaphor, a metaphor for the removal of limits, somewhere between 'permission to...' and 'encouragement to...' experiment, to try something new. I am, for instance, continually struck by my art teacher's insistence on just messing around with something new, and as one participant put it of their leader: 'He gives us permission to be creative'.

> **Somewhere between 'permission to...' and 'encouragement to...'**

Freedom can be seen in one sense as a continuum on which empowerment is at one end and outright anarchy at the other. One team leader described his job as 'Authority and responsibility without domination and control', or seen from the perspective of the members of the team as 'space and trust'; an invitation to 'take the initiative' or 'do it your own way'; as 'freedom of expression,' 'to voice your view', 'to present it your way'; as 'having space where ideas can breathe'.

'Freedom to...' is expressed in a number of ways, including: 'Let's try something new!' 'Permission to go anywhere'; 'to be creative', 'to go into the unknown'; 'be prepared for the unusual'. Creative people also speak about the freedom to exchange ideas; about having a culture which is open, which encourages participation and promotes creative thinking; and where colleagues support, prompt and encourage others to exploit their freedom.

FREEDOM AS DIFFERENT THINGS TO DIFFERENT PEOPLE

Freedom means different things to different people and different aspects of it are important to different people. It can be about:

- their objectives – what they want to achieve;
- their tasks – what they choose to do;
- their methods – how they choose to do them;
- their roles – what parts they want to play in the team;
- their conditions of work – offices, hours of work etc;
- where, when and how they will work.

And there is, of course, that essential freedom, the freedom to make a mistake, as described of one great scientist – 'a breathtaking freedom to be wrong!' Individuals may need their own particular kinds of freedom to help them to be creative.

FREEDOM AS ABOUT...

Different kinds of tasks call for different kinds of freedoms. The larger the number of areas in which freedom is given, the greater is the opportunity for the members of a creative group to work successfully together by using all of those freedoms; but the greater also is the chance that they may fail and the project become disorganized.

Academics and artists are among those who have many degrees of freedom, including over what they will do and how they will do it. While their interests, beliefs and values are what attach them to their field of activity, and while 'you have to go where the subject takes you', the solution to one question tends to lead to one or more others, they do have the opportunity to pursue their own line of development, expression, research or enquiry ('much left to me to decide what to do'). For them, freedom consists first and foremost in deciding what questions one will seek to answer (eg Jonathan Miller asking how to enable modern audiences to understand a play with the feelings and concepts of the period in which it was written); and then in proposing how those questions might be answered, and finally, in testing one's solutions.

Degrees of Freedom – a Taxonomy of Freedom (4)

Areas of freedom	Advantages/Disadvantages
Complete freedom for a team to tackle a project – no task, roles, or methods specified.	Complete freedom allows potential for fluid roles and to find optimum role through informal organisation; but could result in chaos, anxiety or project drift.
Freedom for team to tackle project with neither roles nor method specified, but tasks stated.	Arguably the best potential for worker satisfaction and creativity with freedom over organisation and method, but the defining of goals/tasks supplies a focus.
Specified roles for individuals, but freedom over method, and no stated tasks.	High autonomy for an individual, requiring initiative and commitment. Careful matching of roles to tasks is crucial.
Roles and tasks are specified for each individual to perform, but there is freedom over methods.	Nice balance: efficient and goal-orientated; and the specifying of tasks and roles will mean that there is no ambiguity over who has achieved what, hence rewards can be clearly defined and deserved.
The task, the person to perform it and the method are all specified. The individual is trusted to complete the task.	Productive and likely to meet deadlines, but uncreative and frustrating for the individual.

In the arts, the possible approaches to a problem are many, or even (where the 'process' of creativity is a divergent one) infinite. In a workshop in musical improvisation, there was 'the freedom to take it anywhere, and learn from it'; in radio, the producer has complete freedom (he or she starts with 'an empty page').

In research and in development, in the graphic and the performing arts, the aims and objectives are often clearly defined, but teams have a broad freedom to choose how they can achieve those objectives. 'The supervisor provides overall direction but allows me freedom to work.' 'The responsibility rests with me.' While the aims and objectives may be determined to a large extent by the policies and by the resources (and in the knowledge industries, mainly the human resources) of the organization, there is freedom and a wide possible choice over the roles, methods/approaches and tasks which people may undertake.

In some project groups (especially in hierarchical groups), the members have roles that are more clearly defined, either by their particular skills, or by the hierarchy, whether defined organizationally, or by seniority. 'The staff move the project along, the leader doesn't have to.' In project groups, for instance in medical research and in marketing, where tasks and roles were well defined, there was freedom over methods.

In other organizations there is much less choice over what to do or how to do it: organizations whose output depends on a series of operations which have more or less defined patterns and standards, such as a production group, a construction or indeed an audit group. 'I complied with instructions, working within the group, we generated ideas.' Even in projects of this kind, people sometimes spoke about the 'freedom to choose to act... and where to act'.

'Freedom' can be about a number of aspects of the task: about the freedom that ample funding provides, 'the freedom over how we spend what we earn'; about freedom and trust, in the sense of being trusted to do what made sense or could be justified; about the way the manager does not interfere on a day-to-day basis; and about not being asked regularly about what has been achieved. Freedom is also provided by a leader holding back the normal (commercial or institutional) pressures so as to provide the 'time' and 'space' which are felt vital for creative output ('a womb'). Then there is the freedom to determine your own approach and your own work practices; the freedom to voice one's thoughts and views, to speak one's mind; and collectively, the freedom of 'being thrown together and told to get on with it'.

FREEDOM AS SELF-INSPIRED

Freedom of mind or of spirit is not, by definition, something which comes to order, for if it did, that would be the denial of itself. A feeling of freedom is therefore something spiritual, and something that comes, in some sense, from within: it is self-inspired. Effective leaders succeed in inducing people who work with them to find and use freedom for themselves, *inter alia* by encouraging their natural self-motivation, what Amabile has called their 'intrinsic motivation'.[5]

Those who work in creative disciplines are often very self-motivated: they expect to be responsible for what they do, how they do it, and for the development of their own skills and talents. They want to work where they will have the freedom to develop themselves and their interests as successfully as possible.

A CONTROLLED FREEDOM

Some people say that the best way to manage creative people is simply to leave them to get on by themselves, what one might call the abdication formula. Howard Gardner, in his book *Creative Minds*,[6] a study of seven exceptional creative minds, commented that he had been surprised in his research by the extent to which all of his subjects – from Einstein, to Gandhi and Martha Graham – had 'supporters' of various sorts, 'the intensive social and affective forces that surround creative breakthroughs', who might therefore be seen as exercising influence over, if not controlling the subjects of Howard Gardner's study.

> **Control with a very light touch**

If 'leaving people to get on by themselves' is a way of saying that effective leaders have a gentle and inconspicuous touch, this was emphasised by the chairman of a large advertising agency when he said: 'It is like horse-riding or skiing: the lighter the touch, the better they perform.' The same point is made in an intriguing study[7] of how a faltering R&D project was subjected by its manager to his increasingly tight controls, with progressively worse results, until finally there was no alternative but to abandon it.

THE PARADOX OF COMBINING CONSTRAINTS WITH FREEDOMS

Some of the finest creative work has been achieved against the greatest constraints; yet freedom is an essential ingredient for creativity. How then do managers/leaders succeed in handling this paradox?

One research director aimed to set the tone/the style/the atmosphere, and thus allow people to follow their own motivations about what they would do and how they would do it, but do so within the context of the organization and its objectives. One design house sets it out thus: 'Famous creative briefs are short and imaginative. For Coca Cola's classic bottle it was "Design me a bottle I would recognize in the dark"!' A brief picks out the over-riding priority.

It sets the tone. It hopes to inspire. And of course, it gives freedom by what it omits.

Leaders often use the same metaphor of their leadership style: 'you must not allow them to swim'; and in the words of a leader who ran workshops in musical improvisation: 'I give starting points and leadership. I used to try and shed my responsibility as soon as possible but they do need leadership to channel and focus ideas'; 'later, leaders do emerge in the group'.

> **Authority and responsibility without domination and control**

Effective leaders make extensive efforts to find out about the skills and talents of those who work with them, and the circumstances which suppress them or make them flourish, often using a wide variety of situations (special tasks, unusual visits, 'socializing') in order to understand what motivates, supports or inspires them, including what kinds of constraints act as challenges to them, and what kinds of freedom they seek. And they match up talents and skills to tasks so that the evolution or development of the former is a key factor for the success of the task.

One evidently symbolic way in which leaders encourage freedom (though also one which causes much contention in organizations where groups with different cultures are housed side by side) is by the removal of physical constraints on ways of working, such things as hours of work, time records, office furniture, travel and clothes.

FREEDOM AS NEEDING CONSTANT RENEWAL

Moreover, freedom as a feeling and as relative demands constant refreshment in terms of renewal. As the press never ceases to remind us, we get inured to freedom. So if the feeling of freedom is important for creativity, that feeling needs to be constantly refreshed by renewed feelings of freedom; and this both explains and provides a rationale for this skill in the effective leader of a creative group. He or she must encourage innovative experiences: improvisations and *études* in the theatre; brainstorms and visits; 'escapades' to or from parallel activities; exchanging of views and ideas, what Francis Crick in science described as 'gossip'; asking 'what if...?'; and encouraging people to be astute observers. And in project-driven professions, each new project of course brings a new opportunity for freedom.

To summarize:

- The effective leader has the skill of being able to provide freedom to those who work with him or her.
- He or she will distinguish between, on the one hand, 'freedom from...' the constraints and controls, and on the other, 'freedom to...' do what he or she wants to do.
- Freedom is a feeling and, as such, it is the personal feeling of an individual, and is relative to their other experience.
- 'Freedom to...' is a metaphor for 'breaking the bounds' that limit thinking about the issue in question.
- Freedom means different things to different people.
- Freedom may be about objectives, tasks, methods, roles and conditions (of work).
- Freedom cannot be ordered; it is self-inspired, encouraged by the effective leader.
- The most effective form of freedom is a freedom combined with very light controls.
- The effective leader has to be able to handle the paradox of successfully combining constraint with freedom.

NOTES

1. Abbey, A and Dickson, JW R&D work climate and innovation in semi-conductors, *Academy of Management Journal* **26**, pp 362–68.
2. Andrews, FM (1975) Social and psychological factors which influence the creative process, in *Perspectives in Creativity*, ed Irving A Taylor and J Getzels, Chapter 5, Aldine Publishing Co., Chicago.
3. Fromm, E (1957) *The Art of Loving*, Unwin Paperbacks, London.
4. Analysis of material produced from my research made independently by fellow researcher Neil Conway.
5. Amabile, TM (1996) *Creativity in Context*, Westview Press, Boulder, Colorado.
6. Gardner, H (1993) *Creative Minds*, Basic Books, New York.
7. Jensen, I, Jorgensen, S and Sapienza, A (1994) Skilled incompetence in the management of R&D: a paradoxical, prevalent and costly 'deficiency syndrome', paper presented at the R&D Management Conference 1994.

7

leaders using energy plus resistance to produce light and heat

SETTiNG UP TENSiONS

'An atmosphere that crackled with excitement.'

Tension is often seen as an important ingredient in the creative brew. What is its role in helping to generate creative outputs? One group asked itself how important it was for the success of the group 'to have this ogre, our corporate culture, to stick pins into'. Without clients and the pain, others asked themselves whether there would be any creativity.

Watson and Crick, for example, worked together in Cambridge on the structure of DNA, for which they were certain there was a Nobel Prize waiting for whomever first published a correct description. Their work was fuelled by being in fierce competition with Linus Pauling in America, of whose progress – advances and set-backs – they were in more or less constant cognizance, a competition which seems to have been a continuous spur to their productivity.

How significant was Beethoven's deafness, or Sir Stephen Hawking's disability? How significant is a disability in provoking the development of other faculties? Why do paraplegics become so talented in mastering new skills? Do not 'some teachers work by disorientation'?

The leader of a development project in multi-media, commented: 'People aren't cussed but they do need to have a tension; otherwise life becomes comfortable and easy'. On the other hand, the leader of a new product development group felt that people work better if you take the pressure *off* them. And the leader of a group in medical research sought to turn negative tension into positive by 'adapting the role of one individual, to avoid his abrasiveness.' Evidently different kinds of tension unlock creativity in different people.

TENSIONS IN SCIENTIFIC TEAMS

In one study, Pelz and Andrews[1] concluded that the more productive scientists and engineers did effective work under conditions that were in numerous ways not completely comfortable, but contained 'creative tensions' among forces pulling different directions:

- They were self-directed by their own ideas, and valued freedom but at the same time they allowed several other people a voice in shaping their directions.
- They interacted vigorously with colleagues.
- They did not limit their activities either to the world of 'application' or to the world of 'pure science', but maintained an interest in both.
- Their work was diversified.
- They were not fully in agreement with their organization in terms of their interests.
- What they personally enjoyed did not necessarily help them advance in the structure.
- They tended to be motivated by the same kinds of things as their colleagues. At the same time, however, they differed from their colleagues in the styles and strategies with which they approached their work.
- In effective older groups, the members interacted vigorously and preferred each other as collaborators, yet they held each other at an emotional distance and felt free to disagree on technical strategies.

In a well-known article,[2] Pelz set out eight 'tensions' which he and others found among some 1,300 scientists and engineers in 11 research and development laboratories, and which he summarized thus: 'Achievement was high under conditions that seemed inconsistent, including on the one hand sources of stability or confidence [what he called 'security'] and on the other hand sources of disruption or intellectual conflict [that is, 'challenge']. 'It appears,' he said, 'that if both are present, the creative tension between them can promote technical achievement.'

The tension between security and challenge

I quote the table of tensions from Pelz's article.

Table 7.1 *Pelz's table of tensions*

Tension 1

Effective scientists and engineers did not limit their activities either to pure science or to application but spent some time on several kinds of R&D activities, ranging from basic research to technical services.

Tension 2

Effective scientists were intellectually independent or self-reliant; they pursued their own ideas and valued freedom... | ...but they did not avoid other people; they and their colleagues interacted vigorously.

Tension 3

In the first decade of work, young scientists... did well if they spent a few years on one main project... | ...but young non-PhD's also achieved if they had several kinds of skills and young PhD's did better when they avoided narrow specialisation.

Among mature scientists, high performers had greater self-confidence and an interest in probing deeply.... | ...at the same time, effective older scientists wanted to pioneer in broad new areas.

Tension 4

In loosest departments with minimum co-ordination, the most autonomous individuals, with maximum security and minimum challenge were ineffective... | ...more effective were those persons who experienced stimulation from a variety of external or internal sources.

In departments having moderate co-ordination, it seems likely that individual autonomy permitted a search for the best solution... | ...to important problems faced by the organisation.

Tension 5

Both PhD's and engineers contributed most when they strongly influenced key decision-makers... | ...but also when persons in several other positions had a voice in selecting their goals.

Tension 6

High performers named colleagues with whom they shared similar sources of stimulation (personal support)... | ...but they differed from colleagues in technical style or strategy ('dither' or intellectual conflict).

Tension 7

R&D teams were of greatest use to their organisation at that 'group age' when interest in narrow specialisation had increased to a medium level... | ...but interest in broad pioneering had not yet disappeared.

Tension 8

In older groups which retained vitality, the members preferred each other as collaborators... | ...yet their technical strategies differed and they remained intellectually combative.

Source: Donald Pelz, Creative tensions in a Research and Development climate, **Science 157**, July 1967. Reprinted with permission.

TENSIONS BETWEEN...

Tensions can exist within individuals themselves, their own personal hurdles, or between individuals, up and down the organization (or across it) including within teams. They may be generated between individuals and teams (or organizations); or between teams and the organizations in which they are embedded; and they may be generated between teams and the outside world. There can be tensions between realities and ideals, and there is, of course, always potential tension between the infinite nature of objectives, and the limited nature of resources.

Tensions in individuals

There is the tension generated by the question of whether or not one can achieve a particular objective, illustrated by those who took part in workshops in musical improvisation being invited to dare to do something that they had not done before; also by the producer of an opera at the Guildhall School of Music and Drama, as 'setting hurdles [for his students] at the right height'. One leader commented on the importance of different situations for finding out how people react under pressure.

Tensions in teams

Effective leaders of creative groups make use of the tensions which result from having in the team people with different experience, different approaches, different views and angles. If, in a team, several people play the role of monitor/evaluator/critiquer, each may come at the problem from a different point of view eg one a bench technician, one a theoretician etc; and by doing so, they create a tension. The value of the dumb question, and of acting as the devil's advocate lies partly in the tension that they create. One leader talked about his objective of creating constructive conflict within the team, but focusing it upon achieving one of the objectives for the development of the team itself.

Tensions with the world outside

Creative groups have characteristics which differ from the rest of the organization, especially where small creative groups are embedded in larger organizations. A group of consultants who used psychodrama was embedded in an orthodox accounting firm; a multi-disciplinary 'early intervention service' worked away in a corner of a National Health Service Trust; and the Department of Performance Studies in the Guildhall School of Music and Drama had a culture which was noticeably different from the rest of the school.

Because these groups espouse objectives which are at variance with those of the main part of the organization, they are felt to threaten and be threatened by the organization. This causes tension from, at one extreme, hostility through strong emotion (perhaps a sense of vulnerability), to, at the very least, argued response.

TENSIONS ABOUT...

Professor JP (see page 20) used complexity as a source of tension, inviting his colleagues to supper and then presenting them with a major problem. Others used challenge, one (a psychiatrist) focusing on contradictions and dilemmas, another (a film director) looking for technical challenges. Several leaders used opportunities created by adversity; one, an overseas visit in which the kit to be demonstrated was lost; another, where bad weather imposed a style upon a photographic shoot; and another (a film director) used the pressure of tight time schedules on her film shoots, as she put it, to 'prevent the situation from becoming so comfortable that nothing [creative] happens'. In another case, in broadcasting, it was the difficulties of doing justice to a good idea and of fitting it into the format of a regular programme that had been the mainspring of the creative solutions which eventuated.

Creating constructive conflict

Many, if not most people mention deadlines as the source of tension which has the greatest impact on them,[3] but while deadlines may be important, they are less so in creative groups.

A member of one group commented: 'It is hard to say where the ideas came from – often out of conflict in the group.' One leader commented that 'it is the ambivalence between what kind of organization we are that causes the tension... I have a tension between my roles' which were different in relation to different parts of the organization. 'I see crisis and recovery as a good mythology,' added another.

TENSIONS – AS POSITIVE OR NEGATIVE

Tension and pressure can be negative as well as positive. In several groups which were surprisingly unsuccessful, the tensions were all of a negative kind:

there were personal disagreements, where members of the group did not have the same aims and objectives for the group, and where the group even felt that they had two briefs. There are other groups whose relationship to their organization causes frustration because of lack of time for the job, or because of asynchrony, having to wait months to get approval for the next step. Sometimes anxiety and frustration can be detrimental to a project, and at other times, they can act as a stimulant to creativity.

LEADERS USING TENSIONS

Making conscious use of tensions is of course itself a risky part of the job of leading a creative group: it involves knowingly leading the group into pain and difficulty without any certainty that to do so will be productive. It requires confidence as well as a depth of understanding and empathy with those concerned.

Sometimes leaders seem to be passive recipients of the gifts of tension and pressure; at other times leaders wait for it to happen ('looking for and using crises, milestones'); and there are yet other occasions when leaders court them.

In one group in an NHS Trust, 'differences of opinion are encouraged and shared, and seen as a way of developing the team through debate and discussion.' In another group in the same NHS Trust, the leader, a psychiatrist and self-confessed iconoclast, and his group consciously use 'paradox, controversy and ambiguity, focusing on dilemmas, and challenging assumptions – a culture of contradictions', in which the group engrosses itself, and from which it gains 'achievement and satisfaction', and which 'encourages learning and self-development'. In a third group, working to develop training programmes, the leader makes opportunities for his group to have a bit of fun and go off somewhere on an adventure. He then looks for situations which put the group under pressure and squeezes the opportunity in order to get the best out of it.

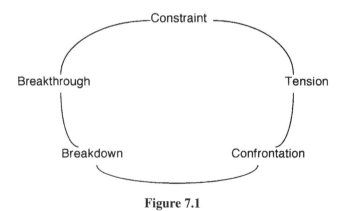

Figure 7.1

As the Head of an IT company put it: 'Out of tensions come new dimensions of freedom.' He saw creativity as the outcome of a cycle, a cycle which led from constraint, through tension, to confrontation (overt but not adversarial); and thence to breakdown, through which came breakthrough (see Figure 7.1).[4] 'I prefer a "let's see what happens" approach,' commented the leader of a workshop in musical improvisation – whereas PW will even let a session grind to a halt [if it is not achieving creativity]. One participant put it thus: 'sometimes the pressures can be so intense, that you need a release from them.'

In summary:

- Different circumstances cause tensions in different people.
- In science, there is a number of 'tensions' whose presence makes for high levels of achievement – tensions between security and challenge.
- Tensions can exist within individuals, between members of teams, or between teams and the outside world.
- Tensions can be caused by problems, issues, adversity, deadlines, crises; anything that makes for discomfort.
- Tensions can be positive or they can be negative.
- While some leaders act like passive recipients of their benefits, others wait for tensions to happen; and yet others court them, in spite of the risks they run in doing so.
- Some leaders orchestrate (or perhaps improvise with) tensions in ways which they believe will bring the best out of the individuals and the team – by making and using situations and opportunities for things to happen, where metaphor and tension will be at their most stimulating, even to the point of potential breakdown.

NOTES

1. Pelz, DC and Andrews, FM (1976) *Scientists in Organizations*, Ann Arbor, University of Michigan Press.
2. Pelz, DC (1967) Creative tensions in a Research and Development climate, *Science* **157**.
3. Amabile, TM, DeJong, W and Lepper, M (1976) Effects of externally imposed deadlines on subsequent intrinsic motivation, *Journal of Personality and Social Psychology* **34**, pp 92–8.
4. Csikszentmihalyi, M (1975) *Beyond Boredom and Anxiety*, Jossey-Bass, San Francisco.

8 *ideas prompters and shapers*

CREATiNG STiMULATiON

'The reason for your complaint lies... in the constraint that your intellect imposes upon your imagination.'

(Johann Schiller)

Many leaders and managers are concerned today to stimulate more creativity, innovation or change in their organizations. Convergence in the information technology, telecommunications and media industries is but one example of how rapid change can beset industries. Organizations respond differently to the forces of change: some are fleet-of-foot, others are plodders. 'Change managers' and line managers alike are increasingly concerned to generate more creativity and to bring about more innovation.

In Chapter 3, I discussed the importance of choosing issues, as questions that have resisted solutions (problems, paradoxes, controversies and ambiguities that are persistent), and of choosing issues that may have widespread impact, that may unlock other issues, and are of public interest. In the diagram below, I have called this task: 'selecting issues that are rich, ripe and rewarding.' Moreover, there is little advantage in solving the problem of how to get from A to B, if for strategic reasons you should not be in that world at all (see Figure 8.1).

I discuss later (Chapter 11) the selection of people to work in creative groups together, including the importance of motivation, of ensuring that projects on which people are engaged also help to meet their own interests and aspirations, as well as their own development. If their ideas are not appropriately recognized or rewarded (see Chapter 13), or are unlikely to be used or put into effect, or are risky and reflect uncertainty on their own future, people will switch off; they will simply not be interested in producing ideas. I discuss how

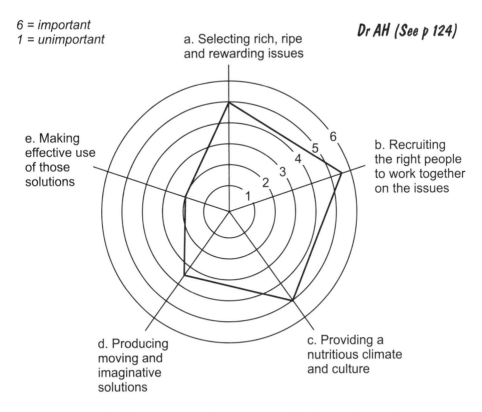

6 = *important*
1 = *unimportant*

a. Selecting rich, ripe and rewarding issues

Dr AH (See p 124)

e. Making effective use of those solutions

b. Recruiting the right people to work together on the issues

d. Producing moving and imaginative solutions

c. Providing a nutritious climate and culture

Figure 8.1 *Issues in generating more creativity, innovation or change*

climates are created in Chapter 13 and in Chapter 14, I discuss what I call 'hostile organizational cultures'; these too can act as deterrents to creativity.

If the problem in the department or in the organization is a lack of ideas, then the skills of the Ideas Prompter come to the fore. Enthusiasm and interest in other peoples' work are what distinguish Ideas Prompters, and then they need to use their ability to communicate a vision of 'where we are going', and to express clear aims and objectives. They need to be aware, whether instinctively or explicitly, not only of how other people feel, but also of how they learn and how they think, as well as what sorts of things stimulate them or act as catalysts for them.

Understanding what kinds of intelligence a person has (Howard Gardner[1] sees intelligence as of at least seven different kinds); which senses and what style someone prefers to use in their learning (Noer[2] has shown how some people prefer to think about an issue, others to feel their way into it, others to talk to people about it, and yet others simply to take action); what sort of a learner they are (in Honey and Mumford's[3] terms activist, reflector, theorist or pragmatist); what kinds of creative thinking they are skilful at (in Kirton's[4] terms, adaptors or innovators); and what thinking styles they prefer.

Robert Sternberg[5] describes four thinking styles which he describes as: the Monarchic, like Scarlett O'Hara, single-minded and driven; the Hierarchic, which is motivated by an hierarchy of goals, between which such thinkers prioritize their resources carefully; the Oligarchic, who are motivated by several competing goals of equal perceived importance; and the Anarchic, who are motivated by a wide assortment of needs, which are often difficult to sort out. He also describes three functions of thinking styles: the Legislative, the Executive and the Judicial.

DeBono, among his many writings about thinking, has used the graphic picture of the six thinking hats,[6] each of a different colour: white hat thinking is neutral and objective and is about facts and figures; the red hat gives the emotional point of view; the black hat covers the negative aspects, like why it won't work; the yellow hat is for positive thinking; the green hat is for creativity and new ideas; and the blue hat is for control and the organization of the thinking process.

There are at least three characteristics that make people good Ideas Generators; and skilful leaders can foster them. Ideas Generators are people who can look at an issue in a variety of different ways, who have a high tolerance for ambiguity, and who have associative minds. People who continue to play with the question, by re-examining it, redefining and refining it are often more successful at finding creative solutions. Being able to tolerate high levels of ambiguity is an important skill that is well recognized in science. Leaders need to keep minds open, and be interested in everything and anything that is going on, so that people remain observant, as was Fleming in making use of the unexpected growth of mould on his cultures on the way to his discovery of penicillin. And minds that do not necessarily follow linear patterns, but (consciously or unconsciously) make links with other thoughts, concepts or ideas, tend to be more expert in generating new ideas.

> **Creativity is the outcome of the free inter-play of differences with equal rights to be different**

Then leaders need to ensure that people have plenty of opportunities for their imagination to 'take a walk'; to experience things that are new or different. There are many approaches for doing this: the physical (visiting new surroundings, reading new material, meeting new people, exploring new situations), and the mental (imagining the strange, the absurd, the impossible).

Among the former are visits to conferences, reading literature from different fields (biology and science fiction are common ones), meeting other people who work in related but different fields, visiting other experts in one's own field, foreign travel, internal sabbaticals, changing roles etc.

Among the latter are techniques for structured problem-solving, such as re-defining the problem, imagining the impossible, using metaphors, similes and analogies, using random triggers, from the immediate environment, from a new environment, from the telephone directory or from specially devised computer programs; and many varieties of brainstorming, whose selection depends on the nature of the problem, the kind of solution that is likely to be acceptable, the process, and the participants themselves (see for instance, Townsend and Favier[7] – for lots of ways of generating ideas).

One project leader commented that in the early stages of their work on any given project, he aimed to flood his team with stimulations. Gryskiewicz[8] has written about the need for organizations to maintain a high level of 'turbulence', an atmosphere in which new information is able to have a creative impact on the organization, to which he attaches two dimensions, difference and speed. The greater the difference between existing information and new information or the greater the speed with which new information arrives, the higher the level of turbulence in the organization.

Some people, especially in the visual/graphic arts – in advertising, architecture and design – see 'inspiration' as a very individual and personal thing. Others find that they work better in groups, that their creative abilities work best when they are working with other people. They find each other's ideas stimulating and encouraging so that they work best by building on each other's ideas.

Begin looking through different eyes at the world around you

Some find their sources of inspiration in one kind of place, others in other places; for instance, some find people either inside their group or outside it, either individually or collectively, as their prime source of inspiration; others find the literature, ie other work in the same field, a source of inspiration; and yet others find events, situations, 'escapades', happenings etc as their best stimuli for ideas. JP's group (see page 20) found their trip to Amsterdam, when they mislaid the kit with which they were to make a presentation, creative and stimulating far beyond their expectations.

An Open University project about sources of inspiration identifies artefacts, images and objects (and, it may be added, happenings) as sources which are commonly used, and a Roffey Park study shows how Directors often get their ideas in neutral locations and non-work settings. 'The artist whose mind is richly stored with impressions suddenly meets something which profoundly stirs him... and what is called a flash of inspiration occurs: he conceives a work of art.'

And then there are several stages to the creative process, which have been described as: 1) information; 2) incubation; 3) inspiration; and 4) selection. Sir Joshua Reynolds, in describing how the successful painter interacts or plays with his subject to bring about an inspiration, says that he: 'first makes himself master of the subject he is to represent...then he works up his imagination into a kind enthusiasm, till, in degree, he perceives the whole event before his eyes, when quick as lightning, he gives his rough sketch on paper or canvas. By this means his work has the air of genius stamped upon it.'[10]

Ideas often come... in a semi-conscious state

What is common to many people who look for ideas is the way they go about it and the way ideas seem to come. Many creative people talk about how they will review the parameters of the problem and then consciously put it to one side. Ideas often come, they say, when they are in a semi-conscious state, either in dreams, or in semi-waking or when they are thinking about or doing something else; and some can identify and move into the kind of mood in which they find this creativity.

Edward Matchett, commissioned by the Science Research Council of Great Britain to research the secrets of the 'creative mind,' once entreated:

> Begin looking through different eyes at the world around you...You must practise for hours getting rid of familiar names and labels... Look at the spaces between and at the shadows rather than looking at what you had considered obvious until now. Mentally crawl inside and amongst these things and also view them from miles away and from every side. Mentally blow them up and delight in watching them explode, collapse and curl over. Play music to them in your imagination. Dance with them and laugh as you enjoy the dance...Work at simply melting familiar forms. Treat it as a game. The act of creation should always be enjoyed... Such is the way of working that our creative giants have enjoyed.

Isaac Newton's approach involved not so much concentration, effort, striving, forcing or wrestling with a problem, but 'relaxing, floating, playing, visualising, mentally becoming part of the situation, joyfully watching and waiting, patiently observing, letting the thoughts think themselves, letting the structure open up like a flower in the warm sunlight of the imagination'.

David Stuart, in his book *A Smile in the Mind*, on design, comments that each of the twenty-six designers he interviewed had their own formulae (or heuristics) upon which they could generally rely in order to come up with an idea of some quality or other, and while some of them would then use that idea, others might set about working up one or more of their ideas.

Some project leaders (as 'Ideas Generators') speak about the integrity of their idea as appropriate for the problem and as whole and complete in itself, and they talk about the importance of communicating and defending that integrity. Others speak about how ideas are built upon and developed as they pass around the group, how the process of being creative is an incremental one, and people often speak about how new technical developments, and how the ideas and perspectives of particular individuals provide the inspiration for their own new ideas.

Projects often go through a number of phases, which can be seen in terms of the feelings they generate, thus:
- scepticism;
- enthusiasm;
- euphoria.

followed by:
- concern about slow progress;
- worry about lack of results;
- questioning of the very project itself;
- depression.

And then the up-turn begins, shakily at first, thus:
- first evidence of results brings encouragement;
- lack of further results renews discouragement;
- general feelings that chances are improving;
- breakthrough!

Scott Isaksen,[9] guru in creative problem solving, lists the skills of the Facilitator of such groups thus: he or she must:
- be clear about the role;
- have people skills;
- manage the content/process balance;
- leverage personal experience;
- manage the divergence/convergence balance;
- have appropriate personal qualities (eg positiveness, self-knowledge, humour, personal integrity);
- manage the logistics (of the group);

- be able to teach and train;
- match style to situation.

This chapter focused on the skills of helping others to produce 'moving and imaginative solutions', whom I have called Ideas Prompters:

- They can frequently see 'where we are going'; and are skilful at articulating aims and objectives.
- They are very aware of what other people feel and think.
- They foster the abilities in Ideas Generators: to look at an issue in a variety of different ways, to retain a high tolerance for ambiguity and to make use of their associative style of thinking.
- They aim to ensure that the atmosphere is one in which the speed and degree of difference in new information that comes into an organization is able to have a creative impact on it.
- They encourage people to understand what kinds of things inspire their creative sides, including whether they create best by themselves or in company.
- They encourage creative people to make use of their own particular approaches to being creative, including using periods of incubation, allowing the imagination to wander, and listening for ideas.
- They need to have a number of skills, not the of least of which are to be what one such person described as a 'process scientist'; and to be aware of the emotional characteristics of each stage of the creative process.

NOTES

1. Gardner, H (1993) *Frames of Mind: The theory of multiple intelligences*, Basic Books, New York.
2. Noer, DM (1997) *Breaking Free: A prescription for personal and organizational change*, Jossey-Bass, San Francisco.
3. Honey, P and Mumford, A (1992) *The Manual of Learning Styles*, Peter Honey.
4. Kirton, MJ (1980) Adaptors and Innovators: the way people approach problems, *Planned Innovation* 3, pp 51–4.
5. Sternberg, RJ (1997) *Thinking Styles*, Cambridge University Press, Cambridge.
6 DeBono, E (1992) *Serious Creativity: Using the power of lateral thinking to create new ideas*, HarperCollins, London.
7. Townsend, J and Favier, J (1991) *The Creative Manager's Pocketbook*, Management Pocketbooks, London.
8. Gryskiewicz, SS (1999) *Positive Turbulence: Developing climates for creativity, innovation and renewal*, to be published by Jossey-Bass.
9. Isaksen, SG (1992) Facilitating creative problem solving groups, in *Readings in Innovation*, eds SS Gryskiewicz and David A Hills, Center for Creative Leadership, Greensboro.

9

leaders as 'angels', midwives and caddies

HOW LEADERS PROViDE SUPPORT

'It's support that gives you the courage to keep going!'

Tackling problems that are persistent is a risky business: they often entail high levels of failure, and they offer no guarantee of success. Moreover, tensions can often run high. Creative people are sensitive people, and while some may be more resilient to failure than others, they need more support than those engaged on less uncertain tasks.

Oppenheimer, who from 1942 headed up the Los Alamos laboratory where the atom bomb was created, was a provider of support in a number of ways. 'He knew how to organize, cajole, humor, soothe feelings – how to lead powerfully without seeming to do so.' 'Everybody had the impression that Oppenheimer cared what each particular person was doing. In talking to someone, he made it clear that that person's work was important for the success of the whole project.'

SUPPORTERSHIP – AN UNRECOGNIZED SKILL

Supportership does not feature as such in management theory; indeed it runs counter to the somewhat individualistic ethos (as authority and responsibility accorded to individuals) of today's organizational practice. However, people work in teams more than they used to: multi-functional teams, multi-disciplinary teams and even multi-project teams.

Moreover, 'support' is a 'soft' area neither tangible, nor logical, nor easy to document. As one action man put it: 'Time spent on [this kind of thing] is nebulous, has no clear action-list, is a waste of time, and little of it is chargeable.'

And if a manager is more interested in the task than in people, as are many of those who lead creative groups (they almost always continue to be practitioners in their own fields), then supportership is less likely to be high on the manager's list of priorities, for among other things, it consists in 'giving time'.

What are the different ways in which leaders and team members support one another? Who gives support to whom? What do 'supporters' do? And where, when and why might they be particularly relevant?

WHO GIVES SUPPORT?

Support is most frequently provided by the leader, though sometimes it comes from a friend, and sometimes from a colleague. Effective leaders are skilful at identifying the support that group members need, and not only do they provide it themselves, but they act as role models in encouraging other members of the group to provide support to each other.[1]

In research projects, people talk of role models as their supporters, often managers for whom they had worked or of whom they had had experience;[2] and in music, in academia (and in industry) of mentors as supporters. In music the leader of workshops in musical improvisation saw his role as a 'Facilitator', as one of support, as did people who led project groups but were not themselves experts in that field. In sport, 'Coaches' and 'Managers' act as Supporters (both of whom often see themselves as acting as facilitators), and in many organizations there are managers whose role as a coach consists largely in providing support. Many 'Team Builders' are Supporters, and in all sorts of organizations. Then patrons, friends, colleagues, and even enemies can also be Supporters. Belbin[3] uses the term Team Worker of those who play all of these roles.

Howard Gardner, in his book *Creative Minds*,[4] expressed surprise at the extent to which all of his subjects – from Einstein, to Gandhi and Martha Graham – had 'Supporters' of various sorts, between whom he distinguished 'affective support' and 'cognitive support'.

HOW DO PEOPLE GIVE SUPPORT?

What constitutes effective support depends upon the context. Mentors help individuals to steer their way in organizations, companies or institutions, as they do in fields (eg academic or professional); Facilitators help people do things; Coaches help individuals achieve performances; Managers (in sport) help their teams by organizing things so that their team can perform at its best; and Team Builders build teams.

Above all, supportership is... giving time

But what kinds of things do they do? Above all, they 'give time'; to be with, to listen to, to see, read, or hear someone else's work. The more creative and successful groups see it as part of their culture and vital to the sustaining of creative process.[5]

Supportership

- Information provider – volunteering information or experience not known or available.
- Shaping ideas – 'why did you do it thus?' 'Have you thought of...?'
- Critiquing – giving criticism, praise or feed-back about a piece of work.
- Building confidence – recognising the qualities in a piece of work, and showing confidence in the originator's ability.
- Developing potential – making ways to explore and develop their skills.
- Speaking for... – supporting a case, a point of view or a piece of work to others – bosses, committees, authorities, peer groups etc; using one's influence on their behalf.
- Emotional support – sympathy or affirmation; acting as a confidante – as someone with whom one can share one's feelings and concerns.
- Physical support – helping someone to do something, or providing materials, space, equipment etc.
- Social support and shared values – caring for the person as a person.

'Information provider'

New members of groups, of departments or of organizations need support in finding out about their new environment, and about how they can get what what they need in it. Finding out takes time and effort, and support in doing so not only helps people in their work, but it also reduces the anxiety associated with joining something new.

New members of groups are often valued for bringing in new ideas, new enthusiasms, new points of view; and, if they are to be successfully integrated into the group, they need to be provided with information about their new environment.

Support received

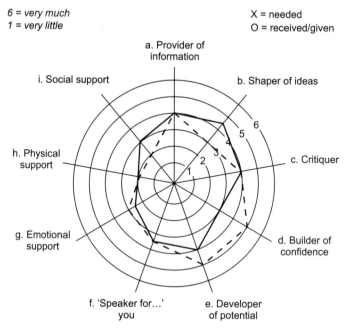

Support given

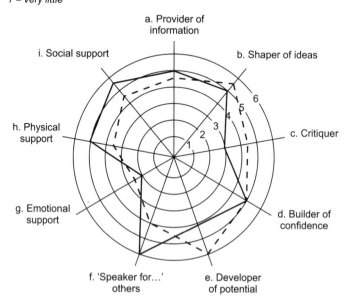

Figure 9.1 *Leaders of creative groups as 'angels', midwives, caddies*

An Olympic coach was seen as an information gatherer and so also an information provider to his team. A mentor (in music) was seen as passing on wisdom, knowledge and experience. A Sister 'presided over a sharing of information'.

... passing on wisdom

If creativity takes place at the point at which people see something differently, in different terms, they must inevitably be or have been exposed to new experiences. The interaction between those who come fresh to a group and those who provide information about the group is therefore a critical one, for, as one participant commented, 'if you look at something long enough, you will see it just like everyone else does!'

There is a balance between providing people with enough information so that they can do the job, but not so much that they do it like everyone else. A marketing controller described it as providing a framework within which her photographer could work. (The art of 'the brief' is course much discussed in advertising and design.)

This aspect of supportership is of greatest relevance in multi-disciplinary project groups, where the different disciplines interact in 'process' terms as well as in technical terms, and where mutual development of the participants in the group is an important ingredient.

Shaping ideas

After their conception, ideas need shaping and developing; they need to be built upon, honed and perhaps adapted. The more successful leaders of creative groups have the skills of helping to shape ideas. '[They] will sometimes bring the group back to reality, by saying "remember, if you do this..." or "what if...?"' And they are skilful at 'building on' others' ideas, and at encouraging other people to do the same. A radio editor commented: 'David just had an idea about that; why don't you go and talk to him?'

Asking: 'What would happen if...?'

Another radio editor – in sports – was described as very good at giving feedback in a way which helped people to develop their skills, as asking questions in a way that enabled you, the author, to think that the resulting ideas were yours.

And the leader of a medical research project was a great discussant – 'it was always valuable, entertaining and stimulating to meet him'; he was 'able to address the practical aspects of a visionary idea.'

Critiquing

When a piece of work has been developed to a certain point, the author can easily become too involved with it to retain the objectivity which makes him or her a good judge of the work. At that point, it can be invaluable to have the support of someone who is a good critiquer.

Constructive critics are people with whom one can share one's responsibility; they are '...available to test solutions with', and often it is something that members of a group do for each other. They adopt the role of the 'constructive critic' or commentator, which is so valuable because it is from a different point of view: the 'third eye' in a marketing company, the 'outside eye' in film making, 'another ear' in broadcasting, the 'third viewpoint' of the coach to an Olympic team.

Critiquers need to affirm what is good as well as being 'good at spotting flaws' (about three compliments before offering even a single criticism, suggested the leader of a design group, is the right sort of ratio for us!). One team member spoke of how valuable she found the Producer's red pen, as this had helped her to become more objective and creative.

Ideas need to have time to develop and flourish before they face the light of full criticism, and they need protection while they develop, what is often described as the incubation period. Critiquing comes into its role once ideas have been developed into a sufficiently tangible form for them to be able to be evaluated. Constructive criticism is helpful both in the development of ideas and for effective learning.

Building confidence

Confidence is a powerful force. Just as those whose confidence is low are less likely to be successful, so also those whose confidence is high are more likely to achieve what they set out to do. Supporters have an important role in helping to develop confidence.

An Olympic sailing coach was seen as a builder of confidence, someone who 'had confidence in our strength and ability', a radio editor as acknowledging that 'everyone that we work with here is intensely creative', and providing other people with a sense of reassurance and support. Other Supporters were seen as giving people opportunities to shine, and giving recognition to people's work (creative fields are awash with awards).

Creative groups are great celebrators of success; drinks and meals together, as occasions which also confirm their confidence in their performance and in themselves.

> ## Confidence as a launching pad

Confidence in people's ability 'makes you feel significant', and gives you a 'sense of security', from which you can perhaps be a little 'crazy'; that mood of spontaneous whimsicality which can produce creative ideas, or as one psychiatrist put it: 'out of structure, spontaneity'.

There are at least three situations in which this form of support is important: first, in groups in which individuals (or indeed the whole group) lack confidence; second, where there is an entrepreneurial element in the group's activities, and they have to be selling their project to others; and third, where there is felt to be a high level of failure, risk or personal exposure; (as in science – where many failures often provide a platform for an ultimate success; and in the arts – where the criteria for success are often various, mercurial and ephemeral).

Developing potential

Creativity and personal development are closely linked, and performers of every kind find it useful to have alongside them someone who can give them support in whatever aspect of their development is of current concern to them.

> ## Putting performers at hurdles of the right height at the right time

Coaches help to develop others by 'creating situations in which they can learn', most commonly identifying talent, setting drills and exercises, putting performers at 'hurdles of the right height at the right time' (Head of Opera at the Guildhall School of Music and Drama), and helping each individual to perform at their best by 'finding the right button' (film director). 'People give you clues,' said one film director, about how to get the best out of them. Of the Head of Opera, it was said that 'he understood what is needed to spur individuals into working harder and to develop their individual talents.'

This aspect of leadership – coaching in the development of individual talents – is especially relevant to projects where the creativity in the output is likely to be the result of one or more members of the group developing their talents and skills (as in the production of an opera by the Guildhall School of Music and Drama, or in their Workshops in musical improvisation, or in a sports team).

Speaking for...

Those who support you by speaking for you are likely to be able to do it better than you can yourself because they cannot be accused of self-interest: disinterested support is more powerful support.

People who work in creative groups need 'support in selling-in their ideas', and see danger in 'losing faith in people who represent you' as you then begin to lose faith in your own creativity. 'You get a feeling he will support a point of view, trust you and show appreciation... that gives you a sense of trust and confidence that you will succeed.'

'I look to you to make decisions and I will support you,' said one project leader. He provided 'approval of initial plans, and trust and faith in people', 'using his influence to get others to act in support of me.' An Olympic track and field events manager saw his role very much as 'influencing without power – consulting, getting support or advice, putting arguments forward'.

<hr>

A word in the right place

<hr>

Creative projects depend upon gaining initial support on the basis of what may be only the germ of an idea. And there may be all sorts of people in all sorts of relationships to the progenitors, who can influence the process of gaining support.

Effective support often consists in supporting someone simply for what he or she is known to be, sometimes a 'blind' support of their talents as seeing something in them that other people might not have seen, and supporting them though difficulty and failure until the uncertainty and the risk are past, and the results of their work can speak for themselves.

Projects of every kind must compete for life with alternatives, and in order to do so, they need to have enough form, shape and style to be able to gain followers and supporters. If the process of selection is heavy or protracted, resulting in many losers or in periods of uncertainty, enthusiasm and creativity are blunted.

Emotional support

Emotions are contagious, and another kind of support consists in the sympathy and understanding of someone else. An athlete pictured emotional support as helping you to pick yourself up when you were disappointed, which he called 'motherly' support; or as affirmation of yourself when you had done well, which he called 'fatherly' support. Athletes, he said, are very self-motivated, and resilient, as are many if not most creative people – their talent is after all their life-blood. Often, he said of motherly support, all you need do is help them by listening, until they have got over their disappointment. 'You need to reassure them that they are not the only person in the world who has failed!'

Encouragement is an important aspect of emotional support. 'He is optimistic.' 'His enthusiasm gives you motivation; helps you generate ideas. It shows you that he is keen for it to succeed.' 'When things are going less well, his enthusiasm to find out why it is not working is a real help.' 'Providing positive feedback is an element in enthusiasm.' 'Being made aware that it is worthwhile is another element in enthusiasm.' 'And providing recognition – by acknowledging people's work; getting them to make presentations is another.' 'And giving the project a high profile, talking about it a lot, both internally and externally.'

Emotional support as a lever

Confidantes help you when you are 'going through periods of intense change' as 'someone you could go and dump on if there has been a bad programme', with whom you could 'let off steam', and 'who would be willing to take the time to talk with you at the personal level'.

Creative tasks are felt to be tasks in which you expose yourself, make yourself vulnerable, in which you are 'naked'; creative people, dependent as they are on their talents, feel insecure. 'You are only as good as your last performance' is every creative person's nightmare.

Tasks which entail high risks, have high failure rates, strong emotional involvement, personal exposure, and critical moments (such as the events at which sportspeople perform, or serious casualties in an Accident and Emergency ward) are therefore likely to be those in which people need emotional supporters and confidantes.

Physical support

'Many hands make light work' and people who give you a hand provide support at many levels. Not only do they share the work and help to get it done faster but they make it all seem easier.

Effective leaders provide physical support – they will go and lend a hand when it is needed – by helping in experiments (on drug research and R&D),

cueing up tapes etc (in radio), filling in paperwork (healthcare), or 'sharing difficult work' etc.

Just giving a hand where you can

Physical support is also a metaphor for emotional support: 'when she is under pressure, I give her some kind of help'. Leaders also provide physical support in an indirect way: they arrange for resources to be available (people, funds, space, equipment), and they do so in ways that best suit the members of their groups: they 'facilitate' their performers.

Leaders who are providers of physical support are usually also Organizers. One was described as like an 'air traffic controller'; another as always there to help when needed; a third as 'managing events to meet athletes' needs and styles'; and a fourth as 'conscious of whether I need to offer help or not'.

Social support and shared values

The effects of exposure to risk are compounded by loneliness: to feel that you are treading a lone path is to make you feel even more exposed and insecure. Effective leaders also provide social support. 'He was as concerned with the social environment (and home) as the task.' Leaders 'talk about personal things.' 'She always started and finished [a discussion] with personal things.' 'People have a home life and home problems, and so... show that you are interested in people as people.' An important element of this consists in 'recognizing that we shared values'.

The closer people are in the group, the more members are likely to care about each other's aims and objectives; and therefore also about the development of their talents ('everyone helping each other... working for each other... wanting them to express their best qualities'). Understanding how people tick helps to show how they can contribute to a creative project group.

GIVING SUPPORT – WHO, WHAT, WHEN AND HOW

If someone who is part of a creative team needs support but does not receive it, their performance will be affected, so it is vital to identify and meet these needs, and to ensure that they are met by the person best able to meet them, and in a way that they need.

Everyone a provider of support?

Creative groups are characterized by the mutual nature of the relationships among their members. Anyone or everyone may therefore act as a Supporter of anyone else. Sometimes leaders are the providers of support:[6] at other times group members provide it to each other. Sometimes subordinates provide it, and at others times people from way outside the group provide it.

Support for what?

It will be clear what it is that a member of the group needs support for; at other times, it may need teasing out. And there are various aspects of individuals' lives in which they may need support; their aims, style, thinking, preferences.

When to give support

Physical support is of course provided in the moment; emotional support is needed when feelings are intense, often when something has just gone right, or wrong, and may need to continue. Help in shaping ideas is required as ideas are evolving, constructive criticism is best given in moments of calm reflection afterwards, and social support, at 'interim' moments.

Moreover, performers are more receptive at some moments than others: you must get the timing right. As one leader commented: 'If you misjudge the moment when you discuss things with them, or don't time your discussion right, or don't give the right time in the right place, you can blow the whole process: save it up for the de-briefing.'

People may need support at any or all of the stages of a creative project, for instance at the stage in which fresh questions are developed, at the stage of looking for new theories and concepts, or later, in looking for appropriate methods. And this is true in all creative fields, whether in science and technology, in the performing arts, in the graphic arts, or in sport.

How to give support

Sometimes support is best provided directly and sometimes best through an intermediary. While one film director talked about how the actor gives you clues about what kind of things will help, an athletics manager had suffered agonies of indecision about whether he should talk directly with the athlete or should offer his feed-back through the athlete's coach. An athletics coach summarized the matter more boldly thus: 'The question of giving feedback is something the athlete should have discussed with his coach before the games'.

People have their own characteristic ways of giving support, just as people tend to want and need particular kinds of support. Some are confidantes, some coaches, some critiquers. There are those who recognize and support your work, and there are those who provide a shoulder to cry on.

Successful leaders of creative groups are those who match up the group and the task in all sorts of ways (knowledge, skills, strengths, roles, styles etc), and it is important for them to match up those who need a particular kind of support with those who are adept at giving that kind of support. Moreover, it is all too easy for this aspect of process to be eclipsed by technical or task issues. Good supporters, like good friends, are good at recognizing what support someone else needs, and how to offer it.

NOTES

1. Kanigel, R (1993) *Apprentice to Genius*, The Johns Hopkins University Press, Baltimore.
2. Oldham, GR and Cummings, A (1996) Employee creativity: personal and contextual factors at work, *Academy of Management Journal*, **39**, pp 607–34.
3. Belbin, RM (1981) *Management Teams: Why they succeed or fail,* Butterworth-Heinemann, Oxford.
4. Gardner, H (1993) *Creative Minds*, Basic Books, New York.
5. Barnowe, T (1975) Leadership and performance outcomes in research organizations: the supervisor of scientists as a source of assistance, *Organizational Behaviour and Human Performance* **14**, pp 264–80.
6. Cohen, BP, Kruse, RJ and Anbar, M (1982) The social structure of scientific research teams, *Pacific Sociological Review* **25**, pp 205–32.

10

leaders as learning psychologists

SUPPORTiNG LEARNiNG

'I can tell you how to get a Nobel Prize... have great teachers.'
(Paul Samuelson)

There is something in masters' working styles and achievements that draws promising young practitioners to them in some way or other: they seem to be natural mentors. For instance more than half the 92 American Nobel Laureates in the period 1901–72 worked as graduate students, postdocs or junior collaborators under other Nobel Laureates. Fermi, for example, let it be known that he wanted to be approached by promising students, and in the end he had served as mentor to six laureates!

There is a close association between learning and creativity. While everything which results in a creative outcome is, inevitably, a learning experience, to be a good learner is no guarantee that you will be creative: you may simply learn things that others know already. Learning is a necessary but not a sufficient condition of creative output. It follows, however, that those who are more skilful as learners stand a better chance of being creative. In order to increase the chances of producing creative output, effective leaders give emphasis to and spend time on the learning/development processes of those who work with them.

Leaders of creative groups need to consider how important learning may be for the success of their project, what the learning may be about, how extensive it is likely to be and how difficult to achieve, and what kind of catalyst may be most effective. They also need to consider whether it is the learning of one or of more individuals in the group that is important, or of the group as a whole.

115

> ## Knowledge, talent and skills are competitive weapons of ever greater significance

It has become clearer to the corporate world that in an increasingly competitive environment, knowledge, talent and skills are competitive weapons of ever greater significance, so managers have focused increasing attention upon learning and personal development. But corporate policies about supporting personal development do not always translate into effective support, and project group leaders need to determine which aspects of this role are important in a given situation (see Figure 10.1).

6 = a very large part of the leader's job
1 = a very small part of the leader's job   *SG (p 169)*

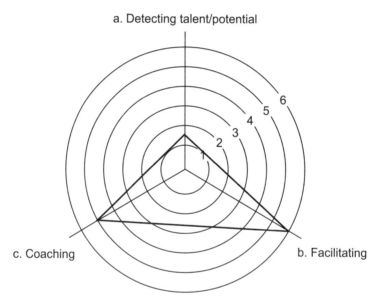

Figure 10.1 *Supporting learning*

This role is clearest in the academic field, indeed it is almost the essence of a 'teacher's' role. It is clearly identified in sport, as that of the manager or the coach. In other fields, the mentor performs something similar. While it is evidently a role that is vital in almost every kind of creative group, in most other fields it is not clearly identified, nor given a distinctive name. The creative director in advertising does a lot of it, as does the film director, and the director of a design project. Yet the fact that the role is not readily recognized suggests that its importance for creativity is not as fully appreciated as it might be.[1]

Even in sport, coaching is often bizarrely amateur; consider, for instance, distinctive characters like Brian Clough or Glen Hoddle in football and Bill Walsh in baseball,[2] sometimes achieving wonders with talents that happened to match the particular needs of a certain situation. The National Coaching Foundation now supports the development of coaching at all levels[3] in a world in which sport itself is undergoing rapid change.

Much of the development of this role has been carried forward by individuals, whose particular experience and ideas[4] have achieved this progress. There have been some parallel developments in the field of organizations relating to developmental relationships,[5] and to coaching,[6] and there are also useful parallels in learning theory.

LEADERS IN SUPPORT OF INDIVIDUALS

Detecting creative talent and potential

The leader of a very creative and successful project commented that one of his roles was to recognize potential: a member of his group commenting that 'a team of complementary weakness was its strength' but a group of people, he added, in whom the leader saw considerable potential. Another leader commented that looking for and supporting emerging talent was a central element of his job (see Figure 10.2).

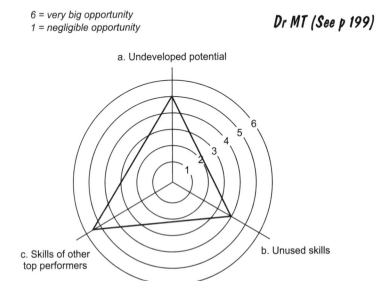

Figure 10.2 *Learning opportunities*

Experienced teachers of music, dance or drama can often 'see potential' in the way people respond, move or present themselves. Moreover their experience gives them the ability to look for (an 'eye' for) characteristics which are important for success in the field. They see skills and talents in people, they see raw material which could be used to build that person's abilities in their own field, and they know about how those skills and talents can be developed and what can be achieved by doing so.

Having an eye for talent

An Olympic manager felt he was 'good at spotting talent because I have that skill in listening and observing, and because I am able to get a mutual understanding with an athlete'. He recalled one occasion when his competitor – who had, in this particular contest, to beat all other contenders – was leading but unable to beat one other contestant. The manager saw something in a third competitor who was regularly beating this contestant, and suggested it to his competitor, who then won, he had seen a skill in another competitor which his own protégé could develop and use.

Facilitating and coaching

Leaders of successful creative groups tend to act as facilitators and coaches. As such they are Supporters (providing mental and emotional support, which they can do because they have a standpoint in which they are mentally and emotionally apart from the team); they are Organizers (whereas performers write the agenda, Organizers help to empower them to achieve that agenda); and they are Evaluators (gatherers of information, observers of the group in action, and providers of feedback, because they are in a position to see what is happening in ways that players themselves are not; a part of the team, yet not). They also act as Objective Setters, Co-ordinators, and Troubleshooters (see Figure10.3).

Facilitating

Facilitators find ways of enabling people with talent or potential to develop it, by setting things up so that they help and support them. 'Sometimes they need help to give of their best.' An Olympic manager 'was successfully devising routes to understanding how to support each individual athlete's aims, style, thinking, preferences, etc; providing support, and showing commitment for doing so.' 'He was continually taking stock, basing plans on circumstances in a

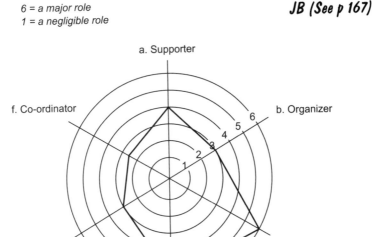

6 = a major role
1 = a negligible role

JB (See p 167)

a. Supporter
f. Co-ordinator
b. Organizer
e. Trouble-shooter
c. Evaluator
d. Objective setter

Figure 10.3 *Rules coaches play*

rational and calm manner.' 'He was good at pre-planning, organizing and arranging in advance.' 'If I can help, for instance, over the logistical obstacles, or help them to take their minds off thinking about their aunt's death...'

> **Continually looking for ways to help**

The leader of workshops in musical improvisation identified as a number of key factors for his success as a facilitator in these workshops:

1. He had to set the session in motion with the right energy at the first moment, so that everything could function successfully for that session.
2. He had to get the right balance between outright leadership and detached support.
3. He had to be aware all the time of what was happening, what people might be feeling, and make sure that the session moved forwards appropriately.
4. The parameters of the workshop had to be clear to everyone, so that they could be comfortable to come up with ideas, and know that they would be utilized.
5. He had to ensure that everyone would get a sense of achievement out of it.

6. He had to assure the quality of musicianship, by briefing the professional contributors well, so as to use their musical skills; and, by leading by example, 'lift all the participants out' to a new understanding.

Coaching

Having identified talent or potential, Coaches must:
- help to motivate and inspire those individuals who have it;
- help to plan how to develop it;
- find and make the right opportunities to do so;
- help to find the right 'button' that unlocks it;
- help to evaluate and discuss performance;
- provide appropriate support all the while.

See Figure 10.4.

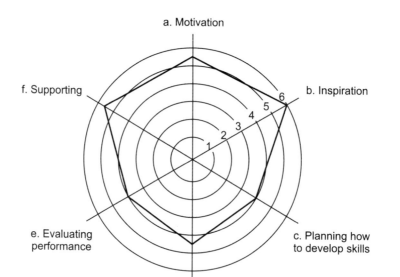

6 = a big part of the job
1 = a negligible part of the job

SG (See p 169)

Figure 10.4 *Elements of the Coach's job*

Said one coach: 'I motivate people by making sure that they know how much it matters. Often people will work on each other in that respect; and sometimes you pick people for the team because they will do that,' 'juxtaposing them with the right people'. 'And the success of one person can help to motivate the others.' 'It is a matter of helping them to know what talents they have and to believe in their potential.' 'Often people do not see the importance of their own performance in terms of their team, to outsiders, or in the development of themselves, and my ability to help them see that is an element in my motivating skills.'

Finding their hot buttons

'If you have been a leader, a captain, you know that athletes can be inspired, and you know that you can help that by creating the right environment. You learn how to help athletes produce their best performances; a captain can go wild in the right environment, and get his team to do the most astonishing things.'

'You recognize that there is a unity of purpose in... groups, and you respond to it so as to get the group to achieve what individuals could not. When things start going well, there is an effect on all the team members, and then your credibility increases and they listen more to the manager.'

'You can't create atmospheres: they just happen... They often don't just happen the way you want them; I can remember one in a Turkish bog. But situations can be unsurpassable for welding a team together; everything is an opportunity.' You recognize the opportunity 'through air and the fingertips. You recognize your heart rate rising, you recognize the stress of the moment, and the fact that you are in charge.'

The Head of Opera at the Guildhall School of Music and Drama commented that he had talent in front of him in abundance, and it was his job to develop it. Several leaders spoke about how it was their job to create the right environment for people to do well, and that they did that first by finding the right opportunities for them, by finding the right job for them, and the right project for them to work on. 'It is a matter of putting the right hurdles in front of people at the right time, and doing that for lots of people.'

They seek to set up challenges that encourage the development of these skills and talents. 'He was setting standards and providing expectations, and generating positive thinking'. 'There are so many practical considerations: the task is to fit each person in a way that will not wreck another person's opportunities.' (See Chapter 5.)

One leader expressed it thus: 'I like motivating inquisitiveness... and encouraging self-exploration, and finding ways in which they can understand for themselves.' 'By giving responsibility and guidance for them to learn for themselves, to learn by discovery, and then by letting them have a go... giving them "the dignity of risk".'

At that stage, it becomes a matter of giving them responsibility, or as another put it, of getting them to take responsibility in the process of which 'I give them achievements, good morale, and then space.' 'You can provide advice, but you have to leave it to them to work it out for themselves.' 'I try and keep discussions in our group as open as possible, not dominated by one person... and I try to get people to take more responsibility for particular tasks.'

Helping to develop their learning capabilities

'I think you learn from thinking about your objectives.' 'I help them to develop their self-critical abilities... becoming more self-critical.' 'The onus moves to them to take control of their work... set their own objectives, and plan and organize for themselves how they will achieve them.' 'I get others to work more independently, with more of my involvement to start with, then increasingly detached. Next time round she will need less help and I may ask whether she wants help on something, and then later, I will simply be responsive to anything she may ask for. Part of it is just being consciously aware of whether I need to offer help or not.'

An Olympic coach 'provided rational analytical de-briefs'. 'He provides feedback on intimate aspects of performance.' 'His appraisals are clearer, more thorough, more broken down.' 'He will say, "you need to work on A, B and C."' 'He has helped us to break what we do down into its constituent parts. Before, we didn't analyse our performance.'

A film director puts it thus:

As a film director, you are looking for keys to unlock the potential which every actor has. How do you find them? First, actors give you clues; and they'll ask how to do something and there may be clues in the way they ask. You may do improvisations; you may ask them to pretend they are someone else; you may ask them to try recall of something past; you may ask them to do some research into some aspect of the part or the play, the situation of the times.

Of another film director, it was said that 'she finds (with the conscious consent of the actor) images of what excites actors, and helps them find themselves in their characters.' 'She deals with people's insecurities in the context of the work in hand.'

The Olympic manager said:

I have found myself being able to make a suggestion that turns something round, that changes someone's perception. I can often put into words what an athlete wants to hear, what stimulates him or what he is not doing, or doing well that he should do again, or do more of. And if you use that skill only when you're sure about it, then you come to have credibility. It is the awareness of an outsider...

'He provided emotional support which matched the needs of the moment.' 'When they were down and their actual achievement had not met their expectations, he seemed to have a way of reminding them of what they had done well.' 'He provided encouragement to help me get through my problems ('motherly' support), as opposed to affirmation after success (or 'fatherly' support).' (See Chapter 9.)

'I regard the creation of that atmosphere in which everyone has their own plan as very important. So I aim to give them overall objectives, provide opportunities and light the blue touch-paper.' 'It's psychology, not music!'

Effective leaders recognize that:

- There is a close association between learning and creativity.
- In order to increase creativity within a group, they must spend more time on creating learning opportunities for individuals and for the group.
- They can achieve this through recognizing untapped or underutilized potential and enhancing it through facilitating and coaching roles.
- In the facilitating role, the leader can help each member to enjoy a sense of personal achievement from the group's performance.
- In the coaching role, the leader can help each member to develop motivation, by setting achievable intermediate targets for performers or by encouraging individuals to set their own objectives and planning how to achieve them.
- Creative output requires learning. Effective leaders need to consider where, what and how much learning may be needed in the context of their project; and then to contribute to learning by helping to detect talent and potential, and by facilitating and coaching the development of that talent.

NOTES

1. Clutterbuck, D (1991) *Everyone Needs a Mentor*, Institute of Personnel Management, London.
2. To build a winning team, an interview with Head Coach Bill Walsh, *Harvard Business Review*, January–February, 1993.
3. Whitmore, J (1992) *Coaching for Performance: A practical guide to growing your own skills*, Nicholas Brealey Publishing, London.
4. Hemmery, D (1991) *Sporting Excellence: What makes a champion?*, Collins Willow, London.
5. McCauley, J and Young, DP (1993) Creating developmental relationships: roles and strategies, *Human Resource Management Review*, **3** (3), pp 219–30.
6. Snyder, A (1995) Executive coaching: the new solution, *Management Review*, **84** (3), pp 29–32.

Dr AH: head of a research team in a medical school

Dr AH was the leader of a number of research teams in a medical school. The aim of this project was to discover the effects of particular drugs on a certain condition, as a contribution towards understanding the condition and so devising ways of treating it, and it involved clinical research with both in-patients and out-patients. AH was a Visionary, Ideas Prompter and Developer, and setter up of projects, who influenced the mutually facilitating style of the team through his own style, a team which was loose and dispersed, but one in which the roles were well defined.

Dr AH was the leader of a team investigating the effects of particular drugs on hypertension: theory-building rather than theory-proving. He was seen as exceptionally knowledgeable and as encouraging the exchange of ideas: he builds on his own ideas as he does on those of others. He listens with 'intellectual honesty and openness' to new ideas, 'responding positively to all input, until it was proved invalid or irrelevant'. 'You don't often hear "Bad idea!" or "Rubbish!".' He was also referred to as a 'Visionary' and as having played 'a major conceptual role' in the project. And he was able to address 'the practical aspects' of a visionary idea. While 'it is always valuable, entertaining and stimulating to meet him, in addition, most conversations end up with a problem solved and directed, and several what-ifs.'

He was described as having an 'entrepreneurial' bent, as someone who generated projects, planned, carried out and completed them, and with 'perseverance'; enabling him eventually to find the funding, after a 'a difficult time' during which the momentum of 'a very good idea' with no official status needed to be maintained. The 'intellectual integrity' which stimulates his research enables him to see the fight for funding as an integral part of the research process, which validates the excellence of the project, and not just as an irritating obstacle which has to be negotiated.

All team members (based in different parts of the building as they were, they might bump into one another regularly, but held formal meetings infrequently) contributed to the development and direction of the research, and worked as a loose association of individuals, maintaining their individual contributions without overt leadership, rather than as a highly organized team. 'We mutually facilitate each other.'

Dr AH felt that while 'finding personnel is the key', the choosing of such a cohesive team was more the result of gathering together people with individual skills and expertise: previous achievement was the overriding criterion rather than any particular behavioural or team-building qualities. 'All of us have strong motivations for success – the project matched these for us as individuals and as a group.' The 'collective spirit' and 'chemistry' were attributed more to the fact that 'we got on and are nice chaps' rather than to any deliberate selection process.

Dr AH's management was described as 'easy-going', and he himself was described as 'approachable, unaggressive and laid-back'. He felt that they would also say that he was always willing to argue vigorously for his point of view at the intellectual level.

When it was suggested that he might have spent more time on the project in order to accelerate its progress, he responded 'Yes, but I might tread on their space.' The project was successful from various points of view, but while not generating any immediate publications, 'Your careful questioning approach has got us there (maybe I have been too careful?)... but our answer will be the right one and the first.'

'In this project, they have assumed [team-]roles along with the management responsibilities that go with them... it is more structured than many other projects.' Thus one member operated as the information gatherer, one as co-guide and another as the completer/finisher; all provided idea-generation and technical expertise. However, at any one time, there was always one person who 'carried the ball'. Dr AH's role changed at different stages of the project in line with the changing needs: initially he was Ideas Generator, Visionary and Entrepreneur; then, in the fieldwork stage, Organizer, Guide and Team Builder; and finally, when it came to assessing the results and preparing for publication, he acted as Evaluator.

Dr AH was very clear about his own management skills and his attitude to management was that of a researcher seeking answers: what has happened before? What good ideas can I take from that? When he first became a manager, he tried various processes to encourage team building, including providing team-breakfasts once a week before official working hours. But 'food didn't seem to compensate for the early hour' and the experiment was discontinued, with a lesson learnt that not all staff had his high motivation and interest. He saw his family situation, his children, even his own childhood, as experiences from which he could learn. He sometimes found it difficult to confront difficult people, and he now felt that his attitude was too idealistic, and he was developing ways of dealing differently with different people.

Everyone agreed on his 'warmth' and his 'always being available'. He was unfailingly supportive of the team: 'he provides "a cushion" to minimize any failure'. He was variously seen as 'teaching/explaining /motivating'. His objective was always to generate a sense of collectivity and when an initiative seemed unsuccessful, he looked for ways of optimizing its strengths before formulating another method to achieve the same ends, the new approach often deriving from listening to other people's views.

Dr EL: senior research scientist in a drug company

Dr EL's objective was to come up with novel compounds for a particular therapeutic purpose. The project started as an unofficial group ('often the way in the early stages'), initially more like a collaboration. The group crossed departmental boundaries and required considerable flexibility. Experiments would be done on hunches, with resulting hands-on work of a varied and less routine nature, giving on to longer-term results, each successful set of results leading on to another, larger wave of collaboration.

Dr EL, a senior research scientist, who was nearing the end of one project, had come together with a chemist who was looking for a new job, someone who saw an opportunity to demonstrate his skills and talents, and who felt that he could be active in spotting opportunities and in the design of the chemistry. They met over a discussion of results ('chemists are always on the look-out for leads'), and, together, they felt challenged.

Initially, they had informal talks and discussions, and the chemist had undertaken to develop some of EL's ideas. EL picked out a different type of compound, in which he observed a different characteristic, and decided to explore and develop that. The hit-rate in their finding of compounds with a particular kind of activity quickly accelerated, to the point where they could predict success in that respect, and they moved up to developing activity at a second level. And other people became increasingly interested in what they were doing.

The members of the group emphasized that this was an unofficial project, and that its work was at a very early stage. And that people play different roles for different aspects of the work: they wear different hats for different occasions. At that moment, roles were changing yet again, and EL was having to rethink both his own role and that of the team. He had now set up a wider informal group because there were others in the company who knew a lot about these compounds whose knowledge would be valuable, and more recently he himself had had to stand back and look at the future of the project. He now had to decide on the relative allocation of resources between different projects, including this one, and to make commitments about resources which he was not sure could be honoured. He found it tricky to change emphasis thus, and was not comfortable with this role.

He felt that the project was the sum of different parts and all of them must work effectively. Co-ordination of the work-flow throughout the project was important, and all, even the indirect participants in the work, must be kept abreast of what was happening and be kept involved, so that when their turn comes for them to play their part, they would be fully involved. Their enthusiasm for 'discovery' must be what retains their commitment to the group, and there must be a logical, clear and efficient work plan (in which the group does not omit something important at a particular stage).

'His role... is an encourager, a persuader, a cajoler.' 'He spends time encouraging people to suggest new ideas, to do new experiments.' 'You nudge,' said EL; 'my initial role was to be the enthusiast, to be impartial and to play devil's advocate (as I see with hindsight); but roles changed very quickly as the project evolved.' 'It is his input of ideas that I value; he is always there to bounce ideas off,' said the chemist.

'Individuals were self-motivated' and 'had responsibility for choosing the project'...'and felt responsibility for their own particular contributions.' 'Yes, I work on that a lot,' said EL, 'my role is as facilitator – to make sure particular pieces of work get done, even when that is in another department.' 'It is a matter of getting people interested in the work.'

'He is a very good communicator: he appreciates the needs of people in our department (chemists) – how we need and like results. We have communicated well and understood each other.' 'It is nice to see chemists take the whole of the results aboard,' reciprocated EL. 'We both appreciate each other's point of view.' 'The weekly team meetings were a useful vehicle for the sharing of ideas.' 'There was a good level of discussion, including on decisions of a scientific nature.'

'It is a matter of having roles and of trusting others to carry out their roles', said EL. 'Drawing the group together, I work on that a lot.' 'Individuals were clear about how what they were doing fitted into the overall picture, and felt that they were working towards a common goal.' 'And there was good recognition from line management.'

'Trust seemed to develop from all the positives the team had and the few negatives.' 'People came increasingly to respect the results, and as time went on would come back more quickly with more.'

'It is a hard job: 90 per cent of the time, it doesn't work, and you go from elation to gloom. It is important to be around: people feel their reputations are on the line all the time, and you need to reassure them when something goes wrong that they are not the only person in the world who has failed!' 'For instance Dr.C floats through his labs regularly – I think that is a good idea, and my office is right beside my labs.'

'My office skills haven't changed at all: they are still dreadful!' 'I know I am dreadful at dealing with company documents, so I'll get J and others to write them up and I'll just correct them!' 'But the wonder of an informal group is that no one knows you exist!'

'I am not particularly aware of the skills I have in the job I do: there isn't just one pattern of skills that is effective, because there are lots of different situations and it is all very fluid. Having a discussion with bench scientists, you use one language, and talking with administrators or with people from other specializations, you use another.' 'You have to say, "yes, of course you are right" even though you have been plugging that idea for some time.'

EL played many team-roles: he was the group's 'Co-ordinator' and 'Planner', and, in the jargon of the organization, he was the 'field[er of] the bureaucracy.' He was also the 'Builder of external relations', 'the Monitor/evaluator', the 'Facilitator' and the 'troubleshooter' and the 'Coach on non-technical matters' (though these roles were rated as less important). Along with one other, he was regarded as the 'Ideas Generator', and (less importantly), the 'Ideas prompter'. These two were also regarded as the 'implementers' – the people who get the work going, and as the people who keep the team together. They were also the 'Spokespersons' for the project. Three people in the group were technical experts and the technical 'leaders'.

'I was surprised that the members of the group were as aware of my roles as they showed: I thought one might fade into the background as a manager, rather like wallpaper.' 'I prefer not to use the term manager of my role in this group.'

MO: brand manager in an international drinks company

MO was a brand manager in an international company. The company was responsible for marketing some 30 brands of wines and spirits. His objective was to produce a Christmas 'on-pack' offer for one of his brands that would capture the imagination, that would be innovative and would reflect the Caribbean image of the brand. As a director, he led a project which was successful and creative: they came up with the idea of a living pineapple plantling, which could be grown to a fully fledged plant.

Before writing the brief, 'he tried to understand the market by his own research.' 'He talked to consumers and read [what they read]'; 'to define new opportunities', so that he 'knew the target market well; and could adopt the right tone from the outset'. 'It was a concise brief, with full knowledge of all the goals at the outset.' 'The brief did not change: we both [the advertising agency and the company] knew what was required and we got it.' The objectives were very clear, yet it was sufficiently open for the agency's brainstorm to be great fun.

He had read out the brief, item by item, to ensure that it was clear and understood, though the members of the agency felt that they might also have liked physical examples of past promotions; some indications of what the packaging restrictions were; and the importance of linking in with the advertising; perhaps also with information from the consumer research, such as videos, murals, and cut-and-pastes of other material. MO commented that the company was a 'challenge' culture, in which no one is of such a level that they cannot be challenged, and he called for more 'challenge' of his ideas next time round.

This was the agency's first project with the company. They felt that their experience with the brand would help them enormously in future, in being able to come up with one recommendation rather than several, because 'we understand better how he thinks'.

One member from the agency commented that 'some people treat you as a supplier rather than a colleague; they do not show the same trust and confidence in you as others do, nor share information as fully.' For his part, MO felt that holding back information from the brief could be justified in order not to push the creative endeavour down a particular road; or in order to match up the timing of the development of the work in an agency with that of the client; or in order to leave the brief open to more creativity. 'My role is not in being creative', he said, 'I pay [the agency] to do that job.'

The project had to tie back into the brand. The enthusiasm for the brand generated by MO carried through into the final creative work. 'We were motivated by enthusiasm, with a bit of help from the brand!'

'Everyone kept to their particular expertise – allowing the creative team to explore the full extent of creativity.'

'He had no need to discuss or gain approval for his decisions, which was speedier [and showed] greater decisiveness.' 'He has a vision/long-term goal.'

'He knows what he wants' and 'You know where you are with him.' 'I knew it,' he said, 'although the agency didn't; but I hope to see that evolve.' 'He knows better: maybe we have got it wrong,' said one member of the team from the agency. 'Some organizations have no challenge and no motivation; nor do they plan far enough ahead,' he said. 'I have more experience than some brand managers here.'

His style was depicted thus: 'He directs discussions, manages differences and controls [the process].' 'He focuses on other people's objectives and requirements and fits them into his own.'

The group saw the importance of the various process roles in the project very similarly: the role of Ideas Generator was seen as the most important team-role ('creative and imaginative'), which was played by the Creative [person] in the advertising agency; and the next most important that of Director – who 'gives clear briefs, sets clear goals and guides team towards them', which was played by MO, and by the agency's account director. The next most important team role was the Evaluator/Realist/Challenger. And finally, the Controller ('manages differences, controls the pace of project progression, and relationships within the team'); and Decision-maker ('good judgement, thinks on the spot, decisive').

MO felt that the role of being the Evaluator etc was an ongoing task, but the account director expressed the view that everyone was involved in that role and that they all made their evaluation from different standpoints.

The other members of the group saw the *account director* in the role of Controller ('I am keen that he manages me,' said MO. 'I gave him the critical path, the budget etc'), but, to everyone's surprise, and seemingly to his own, the account director saw the creative person in this role, rather than himself. MO felt that this was simply a mistake by him, as such a misperception would have been at odds with what he does.

There was a hierarchical structure in the group which meant that the reporting relationships and the main interactions were on a one-to-one basis: for instance, MO as the Director (in which role he saw the brief as key) was very much the authority and the instructor to the account director ('treating him like a supplier'); and the latter, the recipient of that benefaction (fortunate and 'trusted' thereby) and the learner: each complemented the other's style. Likewise, the creative person said that what inspired her was being respected and trusted as the expert in her field and having the interaction she needed when necessary; 'trusting your own judgement and theirs'; and the account director, as giving information and direction to her and asking questions when necessary, complemented her in style.

While one of the important strengths of MO was his ability to do the groundwork in order to understand the market for the brand, he rated himself as making almost no contribution in the role of Researcher.

The project was felt to be innovative, exciting and as charting new ground, and it was successful (though it was early days, sales figures were bearing this out), and the members of the team were certainly delighted with it.

PART IV

FOSTERING CREATIVITY IN GROUPS

11

putting together a good poker hand

SELECTiNG THE
RiGHT TEAM

'None of us is as smart as all of us.'

Creativity is stimulated by the making of unusual connections. The members of creative groups bounce thoughts and ideas off one another, and in the selection of a group, the way in which those members will interact is as important as their knowledge and understanding of the subject and the issue upon which they are engaged.

Xerox's Palo Alto Research Centre is recognized as the cockpit from which today's personal computer sprang, and Bob Taylor headed its Computer Science Laboratory at the crucial time. His approach to recruitment was to seek great people and then turn them loose on projects that reflected their unique talents and passions, but he also sought people who could work collaboratively. To this end, candidates had to give a talk before the assembled staff and field probing questions and comments. 'It was a grueling experience, an ordeal, and thus a time-honored way of creating fraternity.'[1]

While the relevant knowledge and experience are essential for any creative group that hopes to be successful, such things as 'process' skills, the ability to get to know one another, and the ability to use each other's perspectives are at least equally important.

LEADERS CHOOSING THEIR TEAMS

The first task which the newly appointed leader of a group has to deal with is to decide who will be the members of the group, and the effective leader uses criteria which relate both to individuals and to the way they will fit in with other members of the group.

Directors in the theatre, in films and in television regard casting as one of their highest priorities, as do coaches and managers of sports teams; yet in other creative fields, managers/leaders seem too often content to include in their project group as whosoever is available.

The leader's vital first step: acting as the casting director

---

Most successful leaders of creative groups attach a great deal of importance to and take explicit responsibility for the selection of the members of their groups (see Figure 11.1). Sometimes, the appeal of the subject or of the group's activities is such that the leader is spoilt for choice. However, life is very much harder for the leader who has little control over the members of his or her group, and is then lumbered with a 'second choice team'.

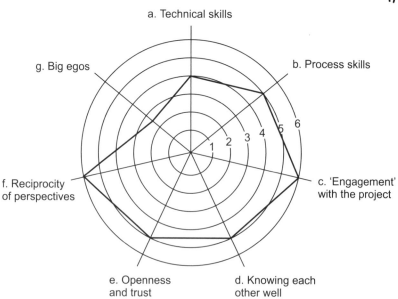

X = Extent to which these are needed for the success of the project
O = Extent to which they are available in the team

6 = *very much*
1 = *very little*

Professor JP's team (p 20)

Figure 11.1 *Choosing teams for creative tasks*

Selecting for technical skills

It is of course essential that the group should include members who have the necessary knowledge, experience and technical skills. The technical skills of team members provide the commonest (and the most obvious) basis for selecting people for a project: is the necessary expertise available in the team, for example, in the techniques of screening, for writing an MsDOS computer program, or in American corporate tax law?

However, individuals have different interests, and those interests take them down different lines of enquiry. It is this that may make it important in certain circumstances to have in the group several people with experience in the same area, for example, of cell cloning ('there are slightly different cooking methods').

Selecting for 'process' skills

The ways in which members of the team interact and stimulate one another is, I suggested above, at least as important as what they know or what they can do. For instance, it is important to choose people who play all the necessary team-roles (see below).

The effective leader will decide which team-roles are essential for the project group, and he or she will ensure that there is at least one member of the group who is skilful in playing each of the team-roles which are essential for this task.

> **The ways in which members of the team interact and stimulate one another is at least as important as what they know or what they can do**

The set of team-role skills needed for any given project will depend upon the task, the organization and the leader. As Belbin[2] has pointed out, it is essential to have a full set of complementary team-role skills available in the team, and this certainly applies to creative groups as much as it does to any other field of work. However, in creative groups, different team-role skills may be important, and different sets of team-role skills important for different kinds of tasks.

Belbin argues that his nine team-role types are appropriate for every kind of team, but other research has suggested alternative ways of looking at team-roles. For instance, one study found that there are six distinct team-role types of burglars,[3] each of which may be necessary for a successful team, depending on the kind of burglary they have in mind; another, that there are four different profiles of Chairman. Galbraith[4] has proposed a set of team-role types appropriate for

'Innovation'; and Souder[5] has proposed another set for 'problem-solving'. In deciding what set of team-roles is best for any given team, it is essential to look at the needs of the task or the project which the team is undertaking.

The most common team-role types which are needed in various kinds of creative groups are shown below, and the effective leader will decide which among these are appropriate for the task in hand (see Figure 11.2).

X = Importance of contribution in that team-role
    for the success of the project team

O = Extent of contribution in that role made by someone
    in the team

6 = very substantial contribution

1 = negligible contribution

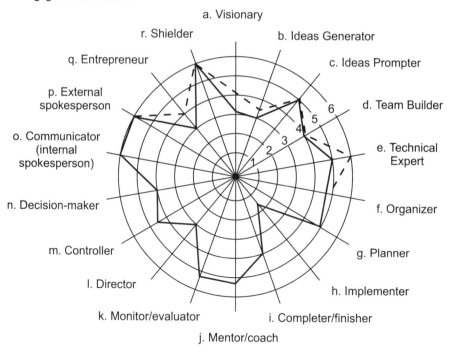

Figure 11.2 *Team-role contributions in creative teams*

By way of illustration, a new product development team in the Research and Development division of a large chemical company included the following:

- Ideas Generator (produces new thoughts and ideas);
- Ideas Prompter (prompts, suggests, focuses and adds to the ideas of others);

- Team Builder (encourages openness and communication within the team);
- Technical expert (expertise in these particular areas);
- Persuader (influential and persuasive with others);
- External spokesperson (develops relationships with collaborators and external contacts);
- Internal spokesperson (voices the views of the team);
- Goal provider (states goals and objectives, provides focus);
- Entrepreneur (commercially aware, seizes and exploits opportunities and contacts).

The cast and crew on a film set included:
- Researcher;
- Visionary;
- Planner;
- Confidante;
- Motivator;
- Collaborator;
- Ideas Generator;
- Improviser;
- Perceptor.

The absence of someone with a key team-role skill will almost certainly render a project less successful, but however careful the analysis of the team-role needs, there can be no guarantee that a team which contains members with all the necessary team-role skills will be successfully creative. Moreover, partnerships in teams are often the result of intuitive rapprochements (eg a designer and a choreographer who inspire one another).

Team members in more creative groups are very fluid in the roles they play; they change their role, adapting quickly to the changing needs of the task as the project evolves and moves through different stages, and to the roles which their colleagues play, almost from day to day.

I have already referred (in Chapter 3) to how we found that 'how to…' types of projects tended to include Visionaries, Ideas generators and Ideas prompters, whereas 'what to…' projects' included Directors, Organizers, Planners and Controllers. I have also referred to the perception that Visionaries are those people who are able to 'see' what problems may be ripe for solving and the ways in which they might be solved (as was the leader of a medical research team), whereas Ideas Generators are more likely to be a part of a group working closely together, producing, developing and testing ideas routinely (like the leader of the new product development group in a chemical company); and

Ideas Prompters, people who may sit slightly outside such a group and are able to stimulate others to help them find their own new approaches (as was the leader of a skunk works group in the research division of a drug company).

Likewise, in 'what to...' projects, Directors tend to take charge, as a brand manager did in a small group responsible for devising a special offer for a brand of spirits; Organizers to produce order our of disorder, as an audit manager did; Planners to devise the way in which something will be achieved, as the manager of a group responsible for devising a computer-based training program; and Controllers to check on how well progress is being made, as did the leader of a project in the NHS to relocate a residential unit. Each of those may be of greater importance to the success of any one project.

Often, in any one group, there will be several players of a role, for instance of the role of technical expert, the role of Implementer, or of Monitor/Evaluator. Of course in multi-disciplinary groups, by definition, there are several Technical Experts, and even where there are several experts in the same field, they usually have strengths in different areas and/or have different perspectives, so that they can, in practice, support each other. In one successful drug research team, there were three experts in cell cloning, and in another successful team – of management consultants specializing in psychodrama – there were three ex-drama teachers.

Often different people act as Implementers at different stages of a project: at each stage in a medical research project, a different person was seen as 'carrying the ball'. In a similar way, monitoring/evaluating can have several aspects: there is the technical aspect (have we failed to take into account someone else's work?), there is the logical/experiential aspect (does our work stand up to scrutiny?), and there is evaluation against expectations (are we meeting schedules, budgets and forecasts?).

There are also roles which are more specific to particular situations: whether the Team Builder or Coach role is more important will depend on whether it is the learning and development of individuals or of the group that is more important for the success of the project. Motivators, Inspirers, Supporters and Encouragers help individuals and groups in risky situations, or who are short of confidence, and/or who need to learn and develop; and Facilitators, Empowerers and Enablers help to provide stimuli and remove blocks which are physical, mental or institutional.

Some people are better players of a given role than others, but to play a role well, you need to know when you have a unique contribution in that respect in relation to the rest of the team; you need to be able to put distance between yourself and the team so as to reflect dispassionately about its 'process', and there needs to be a relationship of trust and confidence in the team so that members appreciate each other's special contributions.

There is no one single set of team-role skills which can be prescribed for every creative group, but leaders need to decide which team-roles are important for their task, and to ensure that the team-role skills of members of the group match with the needs of the task: if it is crucial for the team to have an Ideas Developer, a Constructive critic, a Wrestler/grappler and a Team Builder for that particular task, it will only be successful if it does contain at least one person who makes an effective contribution in each such role.

Selecting people according to the stage of their 'life journey'

Creative people are often more interested in the development of their talents then they are in the task or in the organization in which they are working, and they often see life as a journey on which they seek to find things that are new and exciting that will stretch and develop their talents, and to avoid things that they have done before.

> **All of us were engaged on a happy conjunction which defined our lives, a group of individuals developing together**

The leader of one group sought, for example, to bring together in the team people who would have an 'engagement' with the project. He chose people whose life journey coincided with the project: what they sought to achieve in and for themselves at that moment in their lives should also be key contributions for the project; in the same sense that a talented actor or actress seeks parts which will help to develop their talents, and will not readily seek simply to repeat roles that they have already played. He therefore saw creative groups as having a life-cycle of their own: a birth, a growth and a death, and my discussion with him (about how it had gone) the wake of this particular project!

Selecting people who do or can get to know each other well

Relationships are also very important. Team members of successful creative groups often know each other very well, so that they can be sufficiently relaxed in each other's company for trivial, funny, even silly ideas to be allowed to have time. 'We must know each other so well that the ability to know how another member feels about something changes the conversation in the group'; 'we were able to finish off each other's sentences'; what an Olympic athletics manager described as understanding 'each individual athlete's aims, style, thinking, preferences, etc,' and vividly illustrated by the skills in empathy for members of their team shown by a Sister in the Accident and Emergency Department of an acute hospital.

> ## There was a sort of telepathy between us

This closeness among team members is strong enough to subvert even well-established aspects of culture; one scientist – and progress in that field depends upon one's scientific reputation – said of his team: 'Don't take credit because you might put others down whose co-operation you value.' One leader added that you should select team members who got on with you: he sought not only a closeness in his team, but one which he fostered with food and wine, and with social occasions.

Groups often include members who have known each other or worked together before, perhaps elsewhere; or of whose work they have had experience, so that you could see that they 'had green fingers', and how they worked well together; 'personality and work habits as important as technical skills'. And one group included someone because of her ability to establish relationships quickly.

Selecting people for openness and trust

While the members of creative groups are interested in the development of their own talents, they come together with a common purpose, that of resolving a particular issue; and if they are successful, their reputations will be enhanced. For their common purpose, they must all be able to contribute with openness between and trust towards one another.

Successful creative teams have a high level of mutual openness and trust between their members and/or are capable of bonding quickly. One group described it as a mutual respect and dependency; another put it more strongly, 'Trust is a very important factor... if we could not work with one person on this basis, then he could not become a member of the team.'

Selecting people for their reciprocity of perspectives

The ability to see things in new and different ways is an important skill for successful creativity. 'If you look at something long enough,' said one medical researcher, 'you see it like everyone else.' (Berlioz quipped of Saint-Saëns that he 'knows everything, but he lacks *in*experience'.) People with associative minds, who are fluent with metaphor, simile and analogy are more likely to be able to generate new and fruitful ways of looking at issues; and the perspectives of their colleagues – of those with whom they are in regular contact – are ready sources of inspiration for their imaginations.

The members of more creative and successful teams often have 'a reciprocity of perspectives': the ability quickly to become familiar with each other's approaches, and so to respect and make use of them. As one participant commented of his leader: 'He appreciates the needs of people in our department [who were chemists] – how we need and like results. We have communicated well and understood each other.' 'It is nice to see chemists take the whole of the results aboard,' reciprocated the project leader, 'we both appreciate each other's point of view.'

Big Egos

Creative groups develop their thoughts by playing with ideas, and in order to do this, they need to be bold enough to take risks and to experiment. They often contain people who are arrogant or who are described as Big Egos – perhaps more so in the performing arts and the graphic arts than in other types of creative field. It is in their nature that their self-confidence encourages them to attempt things that others will not. Their very audacity enables them to achieve what others cannot. One proprietor of a film company commented that he could sometimes elicit great creative performances by giving young producers or directors projects in which they were unaware of the extent of the risks they were running.

> **The very audacity of Big Egos enables them to achieve what lesser mortals cannot**

But they have their disadvantages. One film director described the demanding nature of those prima donnas whose talents fell short of their reputation, and, similarly, of those whose arrogance or audacity causes them to meet with more failure than the rest of us. Of the former, she felt that it was their personal fears (of failure) that made them so demanding, and told of how this could undermine and usurp the support which the rest of the cast and crew all required of her. Such individuals may be valuable and important but they are difficult to accommodate in teams.

However, creative groups are mercurial, and their quorum is a changing one. Precisely because the nature of creative tasks is experimental, the having of ideas and trying them out ('let's see how it works'), for that reason it is impossible to predict what the moment-to-moment needs of the project will be, either in task terms or in process terms; whether 'we will need to do this' or 'to think about that' next. Moreover, the high level of motivation and enthusiasm in such groups means that they will not wait until next week for the person who has the necessary skill in the group to become available, they will turn to whoever is handy. And people who work in creative environments understand that need; 'they just do whatever is necessary next'; they are very flexible.

To summarize:

- Effective leaders of creative groups take full responsibility for selecting the members of their groups, and they devote a great deal of care and attention to this task; they use a variety of criteria for selecting their groups.
- While it is essential to have people in the group with all of the necessary technical skills, because creative groups depend very much upon minds working together, 'process' skills are at least as important as technical skills.
- Among the process skills, team-role skills are very important.
- Not only are there different aspects of the same team role, each of which may be important, but different roles may be important at different stages of the project.
- Team-role skills can be learned, and they need the right climate in which to flourish.
- Effective leaders choose members of their groups so that they are all on a stage of their 'life journey' together, so that the project is relevant to each member's own life journey.
- Relationships are also important, and leaders choose members of the group either because they already know one another or because they will be able to get to know each other quickly.
- Members are chosen because of their ability to be open and trusting.
- Members are chosen because of their ability readily to understand and see each other's perspectives.
- They may include Big Egos and people who are arrogant because of the way in which their self-confidence enables them to take risks that others would not dare to attempt.

NOTES

1. Bennis, W and Biederman, PW (1997) *Organizing Genius*, Addison-Wesley Longman, London.

2. Belbin, RM (1981) *Management Teams: Why they succeed or fail*, Butterworth-Heinemann. Also by the same author, *Team Roles at Work*, Butterworth-Heinemann, Oxford, 1993.
3. Natural selection gives six distinct types of burglar, *The Times,* 24 September 1996.
4. Galbraith, JR (1984) *Designing the Innovating Organization*.
5. Souder, WE (1975) Some experiences with idea generation and creativity groups, Technology Management Studies Group study paper, University of Pittsburgh, Pittsburgh.

12

learning to get the best out of one another

DEVELOPiNG TEAM-WORK iN CREATiVE GROUPS

'Many ideas grow better when they are transplanted into another mind than in the one where they sprang up.'

(Oliver Wendell Holmes)

As Warren Bennis has observed, 'people in great groups seem to become better than themselves.' Thoughts and ideas are frequently developed through the interactions between people, rarely more importantly so than when the crew of Apollo 13 were in mortal danger as a result of a mysterious in-flight explosion in 1970. NASA engineers had to figure out how to repair the spaceship's damaged air-cleaning system, using only materials on board, and then talk the imperilled crew through the process of making the repairs before they suffocated.

Creative teams have to develop their ability to interact in ways that bring the best ideas out of the individuals who make up the team, and take forward the nuggets which appear in the course of the team's activities.

In task-oriented groups, the members need to get to know their respective task skills, and in creative groups, they also need to get to understand each other's skills and abilities with ideas, and how thoughts and feelings influence those ideas. It has been suggested that the ability to imagine new realities is correlated with making analogies, with playing, modelling, abstracting, idealizing, harmonizing, pattern forming, approximating, extrapolating. Someone described it as using ideas, thoughts and feelings as the eggs, flour and milk of creativity: cooking is a common metaphor in creative fields.

DIFFERENT KINDS OF GROUPS

Some teams have characteristics which militate against the kind of management/leadership which is needed in creative groups; for instance, if they meet together seldom, or are very much set in the roles that individuals play, in those circumstances, they have less opportunity for contact, or for effective communication. Leaders need to be conscious of the characteristics of their teams in order to compensate successfully for these factors (see Figure 12.1).

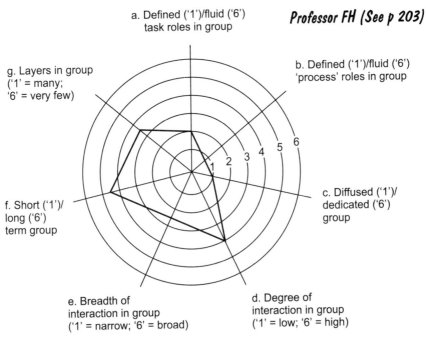

Figure 12.1 *Different kinds of groups*

In some groups, the task and 'process' roles are well defined (in a medical research project people 'had assumed roles along with the management responsibilities that went with them'), and in such groups, members need to support one another individually. In other groups, for instance in the theatre, process roles are very fluid; people simply tackle whatever comes their way, and ideas develop not so much between individuals as when they meet and work together as a group, and they support each other together.

> **Understanding who stimulates whom should influence the way a team interacts together**

Some groups can be regarded as dedicated groups in the sense that they come together for a period of time during which the members of the group are wholly dedicated to the task of the group, such as a theatre company or a sports team.

Often, members are also concurrently members of one or more other groups, groups whose activities are running in parallel. In science and in Research and Development many projects run simultaneously, and most people are participants in a number of such project groups. Often these are organized in a matrix system, in which the management is divided both on a functional and on a project basis (as sometimes it is on other bases as well).

Moreover, the membership of groups usually changes over the lifetime of the group: members leave and new members join. It is unusual for a group to have the same members at its end as it had at the beginning.

There are also short-term groups and long-term groups. Groups often come together for the limited period of a project, as for example did one group of people 'engaged on a happy conjunction which defined our lives, a group of individuals developing together', a group whose birth, life and death were clearly identifiable. There are other groups which work together over long periods, for whom refreshment and renewal comes through the developing nature of the projects which they tackle, a philosophy articulated, for instance, by Pentagram Design.

The activities of groups seldom take place with the entire group; most frequently they take place between twos and threes in the group. Even in dedicated groups, such as a scene in a play, or a move on the rugby field, while the others may have an influence upon what happens, the activity is focused on a limited number of the participants.

DEVELOPING AWARENESS

Two people who are similar in some ways though very different in others can often work together very creatively and successfully. Understanding who works well with whom, who stimulates whom, how, and in what circumstances should influence the leader of a group in his or her thinking about how to influence the interactions of the group.

> **Wanting everyone to express their best qualities**

Successful teams are similar in that they are made up of people who espouse the same objectives, but they are different in that they use the differences between them to their mutual success. And, whether or not the members like one another, it is this respect for one another's talents, perspectives, values etc, and trust in each other's skills and abilities that enables them to work as a team better than each single member can on their own.

John Syer[1] uses a model which proposes five aspects of awareness as important for team development, for which he credits George I. Brown. Whilst these may be a sequence of stages, there are also occasions when later stages (for instance, new awareness of others' skills) generate new insights in earlier stages (eg new awareness about oneself).

The first stage – awareness of self in one's everyday activities, of exactly what one is doing, of what one is feeling, and of how one might have done it differently – is very much a part of the process of developing one's skills and abilities both in the arts and in sport, but less commonly so in science and research or in design and advertising. Understanding one's feelings, one's conflicts and one's personal difficulties is a skill which can be enhanced and developed, and which needs to be exercised continuously as our life journey changes us.

The second stage in this model is described as appreciation of self. Coaches help people not only to understand their strengths, including the circumstances in which those strengths are most effective, what elicits them and so on, but also to accept that we do what we do because it was the best way of dealing with the circumstances that originally faced us when we learned this behaviour. By contrast, 'appraisals' in large organizations tend to focus upon achievements, because all too often they are also used as a measure for pay or promotion, and upon areas for development, as though one ought to be working towards some God-like paradigm model of competence. One of the coach's most important roles is that of encouraging or providing feedback in an objective and non-evaluative way, that helps the performer to understand what he or she is doing and how he or she is doing it, so that they have the option of exploring how to do it differently.

The third stage is awareness of others. Everyone who has worked in a group will be acutely aware of how difficult it is to learn about other people (since, like icebergs, 90 per cent of us is kept submerged). Because people react differently in different circumstances, just as they do with different people, it takes patient, conscious and skilful observation and listening to learn about others, and especially about their thoughts, feelings and ideas. Individuals can develop the skills of suspending judgement, of surfacing assumptions, and of making open and honest enquiries. Moreover, since there are always pressures to get on with the job, there are corresponding pressures for teams to work together on the basis of unverified assumptions about other people's strengths and weaknesses.

The fourth stage is awareness of differences. Syer describes three distinct phases in the making of personal contact: the first is inconsequential chat, the second is meaningful discussion and the third includes shared 'in' references, mocking jokes and a deeper level of personal disclosure. He suggests that people need to find a mutual rhythm for moving successfully through these three phases (as well as through these five stages, it may be added) and to the point where they can contribute to their understanding of one another. 'This means that differences must be brought into the group and then integrated in a way that provides unity while preserving difference. Difference alone is enough to provide a platform for conflict, but the need to unify in the light of differences makes it almost inevitable that conflict will occur.'

The final stage is appreciation of differences: being able to identify with the other person's position, seeing it is right for him or her without necessarily liking it. One team's members described their work together as 'enjoying working with each other'; 'mutual support'; 'wanting everyone to express their best qualities'; 'working for others'; 'looking after each other's self-esteem' and 'gaining sustenance from the group'. Another team's members spoke about the way 'they had a mutual respect for one another, nobody is carrying anybody else'; 'there is nothing magical about it, we just listen to one another'; 'ideas seem to cycle between us'; 'people don't seem to come and seek our advice as much as we seek theirs'; 'success is team-work'; 'we are of course technically complementary, but also we have our different approaches, views, angles etc... and we are always discussing, including for instance our priorities.'

Groups go through a similar progression:[2] first of all they go through a stage in which the members look for similarities; friends and acquaintances, experiences or interests they have in common. In a second stage, they find themselves unable to deny their differences, which often appear first as different work habits and communication styles, later in terms of their different experiences, and later still as their different values and beliefs. In a third stage, the members come to respect and value their differences, and to use and build on their diversity. They unify in their objectives, and they use their diversity as a strength with which to explore new ideas and approaches.

In more successful groups, the leader and the members of the group usually work together as a fluid and equal group, in which 'layers' of seniority seem to disappear. I have discussed elsewhere (see Chapter 4) how the title and position or role of manager can get in the way when groups are attempting to be creative, and groups with fewer layers are more successful as creative teams.

AWARENESS OF WHAT: THE CRITICAL SKILLS

If these models help us to understand how awareness is developed, what aspects of each other might a heightened awareness be focused on?

'Neuro-linguistic Programming' proposes a framework which enables people to explore each other's essences and learn about one another (see Figure 12.2).

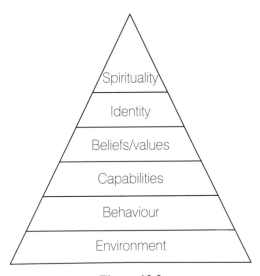

Figure 12.2

In creative teams, the focus should be on how team members think, how they feel and how they do their work.

Howard Gardner[3] has distinguished between four different kinds of creative minds, as: *masters* of their field, among whom he names Mozart and Bach; *makers* eg of a new domain, such as Freud and Darwin; introspectors, who are explorers of their inner life, including Virginia Woolf and Marcel Proust; and *influencers* of others, among whom he names Gandhi and Karl Marx.

In Chapter 8, I discussed some of the ways in which thinking can be explored, thinking styles and skills, and in Chapter 9, I have set out some of the feelings which are prevalent among those who work in creative groups, which I have called kinds of 'support' that they need. Daniel Goleman's book, *Emotional Intelligence*[4] provides a broader and more general palette.

In Chapters 4 and 11, I have gone into some detail about the 'process' roles that people play in creative groups, and stressed the importance of understanding their role skills and abilities.

STAGES OF TEAM DEVELOPMENT

A model of group development, well known as 'forming/storming/norming/ performing'[5] provides another perspective on the process of team development in creative teams. In 'forming', group relations are characterized by dependency, and the major task functions concern orientation. From independence, the group members have to move to a mutual dependence, and in this first stage they tend to rely on the leader to provide all structure. Why are we here, what are we supposed to do, how are we going to get it done, and what are our goals? The leader or the facilitator must take charge long enough to provide a basic orientation, by sharing discussion about the results of the task appraisal, the session agenda and the task summary, and by coaching.

'Storming' is characterized by conflict in personal relations and in the task function. We bring to small group activity a lot of our own unresolved conflicts with regard to authority, dependency, rules and agenda. Who is going to be responsible for what; what are the rules; what are going to be the limits; what is going to be the reward system; what are the criteria? And the issues are often about leadership, structure, power and authority. While it is important for these disagreements to occur, they must be met with effective answers, explanations and modelling. Personal viewpoints must be encouraged without becoming attached to individuals.

In the 'norming' stage, personal relations are characterized by cohesion, and the major task-function is data-flow. In this stage, people begin to experience a sense of groupishness and a feeling of clarity at having resolved interpersonal conflicts. They begin sharing ideas and information, giving and receiving feedback, and exploring actions related to the task. They are open; they may explore and surface each other's judgements and assumptions; and they may look for expanded understanding and alternative ways of moving forward. They feel good about what they are doing. Sometimes there is a brief abandonment of the task and a period of play and sheer enjoyment of the cohesion. It is important for the group to receive some recognition and experience celebration, but only long enough and large enough to recharge and refocus the group's activity.

'Performing' is rarely reached, but is characterized by interdependence in personal relations and in task problem-solving. Members can work singly or together, and the atmosphere is one of collaboration and functional competition, with high commitment to common activity and support for experimentation and risk-taking. Here, the leader or the facilitator can push the boundaries, and his or her challenge will be more focused on selecting appropriate tools to ride the wave. This cohesion is formed round an implicit set of assumptions, and the group will not stay here for ever.

Project groups also go through a series of stages in terms of their emotional reaction to the task[6] (see Chapter 8). They start with scepticism, followed by enthusiasm, which can spill over into euphoria, but this is soon followed by concern, worry, disillusionment and even depression, as the task fails to yield to the efforts of the team. Then, at last, some good results begin to arrive, though often followed by discouragement, then some more good results come through, and finally, the problem is cracked, and the team basks in the satisfaction of its success.

HOW LEADERS DEVELOP THEIR GROUPS INTO TEAMS

Lots of contact and high levels of discussion and debate are closely associated with creativity. As well as providing the opportunity to come to share understandings about the task, meeting and talking also provide the opportunity for (though they do not guarantee success in) learning about each other's strengths, coming to respect each other's ways of working, and coming to make use of each other's ways of looking at things (see Figure 12.3).

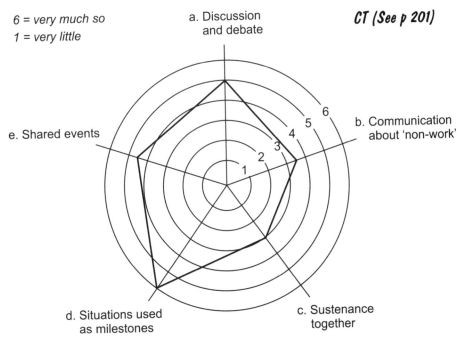

Figure 12.3   *Developing groups into teams*

Leadership as using serendipity to influence 'process' in creative teams

In successful groups, the leader and the team members tend to talk more about 'non-work things', and this provides the opportunity for members to learn about each other's values, and to understand where they share values (the members of more successful and creative groups often refer to their 'having shared values'). Many, if not most successful creative groups talk about how they regularly have food and wine together, or meet to celebrate a milestone with such an event.

Leaders of many creative groups talk about how they make or use situations as opportunities for them to influence process in their groups. Discussions of 'what ifs' and alternative scenarios, experimental situations, studies and role-playing exercises provide similar opportunities. While sports teams not only demand team-work, but also provide continual opportunities for its development, team-work in the performing arts is developed mostly in rehearsal, and there, the warm-up – deliberate and often physical – provides a model (as attunement to oneself, to others, to the team, to the purpose and to the agenda), as does the theatre, including 'performance' theatre, for improvisations and studies. Improvisations have the ability, in their own right, 'to encourage spontaneity and creativity by catching the subconscious unawares'. And there is experimental evidence that prior activity that helps towards engagement in a creative task has positive effects upon the creativity of the outcome.

One leader of a development project, for example, welcomed an opportunity for his group to go to Amsterdam to make a presentation of their 'kit'. The kit which they had been developing broke down, and they created a presentation in which each one of them simply represented a part of the kit; a situation in which they shared a difficult problem, they shared the problem-solving, they shared the learning, and they shared in the success. 'As well as coming up with a new product, we understood the project better and we got a standing ovation for it... it kept us going in enthusiasm for eighteen months!' As an Olympic manager put it, 'You recognize that there is a unity of purpose in such groups, and you respond to it so as to get the group to achieve what individuals could not. When things start going well, there is an effect on all the team members, and then your credibility increases and they listen more to the manager.'

As I have discussed earlier, one film director, before starting filming, had first put her team of actors through a three-day team-building course, so that they would quickly get to know each other and thus save rehearsal time.

To summarize:

- In creative groups, the members need to get to understand each other's different skills and abilities with ideas.
- Some teams have characteristics which reduce or avoid the contact

which is necessary for creative groups to achieve this, but effective leaders make and use different kinds of opportunities for contact and for generating discussion and debate, which help their members to get to know more about each other.

- Groups go through a number of stages in the process of getting to know one another, and their members develop an expertise in the process of doing so, which enables them to expand their awareness of each other and of the team.
- Above all else, they need to understand each other's skills and styles of thinking, feeling and doing their work.

NOTES

1. Syer, J and Connolly, C (1996) *How Teamwork Works*, McGraw-Hill, London.
2. Ellinor, L and Gerard, G (1998) *Dialogue – Rediscover the Transforming Power of Conversation*, John Wiley, Chichester.
3. Gardner, H (1997) *Extraordinary Minds*, HarperCollins, London.
4. Goleman, D (1996) *Emotional Intelligence*, Bloomsbury Publishing, London.
5. Jones, JE (1983) *An update model for group development*, paper presented at the 29th Annual Creative Problem Solving Institute, Decker Memorial Lecture, Buffalo, NY.
6. Ceserani, J and Greatwood, P (1995) *Innovation and Creativity*, Kogan Page with AMED, London.

13 *mixing, kneading, leavening and simmering*

CREATiNG THE CULTURE AND THE CLiMATE

There is a theatricality about managing creativity. Herbert von Karajan, the conductor, was an elicitor of performances, perhaps like no other. In rehearsal, he was once depicted by Winthrop Sargeant as:

> nervously appraising the action from different parts of the house... [he] seats himself momentarily at the piano, where he thumps out a passage... perches on top of one prop or another... prowls around the leading soprano while she sings, sometimes stopping the performance to pantomime her role so that she will understand it better... he assumes the role of one singer so that he may get the response he wants from another... putting on a demonstration of acting that shows him to be a better practitioner of his craft than most singers are.[1]

In creative organizations, leaders tend to express their aims and objectives through the climate and the culture which they create. In a great performance, as someone once said, it is difficult to tell the dance from the dancer or the managing from the doing. So, if leadership consists in making a contribution when one has something worthwhile to contribute, and making that contribution have its due influence upon the group's performance, it can perhaps best be seen through what have been called acts of leadership – by identifying what effective leaders choose to do and how they choose to do it.

Messages are conveyed by those who have power and influence by what they reward with their attention, or with promotion or pay, by how they do things themselves (as expressing their values), and by the environment they create (as conducive to certain ways of doing things).

WHAT DOES IT FEEL LIKE TO BE WORKING IN CREATIVE GROUPS?

The atmosphere in successful creative groups is very challenging, supportive, trusting/secure, friendly/warm, and fun/enjoyable; it is also somewhat risky, tense and unrelaxed. The more creative the project, the stronger these feelings are likely to be, especially as regards supportiveness; but also the riskier and the more tense it is, and the more fun! (See Figure 13.1.)

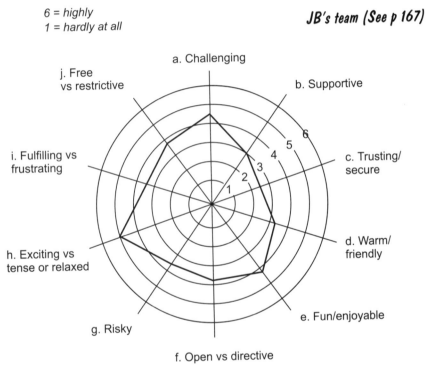

Figure 13.1 *Project climate*

Less creative project groups are often more directive and involve 'no risk'; sometimes they have more of a team approach/feeling, but this is probably because there is less discussion and debate, and less rigorous thinking, and they are often felt to be more frustrating/restrictive. While creativity is not the only source of excitement in this world, if your project requires creativity and the group includes creative people, you had better make sure that it is exciting to them!

Humour is recognized as being closely associated with creativity. The way one group worked was 'more like the film *Carry on up the Khyber!*' One leader, who spoke of his family as 'always either wits or half-wits,' commented that humour in science is important: 'only for 5 or 10 per cent of the time does science do what you hope, so it is important... to have a sense of fun and see the funny side of it all.'

Points of direct influence

There are a number of different points at which leaders exercise their influence, and the importance and advantage of each varies in different circumstances (see Figure 13.2).

6 = *a very important point of influence*
1 = *an insignificant point of influence*

DS (See p 172)

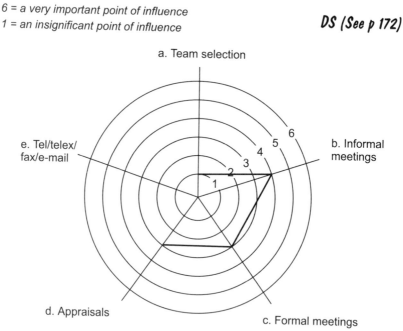

Figure 13.2   *Points of influence for leaders*

First, effective leaders take a great deal of care over the selection of the team, though in some situations team members can be self-selecting, and are attracted either by the value they can add, by the style of the group or by what they can get out of it in terms of their own development.

Second, leaders see the members of their team frequently; they regularly wander round, to have coffee with them or visit them in the lab or office.

Third, there are the more formal events: 'the weekly team meetings [are] a useful vehicle for the sharing of ideas', when members are encouraged to make presentations, 'new data received, ideas generated'. There are presentations to other parts of the organization and to other institutions; meals taken together, both regularly and as occasions to celebrate mile-stones and successes; brain-storms, discussing and debating; and escapades to 'get away from the work-place' and to other settings 'to talk about issues and scenarios'.

Fourth, there is the appraisal, associated (at present) more with companies than with other types of institution, to which most of the leaders in organizational settings now attach considerable importance, and for which they usually receive some training.

And finally, there is electronic communication, from telephone to e-mail etc. One leader of a group working thousands of miles away said, 'I have often just been a hot line [down which the team members could simply vent their emotions]'.

FREQUENT CONTACT?

Good leaders give careful thought to when and how interactions take place between themselves and team members. Discussion and debate may be stimulating, but people need to have time and space to work out their own contributions, and different people have different ways of working.

Be careful not to tread on their space

Leaders are often concerned at the possibility that their visits are seen as interference: as one leader put it, 'I must be careful not to tread on their space.'

Members meet one another more frequently in some groups than in others: while one leader visited his laboratory every day, in another group, although members might bump into one another regularly, formal meetings were infrequent.

One group commented that 'we experiment and we learn from what we do... and we take it and use it with... others. The common theme to our work is that of learning, so the role of the team is to share that learning, and difficulties in communication make it difficult to do so.'

One leader commented that he was now less interventionist, and gives more freedom, though it is not easy, he said, to dissociate oneself from the task of getting to know people more. The larger the number of projects and the more people he found himself managing, the more effective and focused he felt his interventions had to be.

HOW THOUGHTS, FEELINGS AND IDEAS ARE CONVEYED

The members of successful creative teams tend to know one another very well; 'well enough to be able to finish off one another's sentences', 'telepathy told you when it was and wasn't working', 'behaviour as expressing attitudes', and 'the ability to know how another member feels about something changes the conversation in the group'.

> **Creative groups shape and use each other's thoughts, feelings and ideas**

Successful creative groups shape and use each other's thoughts, feelings and ideas just as other groups use each other's hammers, pencils and computers (see Figure 13.3).

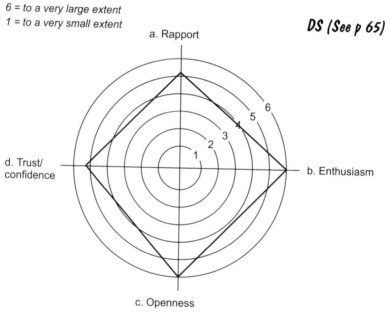

Figure 13.3 *How leaders influence climates*

Rapport as a successful relationship is, of course, a prerequisite. One leader spoke about how he liked developing relationships, another as seeking to build up a relationship, a third as keeping up a rapport. This was achieved through meeting and talking about everything and anything: 'he cared for the person

158

and the project, but the person came first'; 'he was as concerned with the social environment and home as the task'. They achieve rapport through exploring each other's understandings, beliefs and values; through friendship, laughter, trust and shared values.

Enthusiasm is conveyed by interest in the work. 'Enthusiasm makes for a creative atmosphere about the science: if you are inspired by what you are doing, it becomes fun.'

Let's try something new!

'If you were not enthused, you would simply go away and do something else!' A leader who shows that he is keen for the project to succeed, does so by making people aware that it is worthwhile, telling people of its value, of how important others see it, and by giving the work a high profile, both internally and externally. He or she will be 'hyped about success', provide positive feedback and recognition when it is going well, is always interested in finding out why, and providing support when things are going less well.

Openness is conveyed by 'asking the right questions', by talking around widely, ('treating the world as one big coffee shop') by seeking the advice of others and being 'willing to take ideas and contributions from others in the team'; 'a partnership in which we did things together'. 'He is open to any ideas, however trivial.' 'He actively encouraged the exchange of ideas and listened with 'intellectual honesty and openness' to new ideas, responding positively to all input until it was proved invalid or irrelevant. 'You don't often hear "Bad idea!" or "Rubbish!". He rarely overtly expresses any negatives'. 'He treated it as an adventure: "Let's try something new!"'

The *trust and confidence* of one leader were evident from his comment that 'with the right people in the team, whatever they do is right'. One member of another team commented: 'Just as the team were drawn to the leader to help them shape their ideas, so he was equally drawn to the team to help shape his own ideas, each acting as a sounding board to the others.' Another leader felt that it was critical to select team members who would have a particular [high] level of trust. His team members commented that he 'trusted the team to use their skills as they thought best, and was prepared to be driven by them.' 'Trust is not a traditional leadership function', but 'given trust and scope, you have the opportunity to go as far as you can'. 'He demonstrates in his style a sense of worth.'

A question can serve as an invitation, a stimulant or as a challenge. Leaders often ask questions as a way of maintaining alertness, thoroughness and good observation in team members. One leader used ('what if...?') questions as a way of getting groups to retain options in their approaches; another as inviting members to explore their mental workings, and/or justify their results so as to ensure that the conclusions were robust in the face of all possible lines of questioning; another for playing devil's advocate; another as a way of making suggestions without being seen to be interfering or dogmatic; and another as a way of ensuring that the focus remained in the right place ('have you considered...?').

The National Coaching Foundation's Course 'A Question of Style', uses questions as a way of helping athletes to explore their performance through their successes and their failures, in order to develop their own performance. 'I have an intuitive ability for stimulating people,' said one leader.

MOTIVATION AND REWARDS

Most people who work in creative disciplines are very self-motivated, and success is seen as its own reward. Leaders take care to match projects to team members' needs and aspirations, as providing them with a challenge whose achievement will help to develop their skills and talents. 'He recognized that those who were involved were best helped by having a worthwhile work success' (see Figure 13.4).

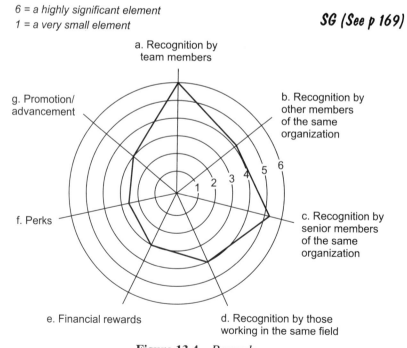

6 = a highly significant element
1 = a very small element

SG (See p 169)

a. Recognition by team members

g. Promotion/ advancement

b. Recognition by other members of the same organization

c. Recognition by senior members of the same organization

f. Perks

e. Financial rewards

d. Recognition by those working in the same field

Figure 13.4 *Rewards*

If people are to be encouraged to venture, to risk and to dare, their successes must be recognized. As the Nobel Prize winner, Julius Axelrod's biographer observed (see page 17), those in his group who produced interesting results had his ready attention. Effective leaders always 'give time' to creative people: they are interested in what is happening, they are readily available to comment and offer/provide feedback, and they show their appreciation. 'He perceives well the kind of impact people have on one another, and when they have done well or had a problem.'

If feedback is focused on *failure*, then people become more averse to risk and more concerned to ensure that their reputations are about success and achievement than about risk and creativity; where feedback is more about *effort*, people are less interested in problems and 'process' and more interested in showing how busy they are. Where feedback is *not available* at all, people feel dismissed, even embittered at the silent criticism.

Given that people who work in creative groups tend to be very self-motivated, the prospect of a pay rise or of promotion can easily divert effort in misconceived ways, for instance by encouraging the need to be seen to perform in a particular way. The best form of reward is of course help in achieving your objectives; first choice of project team, the opportunity to work on projects which are high profile, or even the opportunity to be a delegate at an overseas conference (see Figure 13.5).

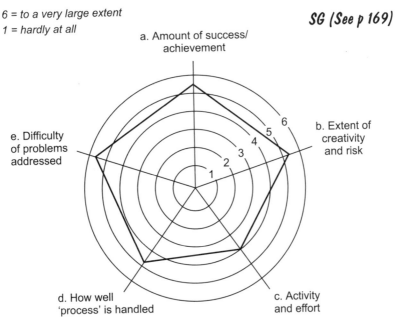

Figure 13.5   *What gets rewarded*

MODELLING THE CULTURE

Just as leaders learn more about leadership from other leaders whose leadership they have experienced, so they act as role models for the members of their teams. They behave in the way they expect every one around them to behave, by contributing their knowledge and expertise, and by contributing in their team-role, each person taking the lead when it is appropriate.

> **I anticipate that people will take more notice of what I do than of what I say!**

One research director saw his task as setting the tone/style/atmosphere, and thus allowing people to be self-motivated (in their freedom) about what they would do and how they would do it, and yet remain within the envelope of the organization's culture and objectives.

STYLES OF PERFORMANCE (SEE ALSO CHAPTER 3)

Whatever the choreography, whatever the context of the piece, the essence of a work is found in the performance, and leaders influence the performance in subtle, often intuitive ways, and frequently in ways which come to them in the moment.[2] In earlier chapters, I have described some of the roles leaders (and members of their groups) play, as well as some of their characteristics and styles, and here I can do no more than *suggest* the theatrical and spiritual aspects of what they do.

Leaders of more creative and successful projects are seen as non-dictatorial and non-directive, and as democratic, fluid, and participative. Autocrats are only successful as leaders of creative groups in certain circumstances. And to be a manipulator is useful for achieving certain effects, but people have to be able to forgive you for it! 'Individuals had responsibility for choosing the project; and... felt responsibility for their own particular contributions.'

In one group (in Research and Development), decisions had to be taken unanimously; in another, they were expected to be made democratically; and in another, one member commented that 'decisions were based on context, not on status'.

Effective leaders are frequently seen as facilitators; helping and enabling others to get on, 'acknowledging and deferring to individual members' styles', 'building on strengths and controlling weaknesses'. They are often seen as co-ordinators, among other things bringing together people who come to understand and use each other's points of view. And sometimes they are seen as organizers and planners, providing a structure out of which they then 'give people the colour'/the feel, and help them to find a performance.

Leaders of project groups are often seen as charismatic either because they are heroic (very successful in their field), personable (a 'star'), companionable (he 'persuaded people almost by good healthy spirit'), or inspirational ('challenging' and 'stimulating').

Charisma is no guarantee of success, but it can of course be used to encourage such useful characteristics as team-work and inter-activity. Sometimes project group leaders are successful contributors in all of the team-roles in a group, and they may act as the hub of the group to which and through which much of the communication in the group takes place. Autocrats can of course use their power to influence and encourage team members to contribute their knowledge, skills and talents in a democratic and participative way. One 'star' was an iconoclast, and confronter of paradox, dilemma and contradiction, and another, the leader of a team where one of his skills was described as 'allowing ideas to breathe'.

CREATING THE RIGHT SURROUNDINGS

Environments all carry messages: they epitomize the culture. Big meeting rooms betoken big meetings; plush premises imply generous budgets; well-equipped canteens encourage people to meet and talk (see Figure 13.6).

One film company has big toast and coffee rooms on every floor where team members eat and drink together. The majority of effective leaders of creative groups make opportunities for social events and celebrations.

Taking food and wine together

People then see each other in different circumstances and thus they 'see' different skills and abilities in each other; other people's angles inspire new thoughts and ideas.

Most scientific organizations ensure that the results of successful projects are on public show, by being presented on panels in public spaces: receptions, meeting rooms and corridors. Marketing organizations ensure that their more successful advertisements are framed and put on public display. Advertising agencies do likewise, and broadcasting organizations ensure that photographs of their more popular presenters are displayed in public areas. (Notice boards are also opportunities for humour, an ironical commentary, perhaps, on the role of authority in creative organizations.)

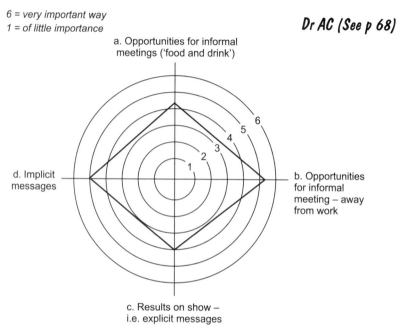

Figure 13.6 *Ways of creating environments*

THE CONTRIBUTION OF THINGS THAT CANNOT BE DISCUSSED

Some people feel that if you analyse a performance too much, the magic of the art may just disappear. To use Wordsworth's words 'we murder to dissect'. I have already quoted the composer, Aaron Copland's comment, that:

The inspired moment may sometimes be described as a kind of hallucinatory state of mind: one half of the personality emotes and dictates while the other half listens and notates. The half that listens had better look the other way, had better simulate a half attention only, for the half that dictates is easily disgruntled and avenges itself for too close inspection by fading entirely away.

And the theatre director, Peter Brook, talks about how the director 'day after day as he intervenes, makes mistakes or watches what is happening on the surface, inside he must be listening, listening to the secret movements of the hidden process'.[3]

Many leaders just do, as leaders, what they feel appropriate at the time. Experience, reflection and intuition combine to give them their instinct for what they do, and often they find it difficult to articulate things about their performance. Some said that they would not normally analyse things in the ways in which we invite them to do with us and some feel uneasy about doing so. However, without trying to articulate aspects of performance, it is harder to subject them either to reflection or to teaching.

Some elements of the creative process are unable to be discussed. Among these are intuition[4] (as the mind's ability to make connections and produce ideas without a logical or intelligible basis), 'ego' (as a form of arrogance, an irrational but self-fulfilling belief in self), and freedom/challenge/tension (as personal feelings). Creative groups have values and beliefs that are implicit rather than explicit.

> ## Ambiguity and the role of the unconscious are important

In the words of one leader from the field of drama: 'Ambiguity and the role of the unconscious are important elements of what we do.' Sensitivity and feelings are important because realism and self-analysis at the wrong moment can be destructive.

REFLECTORS OF MOOD, 'PROCESS' AND PROGRESS

Effective leaders, like their team members, are very sensitive to atmospheres and feelings, even to those inaccessible to others, and they are sensitive to moods and to how they may affect the group. They are conscious that the changing phases of a project entail different roles, skills and moods.

Effective leaders of creative groups look for, and use opportunities to influence, the thoughts, feeling and ideas of members of their team creating different environments, using different styles and responding differently in order to sustain an atmosphere which will elicit the best out of their team for the task in hand. One looked for opportunities for 'escapades' for his group, as he did for milestones which he could make use of, another reflected upon the most effective use of such opportunities, and the chief executive of another organization saw his main role as that of 'setting up conversations between people'.

NOTES

1. Osborne, R (1998) *Herbert von Karajan: A life in music,* Chatto and Windus, London.
2. Letzler Cole, S (1992) *Directors in Rehearsal*, Routledge, London.
3. Brook, P (1993) There are no secrets, in *There are no Secrets*, Methuen Drama, London.
4. Nadel, L, Hiams, J and Stempson, R (1990) *Sixth Sense,* Prentice Hall/Prion, London.

JB: editor of an arts programme on radio

JB was the editor of a regular daily arts programme on radio, for which certain objectives had been set. He was very interested in the arts and in their presentation on the media, and while he always found time to listen to the output of members of his department, he now found himself stretched, and the members of this team found themselves working very much on their own. Whilst he had a strong personality, he gave others the space to speak in an organization with a long-established tradition in broadcasting.

To increase audience participation was one of the objectives for the network, and this item in one series of programmes was to enable listeners to express their views about architecture, through discussions about individual buildings, culminating at the end of the week in a discussion with a number of experts about listeners' views.

While JB did not see himself as 'having thousands of ideas', he suggested the idea/concept and he proposed how it might be done. 'The idea started as the leader's, and became "you run with it"; you have the little ideas.'

He 'left the brief vague about how to do it, what might come out or how it needed to fit into a context'; it 'was... very much left to Producers, and not followed through by the leader', 'unpredictable events and contributions changing the shape of the project'. 'Producers of course have all the freedom in the world'; yet 'producers feel trapped; they are threatened/imposed on.'

Producers, he suggested, are self-empowered and all prefer to delegate the task to themselves! 'A delegator opens the door and says get on with it.' And they were all evaluators of their own work. While JB felt that he had inherited a department in which there was a tradition of mutual support – above one's own ego – in which people were happy to give their best idea to someone else; 'but I made sure that I encouraged it by example, (and) by asking others for their ideas.' One member of the group commented: 'More awareness of people around is needed and people would then open up more. Creativity is people throwing ideas off each other. Although there is less tendency for people to do so now, people used to hide their ace cards.' 'A closed door is incredibly powerful, even to your fellow Producers, who themselves form a hierarchy, even though at the last moment of pressure (ie immediately before a programme), space to yourself is vital.'

JB commented that there was what he called a corridor culture: if you asked a question in the corridor, there was always someone there who would know the answer. JB does a great deal of walking around. 'It is surprising what happens, and it takes a great deal of time, but it is well worth it,' he said.

He made himself available to his staff and responds to their needs. He 'actively responded if you wanted to see/discuss with him.' He 'indicated at the outset: if there's a problem, come back.'

He took time to explain why things have to be done and provided constructive feedback on performance, helping team members to learn from the experience. To an extent, he was seen as 'providing people with positive feedback, and in detail, so you could learn from his experience for next time'; and he 'kept me informed and involved me, explaining why.'

Roles were seen sometimes as static: 'there are traditional divisions of labour' and 'you are seen in a box in some jobs', and sometimes as fluid: 'we were re-learning roles in relation to each other.' He took upon himself the 'ultimate approval', of 'signalling stop/go, or no/yes to Producers' ideas (ie my deciding whether something will fit well into the overall schedule)'; and he 'imposed adherence to programme style/pattern: "no cutting".' 'I was a bit dictatorial.'

He holds a weekly 'back-stabbing' meeting, which aims to provide an opportunity for members of the department to discuss its recent output. While he generally initiated discussions, others were given plenty of space to speak. He says that there is not normally a great deal of criticism, but they do find it easier to discuss the work of members who are absent. He seeks thereby to ensure that they do listen to the department's output.

'I have a strong personality. I should talk less. Some of the less outgoing staff might find me threatening; so muting that might help. But I do make sure that I don't take all the meetings, so that others can see their colleagues threatening (sic) their ideas.'

He jokes and uses his sense of humour freely, at times to make light of more serious or 'difficult' aspects of the department's work, and had adopted the term 'the running sore' for this item of discussion.

The group saw itself as working informally together and as hard-working, though described from outside as 'a bunch of individuals who sometimes come together.' Whilst the atmosphere was stimulating and interesting, it also contained paradoxes and contradictions; at times positive and purposeful, and at times restrictive, there was anxiety and tension, sometimes resulting in stress.

He was particularly interested in idea generation and in the managing of ideas: 'everyone in the hierarchy has a different weight and a different capacity for generating ideas. Are enough doors open to ideas?'

SG: leader of workshops in musical improvisation

The Guildhall School of Music and Drama's Department of Performance and Communication Skills aims to broaden the environment within which musicians develop their skills, personalities and powers of communication. Its objectives include a commitment to the development (or rejuvenation) of creativity, and its programme acts as something of a laboratory in cultural change and social action. Among its activities were workshops in musical improvisation, some of which were carried out with local schools. SG was a leader of these workshops: he led groups of people in devising performances of music by a process of music-making; his task was to induce people to make a performance. The objectives of each session included giving participants the experience of being more creative in music, of illustrating how to be, showing how to become, and helping them to become so. SG contributed to these by virtue of his 'ability to just make things happen'; his 'sense of generosity to others in his groups'; his ability to 'protect people and provide security'; his ability to 'satisfy too many constituents at the same time'; and his superb skills as a facilitator.

'I look for a space which can give warmth and focus to the group. At the outset, I want to get some awareness of their personalities. I look for a bit of delay, so I can get more of a feel for the group and they can meet one another and relax. To start, I get them in a circle. I don't know what I am looking for. I am nervous inside. I try and put them at their ease. An element of me wants to hold back, and an element wants to get stuck in.

'I start by saying what we are going to do. One minute I am talking and the next minute they are doing something physical, and together, so that no one is exposed. They are looking at me. First, we do something very simple. Warm-ups are always identical and I talk people through them. I generally make mistakes, though not on purpose. I mention my mistake and we all laugh. 'Do you notice different sounds in your body?' I ask. I try and pre-empt their questions. I have planned what I am looking to achieve, but I do adapt a bit.

'Then I move to individual tasks, like speaking your name in a space in the circle, getting people to give a bit of eye contact, then perhaps to speak their name musically. Then I go on to an exercise involving moving around. There is of course a musical aspect to it. A lot of it is being centred (Thai Chi), at one with yourself, being comfortable with yourself and comfortable in making a mistake; focused enjoyment. To start with, I used to seek a real "buzz", now just a focus.

'I now invite less feedback than I used to, perhaps short moments, after each section, but not a long discussion. Sometimes strong groups will start chipping in. Initially I aim to set up a rapport with me. I might get people to emulate someone's success.

'I generally run sessions so that at the end, groups have come up with a piece of music that makes them feel good, a very simple piece. And which broadens their horizons, perhaps not quite realizing what they are doing.'

'Sessions are built entirely on ideas; people coming up with ideas. I give starting points and leadership. I used to try and shed my responsibility as soon as possible, but they do need leadership to channel and focus ideas. You may yourself give them an idea, but you do it in a way that is open to rejection. You can ask them if they are comfortable with that. Do they like it? Is it too difficult? There might be certain ideas that come up where I would be more directive. Where I have the idea, I am none the less open to other ideas, or they can elaborate mine. It must be open to their ownership.

'Sometimes conflicts happen between people inside the group, and then it becomes a problem-solving exercise. My problem is where to intervene. I'm working on this. You have to set up a situation where they trust you, but not trust you to sort it all out. Leaders do emerge in the group. The more forthright ones may give you lots of ideas to start with, then the quieter ones come in. I may encourage that if the group isn't doing that itself.

'If the group doesn't deliver, I won't ask, "What went wrong?" but, "Is that what you were looking for?" If they weren't clear, it may have been your fault; maybe I gave them too many things at once. If they wanted to be hand-led, you may try and give pointers as to how they might have done it.

'Adults are more comfortable talking than doing. I say: "Try it! Don't be afraid." This stage is very different every time. There is a point where they need to take bigger decisions: have they got a leader, or should they deal with it in steps, and how big should they be? Each person has their own way of dealing with it as a facilitator.'

'My [paramount] skill is being able to walk into a situation and get something going.' 'You make creative things just seem to happen.' 'I have an ability to pick things up and fire things in.' 'I have and give an up-lifting energy.' 'I enjoy just making things happen through my personality.' 'I try not to make things into a problem; my way is: let's just go and do it.'

Professor Renshaw, his boss, commented: 'There has to be an openness and sense of direction within the group, and to hear that, there has to be a generosity [in the leader] to others in the group.' SG said: 'There is a lack of ego in me: I like allowing others to shine, and I enjoy getting that to happen.' 'I certainly felt that what we were doing was not safe. Perhaps I gave an impression of security. Maybe I was able to give the task a context and a sense of mystery, which helped to remove the feeling of insecurity.'

'Satisfying too many constituents is one of his skills. He is very good at dealing with the difficulties of a compromise.' 'I always over-commit myself.' And he later commented that he liked the edge in situations, and relying on his wits and personality to get himself out of it.

'I enjoy facilitating.' 'I suppose I am a musician-and-facilitator.' 'People often say to me that I am a very good teacher, but I don't think of myself as a teacher.' 'People are learning without realizing from you.' 'I have often wondered if by being a facilitator, I was simply covering up my inadequacies as a musician and composer.'

What he liked was 'a broad range of people: I love people'; and a broad range of music: 'I'm into music of all sorts, and I like to build from where people are at.'

SG's role was that of the 'artistic director'. In these groups, he was seen as a charismatic leader: he was the inspirer of ideas, and the creator of enthusiasm. He created a climate that was described as challenging, risk-taking, anxious and playful.

'Often, there must be a creative tension,' said Peter Renshaw. 'There are some projects which are safer,' said SG, 'but they are not always inspirational. I prefer a "let's see what happens" approach at present.' 'X [another facilitator] will even let a session grind to a halt [if it is not achieving creativity]. I can't do that yet. I have moved from "have a good time" to a position in which I aim to give them my energizing qualities. I think I will push people more in the future.' 'Facilitating someone to do something which you yourself cannot do, that would be a risk.'

'To have a vision is crucial; your main role is as over-viewer, and keeping everyone in the picture. One person must always pull the whole thing together; you, as leader must give a context to all the decisions.' 'There needs to be a clear vision.'

SG commented on how other members of his group – from the Guildhall School – had complementary skills that supported him in his work. Of one person he said: 'You give me an edge; you are a challenge because you spot things; you are an evaluator; you give something I haven't got. I didn't necessarily feel good afterwards, but I do feel helped, or wiser.' And of another: 'You were a real safety net for me. My concern was not to cross our roles, and for my role not to be shifted by virtue of you taking yours, but maybe it was.' And of another: 'You again were more direct; it is something to feed off; it was ultimately rewarding.' 'I'm always amazed that R's presence makes something interesting happen; he gets results but he has a very different approach.'

DS: leader of a design group

DS led his design team as a Visionary and Ideas Generator, and as the guardian of his organization's style. He spent a great deal of time in eliciting the brief from an inexperienced client, and in distilling it into its essence. An established and well matched team in 'process' terms, the other members played counterparts to the team-roles of the leader, 'digging out' and elaborating his ideas, and developing them for the various applications for which they had to be used. His approach with them was forcing options upon them, and then guiding, defending and encouraging them.

DS was the leader of a graphic design team on a project to design an image for a new network marketing concept, a 'buyer's club', which by virtue of its being a service-by-mail, had to 'say it all' through the image it presented: 'making the intangible tangible'. The task was, therefore, to design a corporate identity, which had to be applied across all key communications material.

While time was very short, 'we were writing the play at the same time as fitting the costumes', the client was very trusting and responsive. As a brand new business concept it presented a great challenge, but shortage of time and money, and the inexperience of the client, were unhelpful.

The leader was mother to ideas: he had a clear view of the end-objective, what he saw as the deliverables, which he articulated by analogies. He was the source of the central concept and of ideas; 'the identity and the tone of views'. 'You believe you know which road to take, and we're in a rush anyway!' Another member of the group added 'not knowing whether you were going to go by bus, train or bicycle', and another adding, however, that 'by knowing where you were going to end up, you might miss a useful opportunity to deviate'.

'He was the leader, giving directions, talking to and relaying things from the client, telling team members what to do, and providing feedback.' 'He... had a clear relationship with and understanding of the client.' 'They were helpless and needed foster parents.' 'Under a veneer of organization, they were chaotic.' 'We had to think clearly about their business process, almost designing the company.' 'They used us as a security blanket and as adviser, because they knew, trusted and relied on you.' The client was a friend of a friend of the leader, and the latter expressed concern about failing in front of your friends as well as failing in front of your peers: 'You would have nothing left!' he commented.

One of the team produced a detailed form for the client to complete as a brief, who then came with a clear view because she had done the thinking and the preparation before she came and talked to us.' 'I [the project leader] would bounce a question back and then wait twenty minutes while they effectively decided the policy; ten questions like that, two hours gone and no designing done. We are always questioning, distilling the essence. And then, after discussing with us, she would go away and revise the brief for our subsequent amendment.' The leader spent a lot of time analysing the problem and reducing it to a minimal brief about how to achieve the objectives.

The leader was the dominant source of creativity and ideas. He is 'the policeman of (or the helicopter over) the organization's style, as clever, "tricksy" and "ideasy".' He exercised strong guidance and control throughout over the concept and the details of its development.

'He wanted the end-result to reflect his own creativity, as different to pre-conceptions, to the past, and to competitors, and as humorous, friendly and well thought through in terms of the user's mind.' 'With so many component parts,' he said, 'if you lose some, the whole is diminished or fragmented, so you spend a lot of time trying to convince others of the benefits of what is important in your idea.' 'The creative beast wants to oppose, not to comply.'

DS's approach with his team was more reflective, hinting at solutions ('a bit like a magician inviting you to choose a card') and then giving them confidence and acting as their 'shielder'. He quoted Alan Fletcher's comment that 'being a graphic designer is like taking your clothes off two or three times a day'. He would give strong support, guidance and encouragement concerning concepts and ideas, as well as tuition in the form of clear and frequent approvals.

'All of our roles were well defined, where often that is not so, or there is a pecking order'; and 'there was a common understanding of people's roles and capabilities,' just as there was one (and sometimes more than one) team member who made a full contribution in all of the key team-roles.

The role of Ideas generator (source of creative concepts and ideas) was seen as the most important team role for the success of the project, and the leader contributed this role. The roles of Organizer (planning and organizing work), Intermediary to Client (handles client relationship, talking to and relaying from client) and Implementer (developer and applier of concepts and ideas) were rated next in importance. These were contributed by other members of the team (with the leader making an important contribution to client relationships), as was the Controller (exercising guidance and control – the next most important role). The Visionary has clear view of end-objective/destination; paints end-picture, the Problem Analyser (reducing it to a minimum as brief) and the Policeman (of the organization's style) were also important. The leader was the main contributor in each of these roles. The least important role was felt to be that of Supporter and Guide (gives encouragement and approval), although this role was still rated relatively highly.

Although successful in terms of meeting the client's brief, gaining his approval and getting feedback, and in terms of the solution's 'ability to gain notice', and 'to communicate its essence', the work had not yet proved itself by the success of the product in the market place, nor through peer approval, nor personal satisfaction.

They felt it had been fairly creative, especially in terms of its open brief, the uniqueness and innovatory nature of the project, the opportunity to find ways to communicate and gain notice, the openness of the client and the freedom and breadth of scope in the project. It was an exciting project, tense, even manic.

The team felt it had been striving for unique, bespoke and original solutions; hierarchical in the way its work is organized, disciplined and ordered in its own terms, with a great sense of craft and detail, in an organization committed to creative excellence and concerned to maintain its high reputation (every project an award winner), and in which, while attention is paid to internal communications, they do not always work as well as they might.

PART V

PROTECTING ONE'S TEAM

14 *removing road-blocks*

HOSTiLE ORGANiZATiONAL CULTURES

It is often argued that if necessity is the mother of invention, adversity is its father: small groups, working in shabby surroundings, the argument goes, are more likely to produce creative outputs.

Walt Disney, Hewlett Packard and Apple were all born in garages; the original skunk works in Hughes Aircraft was housed in a windowless and unprepossessing building in Burbank, California, 'about as cheery as a bomb shelter'; radar was developed in a hut in Malvern, and the Enigma machine in isolated and unamenable circumstances at Bletchley Park.

However, in the last decade, SmithKline Beecham, the Wellcome Foundation and Hewlett-Packard are only a few of the organizations which have all built huge, modern and plush research centres in the UK, despite the fact that Nobel Prize winner, Sir James Black decreed that his Foundation for drug research should never exceed 20 staff.

What is certain is that while there are lots of ways of killing ideas, you have to get lots of things right in order to nurture ideas successfully (and there are times when effective leaders manage to shield their teams from the disabling effects of hostile cultures, see the next chapter). In this chapter, I discuss some of the ways in which organizations create cultures which are hostile to creativity: they are felt to be negative as disabling creativity, rather than positive as a stimulating challenge.

DIFFERENCES AND TENSIONS

Creative groups have characteristics which differ from other parts of the organization, most conspicuously from production people, the accountants, or administrators. In some organizations, the creative side may predominate, as in a TV company or a design company, whereas in others, the research and/or development section may be a minority (though sometimes a large one), and the operational side of the organization is the larger part.

There is often a tension between the two and the sharper the contrast, the greater the tension. In a large accountancy firm, a specialized and idiosyncratic form of management consultancy (psychodrama) was regarded as risky, and was seen as an inappropriate bed-fellow for the mainstream activities of the organization, and the members of the group, in their turn, felt alien to the rest of the firm. In a large drug company, a small group whose task was to look for compounds with particular therapeutic effects was described as a 'skunk-works' (something that goes on without management's cognizance), not only by the group itself, but also by senior management!

Large organizations are unified (and identified) by their missions, objectives, policies and plans, both in the minds of their staff, and perhaps more importantly, in the minds of their clients/customers. By contrast, creative groups demand to be different whatever the policies and practices of the parent organization.

> ## One of the most powerful metaphors is to be different

If creative groups need to be surrounded by mental metaphors to do it differently, then one of the most powerful such metaphors is, of course, to *be* different: different dress codes (suits versus sandals), office lay-outs, notice boards and notices, patterns of work, rewards, food and drink, office humour, styles of discourse, language etc. The whacky scientist, the creative department in an advertising agency, the working style in a film company all express a need to be different, both 'to do it' in varied ways, and 'to do it' in ways that are different from others.

Creative groups need freedom and 'space' within which to experiment; they need to try things out, to do things their way, to do things differently, and to take risks, and to do this effectively they need to be without continual pressures to do it like everyone else. They need 'a context for freedom – a protected vacuum', in which the leader 'holds back the normal pressures, to give a space – a womb'.

There is thus an inherent tension between creative groups and their parent organizations, just as there may be between one creative group and another in the same organization, and between a creative group and its outside world.

MUTUALLY THREATENING

Groups talk about the mutual 'threat', 'danger' and 'challenge', and even of being 'under siege.' One leader felt that the style of leadership in his group was 'at best to be tolerated, not to be facilitated, encouraged or developed'. If a group was seen as having a high profile, it was also seen as being a greater risk to the organization. Creative groups feel that these tensions and pressures are insidious and undermining; they feel that they need constant and continuous protection against them, giving rise to what one group called 'an uneasy peace'.

Parent organizations feel threatened because values and objectives in creative groups are invariably different to those in the rest of the organization: creative people tend to be self-motivated and have a strong interest in the development of their own area of expertise, and their own skills and talents, because those are their life. They participate in the development plans of the organization only to the extent that their life journey coincides for a period with that of the organization.

> **Uncertainty, ambiguity and risk may contrast with an organization's desired reputation for solid steady progress**

Moreover, creativity is marked by uncertainty, ambiguity and risk, and these may contrast with an organization's desired reputation for solid, steady progress, which is what patrons and financial markets demand. Organizations therefore feel that their main activities, their progress and their reputation may be threatened and put at risk by the unorthodoxy and volatility of their creative side.

'Parent' organizations are seen as disabling where the following is the case:

- Their missions and objectives are excessively dominant.
- They keep a close hold over authority or legitimacy.
- They are tightly structured.
- They are paternalistic.
- Jobs are closely defined or circumscribed.
- Office spaces are arranged in divisive ways.
- They do not focus on soft issues, like risk and failure as well as success or other aspects of how things are done (as 'process').
- They are restrictive/tight with time and space.
- They are not receptive to or users of ideas.
- They take little account of individuals' aims and objectives.
- They take little account of personal development.

CLIENT- AND TASK-ORIENTED VS 'PROCESS-' AND 'PEOPLE-ORIENTED'

Organizations often place a strong emphasis upon achievement, a customer- or task-orientation, articulated as the importance of identifying customer needs and/or 'delivering' the goods. While in some organizations, this is balanced by a concern for people, in others, there may be little interest in people, their feelings, their development and their futures.

The development of skills and talents in team members is frequently an integral part of successful creative process, and to the extent that organizational effort is drawn away from it, to that extent such groups may be less likely to produce creative outputs.

POWER, CONTROL AND BUREAUCRACY

Some organizations exercise extensive power and control over those who work in them.[1] Organizations have at least two reasons for exercising control: they seek, of course, to achieve certain specific aims, as expressed by their mission and objectives, and they are expected or required to meet certain standards in the way they carry out their business eg employment standards, environmental and safety standards etc. Organizations that have reason to be concerned about dilution of effort away from their mission and objectives are likely to be more concerned with control, as are those organizations whose mission is about standards eg of accounting. In one large organization, the culture was dominated by plans and budgets; in another, planning and accountability ('strategy and finance') were now being given increasing prominence.

The carrying out of staff appraisals is another task that is frequently mentioned as taking a great deal of time and/or being an irksome administrative task. While these were undertaken by one group leader in a media organization because otherwise he felt he would be 'failing in his duty', it was dismissed by the head of a large research division in a drug company, who simply said that he asked people to do their appraisals for themselves!

Demands for accountability, monitoring and control have had the effect of diminishing freedoms

---

The heads of two interdisciplinary research centres complained that in today's contractual/performance society, they spent too much of their life with such things as evaluations, the University Funding Council's research selectivity exercise, and submissions for funding. The way in which, in today's world, trust has been displaced by accountability, monitoring and control has had the effect of diminishing freedoms, to the potential detriment of creativity.

Dealing with the bureaucracy, responding to requests for information, completing returns, carrying out appraisals, are all aspects of working in large organizations, and tasks which leaders of creative groups often carry out on behalf of their groups in order to enable the members of the group to 'get on with their jobs'.

Power and control can also influence the way in which the organizations handle differences of opinion and view.[2] In some groups, people freely and openly express opposing views about the culture of the organization: in others, differences and difficulties can be felt to be divisive, to the point where some members of one group admitted that they simply kept their heads down.

Successful creative groups are characterized by freedom, discussion and debate, and self-direction.[3] Power and control are the very opposite of these characteristics; and organizations whose cultures are concerned with power and control will be less fertile grounds for creativity.

PATERNALISM

The culture of one organization in the field of drug research was depicted as both 'hierarchical' and 'paternalistic'. Both of these aspects of its culture seemed to dull the adventurousness of spirit which is the essence of successful creativity. While many people in the organization felt that there was a great deal of encouragement, support, openness and trust in their unit, it was also felt that to some degree idea-generation was *not* supported, and that there was *less* risk-taking.

ORGANIZATIONS WITH HIERARCHICAL VS FLAT STRUCTURES[4]

Some organizations have a large number of layers of management between the project leader and the top of the organization, whereas others have either simple, short and direct lines to the top, and/or give a great deal of freedom to departmental heads as in universities, post-graduate schools and medical schools.[5]

Hierarchical organizations are more authoritarian

In hierarchical organizations, the processes of gaining authority, obtaining funding and other resources for projects involve more layers of authority, and such organizations therefore tend to be more authoritarian than organizations with flatter structures. They require more fulsome representations to be made and more time to get answers, with the result that projects run a greater risk of death by attrition.

The situation is worse in arts and other organizations where the criteria for support admit a large variety of candidate projects (see Chapter 3) or where an organization's mission and objectives are vaguer or broader. In these circumstances, the scope for dispute is even greater and the impact on creativity is potentially even more serious.[6]

In one media organization, a group was making representations about what it would 'sell' to other parts of the organization and then waiting for months before hearing what had been 'bought'. The results were that those who had created the 'products' waited for answers with diminishing interest and increasing aggravation, and everyone found it difficult to pick up the projects again when the answers were eventually handed down.

Similarly, in a medical school, where proposals were submitted to outside charitable bodies for the funding of particular research projects, there was an interval of two years between the conception of the project and the time when funds were eventually forthcoming. The leader commented that it required considerable ingenuity to keep the project alive.

ORGANIZATIONS WITH 'BOXED' THINKING

Members of creative groups tend to be flexible and fluid in the ways they think and work: ossification and inflexibility in organizations tend to operate against the interests of creativity.[7]

Ossification and inflexibility operate against the interests of creativity

The structure of one organization was such that jobs had contents and boundaries that were firmly established. Whereas in comparable organizations 'you did everything', by contrast, in this organization the jobs of personal assistant

and researcher were firmly at the bottom of a hierarchy, with their contents and boundaries well-defined and their status clear (recognized as 'dogsbodies'!). And, in the same groups, at higher levels, the established ways in which people worked seemed to act as an obstacle to thinking about 'doing it differently'. In the Research and Development division of another company, there was an established way in which the company did things, and this seemed to box in the freedom of people in the group in their approach to their work.

By contrast, in a medical school, though the roles of the members of a research team are strongly structured, the fact that doctors are expected to undertake research if their careers are to progress seems to make the culture one which anticipates and facilitates that.

PHYSICAL SPACES

Spaces can exercise a strong influence over the creative process. One group commented that the move to new premises had had a striking effect: 'It made us feel uncomfortable: this physical environment is getting at people.' 'The solution has been to put wagons in a circle – make it like a home.' Another group felt that using a bigger meeting room would enable all the members of a team, including researchers and production assistants, to attend meetings. They were concerned about how the huge book-shelf down the centre of the office locked people away and closed down their vision; about how a closed door is extremely powerful (even though at the last moment of pressure – before a deadline – having space to yourself is vital); and about what was described as a corridor culture: if you asked a question in the corridor, there was always someone there who would know the answer.

In another field, individual scientists worked away by themselves, each in a separate laboratory, with no focal opportunities for them to meet and talk together. The leader of a group in this environment commented:

We meet together [as a group] twice a week offsite. Where you hold meetings is important. I like to have meetings over food – it contributes to the atmosphere. There is a small sandwich bar which we all like, which is just far enough offsite, but quick to get to, cheap so we can all afford to go quite often, and where the atmosphere is completely different. I realized that I was not good at getting out of here, that we needed to get together and that doing so would provide us with a sense of identity.

A film company provided a large number of extensive toast-and-coffee making points so as to increase the chances of idle discussion generating useful ideas, what the scientist Francis Crick called 'gossip'. And there is of course a consid-

erable body of knowledge and experience about the lay-out and design of scientific laboratories.

Creative projects are distinguished by interaction, and by discussion and debate: encountering things that are new and different helps people to see things in new and different ways. Where physical spaces do not encourage interaction, they are likely to be unhelpful to the creative process.

ACCEPTANCE OF RISK/FAILURE VS SUCCESS

Some organizations are more client- and task-oriented, more concerned with 'delivering': others are more conscious of how things are done and what it feels like to be working in the organization. In the former, people tend to be less aware of feelings about success (or failure).

> ... they would often not hear about how the client had responded to their efforts

In one particularly client- and task-oriented organization, the culture was one in which success was presumed. The result was that team members would often not hear about how the client had responded to their efforts, nor expect to enjoy praise or the celebration of success (as frequently characterized more creative groups). In a culture described as 'risk-averse' and in which progress is 'up-or-out', handling feelings of failure was a need which the organization did not acknowledge.

By contrast, in organizations where people are close to intense emotions and where there are high levels of risk, exposure or failure, the culture will tend to be one in which there is a great deal of emotional support, just as there is a need to celebrate success: milestones celebrated with wine and food together.

Creative work involves high levels of risk, and those who face risks need to be in a situation which recognizes the importance of both providing support and a cushion for failure, as well as affirmation and celebration of success.

HAVING TIME AND SPACE VS BEING PRESSURIZED

Experimentation is a vital part of the the creative process, and creative work requires 'time' and 'space'. Freedom over time helps to provide the right atmo-

sphere in which creativity can flourish, just as protected space is seen as essential (what one group described as a womb).

By contrast, some groups have budgets and schedules which are so pressing that they do not even have time for reviewing how they carry out a project, or to reflect upon 'process' in general. In one organization (in broadcasting), editors normally listened to every programme made by their staff; they then commented to the producer about it, and made themselves available to discuss it. Most of them also pointed out that increased responsibilities and larger numbers of staff were putting pressure on their ability to do what they evidently regarded as an essential part of their job.

Some creative organizations have set aside special spaces: for being silly, for playing, for humour, and for trying out 'mad' ideas etc; where the culture is, as it were, suspended. IBM and Kodak are among those organizations which have recognized this need, and the most distinctive 'reservations' are Walt Disney's famous three rooms, the first, the ideas room, the second, the sceptics room, and the third, the commercial room – each reserved for applying a different type of thinking. Time and space are vital for successful creative output and excessive pressure on them can destroy the creative process.

RECEPTIVE TO AND USERS OF IDEAS

Creativity is fragile, and people do not sustain their interest in producing ideas unless those ideas are welcomed and unless they are used. Organizations need to make it evident that they want ideas, and they can only do so if it is obvious that they make effective use of them: suggestion schemes quickly atrophy if the suggestions just disappear into a morass of bureaucracy.

Moreover, ideas need to be rewarded. In intimate atmospheres, the very production of ideas can itself be rewarding, where the organization evidently wants to make use of the best of them, and in more diffused organizational atmospheres, it is often necessary to make rewards more explicit.

RECOGNITION THAT PEOPLE HAVE A VARIETY OF DIFFERENT OBJECTIVES

Those who work in creative fields are as concerned with their talents and skills and with their development as they are with their job or their organization. However, as Kuhn pointed out in his book, *The Structure of Scientific Revolutions*, groups and their leaders operate in a context, and performance is affected by the way that context influences both the group and its leader.

A leader has to bear in mind the objectives of those who appointed him or her:

- how much do they want to influence him or her;
- and to what extent do they in fact do so;
- how explicit are their expectations;
- how much power do they have over his or her future;
- and how much do they use it?

For instance, a coach appointed by the British Olympic Association will be influenced more by the objectives of that organization than will a coach appointed by the team itself (as is increasingly happening in top class sport).

A leader in industrial research and development who wants to make his or her career in that organization will be more influenced by organizational objectives, plans and policies than will an academic, whose future will depend more on how his or her work is judged by peers elsewhere in the discipline. In a world in which careers are becoming increasingly hard to plan, people will be more concerned about the development of their skills and talents than about the objectives of organizations for which they work.

> ## You are not a respected Head of Department if you are not also a practitioner

This dilemma was illustrated by the head of a department in a university, who commented that 'one needs to retain a research momentum, and my responsibilities as Head of Department draw me away from my roles in research, and consequently I am losing my research momentum and credibility.' 'I am recognizing that I have a problem, which in turn means that I do not know in what direction I might aim to develop myself. And there is no institutional career development structure.' 'I feel that I am not failing my department as much as I am failing my research group.' 'However, you are not a respected Head of Department if you are not also a practitioner, and if I continue to be a practitioner, when I criticize someone, I do so from a position of strength – as someone who is getting a lot of research grants.'

In many research-based companies, dual career ladders have been established, and sometimes triple ladders, enabling specialists to secure promotion, seniority and rewards in parallel with other specialists, and of course, parallel to the management stream.

And in science, fundamental research must go where the subject leads it rather than where the market takes it, although, as I have suggested, what topics appear sexy at any one time also depends on how great an impact the results would have, and on public interest: cures for cancer are both of public interest *and* make markets. People who work in creative disciplines seem to espouse a wider variety of objectives, including especially the development of their own skills and talents.

ORGANIZATIONAL SUPPORT FOR PERSONAL DEVELOPMENT

Successful leaders of creative groups are active supporters of those who work with them as regards their personal and professional development. Some creative organizations leave issues of personal development to local departments within an overall policy of 'providing material and a ration of time, and then it is up to them', with the result that support can be described as 'patchy'. Some provide support through central training departments, sometimes offering courses on key subjects, like budgeting and appraisals; others offer a fuller range of courses, including such topics as 'project management', 'presentation skills' and 'influencing skills', from which people are invited to choose those which interest them. Sometimes, it is very much left up to individuals, who might not take up the offer without being encouraged to do so and, at other times, would be very selective on the basis of their current needs.

While one project group leader in a large chemical company said that this was more a matter for the personnel department, most leaders of creative groups feel that the development of the members of their team is an integral part of the team's work.

One leader commented that courses had 'helped me to become more aware of my existing skills, and of when and how I was using them'; 'to develop strategies for...' using strengths and overcoming weaknesses. Another that: 'Some courses are very good, where the information content is good or the role-playing is quite realistic, but mostly they do not relate well to me: they are either a waste of time or else very good.' Other leaders commented about the learning atmosphere, and the extent to which there was an active support system for personal development. And people commented about making effective use of training/development activities: 'You feel good at the time, but when you come away, you don't feel you have learned very much. Or if I have learned, I don't implement it well.'

Personal development and creative output are closely connected, and team leaders of the more creative teams concern themselves with personal development in their teams. There is, however, a much less consistent pattern in the way their organizations support personal development (see Figure 14.1).

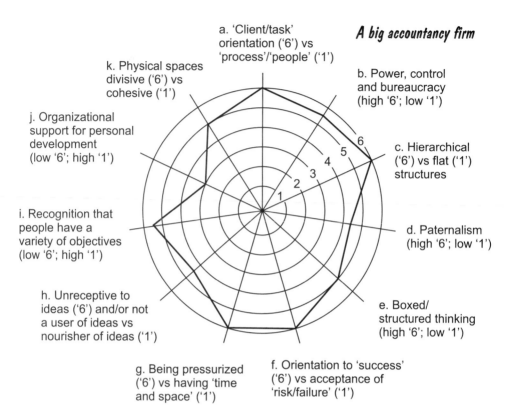

Figure 14.1 *Disabling organizational influences*

To summarize: organizations often have characteristics which are hostile to creativity: if they identify very strongly with the customer or with the task, if their cultures exert power, control and bureaucracy, if they are paternalistic, if they are hierarchical and compartmentalized, they are less likely to focus on the factors that influence creativity; if they do not manage the climate and the culture, if they exert 'pressure' without recognizing that creative people have a diversity of objectives and demand support for their personal development, if the culture is not one that welcomes ideas and makes use of them, they will be less fertile greenhouses for creativity. By ensuring that their cultures are not hostile to creativity, creative organizations can provide an atmosphere in which creative people can hope to work successfully together.

NOTES

1. Hackman, JR (1990) (ed) *Groups That Work (and Those That Don't): Creating conditions for effective teamwork*, Jossey-Bass, San Francisco.

2. Pelz, DC and Andrews, FM (1976) *Scientists in organizations: productive climates for Research and Development*, University of Michigan, Ann Arbor, Michigan.

3. Jain, RJ and Triandis, HC (1990) *Management of R&D Organizations: Managing the unmanageable*, John Wiley, Chichester.

4. Clegg, SR (1990) *Modern Organizations: Organizational studies in the post-modern world*, Sage, London.

5. Ekvall, G (1990) The organizational culture of idea management, in *Managing Innovation*, eds J Henry and D Walker, John Wiley, Chichester.

6. Holbeche, L (1997) *Motivating People in Lean Organizations*, Butterworth-Heinemann, Oxford.

7. Lessem, R (1985) The enabling company, in D Clutterbuck, *New Patterns of Work*, Gower Press, Aldershot.

15 *the leader like a cell membrane*

SHiELDiNG THE GROUP

Because creative groups are different from other sorts of work groups – the kinds of people they are, the kinds of things they do and the way they do it – they need to be shielded.[1] Kelly Johnson, head of the original skunk works at Hughes Aircraft was described thus: he 'did everything he could to protect his group from the meddling of corporate 'suits', the bean counters and go-by-the-book types who can so easily undermine a creative enterprise by trying to tame it and bring it under corporate control.'[2] In other words, he was a Shielder.

WHERE DOES SHIELDING TAKE PLACE?

Creative groups may be shielded by the leader at the level of the group itself, but they may also be shielded at higher levels. Brand management groups in the marketing division of an international drinks company are shielded at the level of the division itself, as are technical/development project groups in an international telecommunications company. And academic groups are shielded at an even higher level, in the sense that they are part of an entire organization whose mission is to be creative.

Where a creative group is operating in an alien environment, it is the project group leader who has to shield the group against the disabling influences of the rest of the organization.

190

HOW DO YOU SHIELD?

Shielding is achieved by almost any kind of distinction that keeps people apart: the laboratories of a drug company or the research facilities of a commercial or industrial group may be located at a distance from the rest of the organization; skunk works only exist some of the time; the activities of a creative department are completely different from those of the accounts department; dress codes (suits versus sandals) keep groups apart; as do the ways in which people work (action versus reflection), and the ways in which groups are organized (democratic versus hierarchical).

> **Shielders keep feelings and/or people apart**

Groups may also be divided by more subtle distinctions: one group may be funded by a client, another by grants and subsidies; one group may be all female, others predominantly male. All of these differences can keep creative groups apart from the rest of the organization.

However, keeping creative people apart from the rest of the organization also creates difficulties. Where people in the rest of the organization do not know about what creative people do, or where they do not get assurances about or do not understand what is happening in the creative groups, rumours and stories will abound. Other people will feel threatened and in turn be anxious to control the activities of those groups, which means ensuring that the creative groups behave like the rest of the organization!

WHAT DO SHIELDERS DO?

The descriptions which people use of leaders of creative groups illustrate many of the ways in which they do their shielding (see Figure 15.1).

The 'Internal Spokesperson'[3] has several roles: one of them is to explain to the rest of the organization what is happening in the group (as one leader said: 'I have to speak in two different languages and translate between the two [the organization and his group], having a discussion with bench scientists, you use one language, and talking with administrators or with people from other disciplines, you use another').

> **I have to speak in two different languages and translate between the two**

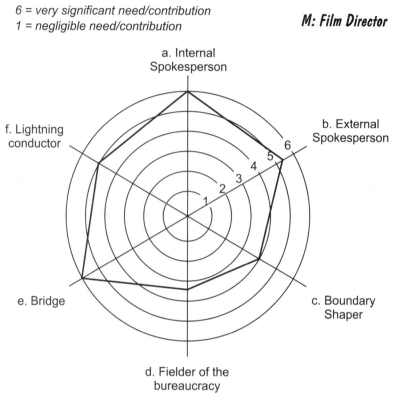

6 = *very significant need/contribution*
1 = *negligible need/contribution*

M: Film Director

a. Internal
Spokesperson

f. Lightning
conductor

b. External
Spokesperson

e. Bridge

c. Boundary
Shaper

d. Fielder of the
bureaucracy

Figure 15.1   *The roles of 'Shielders'*

Another role is that of 'selling' to the rest of the organization. In many organizations, the creative group(s) (eg research and development/marketing) constitute a vital service to the rest of the organization, and it is important to
ensure that what they produce matches the needs of the organization. And a
third role consists in obtaining support and resources (people, funds and
equipment) as well as help from the rest of the organization. This role – of
Internal Spokesperson – is characteristic in 'mutual' organizations, such as
partnerships, professional, knowledge-based and democratic organizations.

Then there is the 'External Spokesperson'[4] role. This role consists in developing relationships with collaborators, clients and customers, and with external
contacts who may be people in similar or parallel activities in other organizations, or other types of organization (eg academics, as opposed to business).
The task is to get them to understand the objectives, needs, interests and
approaches of the group, so as to orchestrate productive communications
between them and the group, and this includes making presentations. 'He was
honest, but would put a positive gloss on team performance.' 'When things

were going wrong, he portrayed success to the system, to keep the system happy!' (This role has many similarities with the role depicted in scientific research as the 'Gatekeeper'.)

> ... he portrayed success to the system, to keep the system happy

This role is typical of projects which have a specific user focus and where stimulation or feedback from outside sources is important.

There is the 'Boundary Shaper' or 'Cell Membrane'. One person has to act as the 'creator, maintainer and terminator of the membrane' which provides the boundary around the group; he is 'a process, a weaver of boundaries, a skin... which keeps the group insulated but not isolated... from the outer public environment.'

> The cell membrane ensures equilibrium between energy and emotion between the inside of the cell and the external environment

'Cell membranes have a bias towards verbs/processes, whereas the elements inside the cell have a bias towards nouns.' 'If the elements or the membrane think or act like the other, there can be disease in the cell; if the membrane becomes over-blown, the cell over-generates, disregards its environment and becomes too self-important. Alternatively, if the membrane is decaying, the cell degenerates, the team is stifled by the environment, and there is a loss of confidence.'

The creative process often requires a period of 'incubation', and if ideas, as artists will say, are articulated too soon, or see the light of day too early, they can lose their power or their fascination and evaporate. One leader talked about the need for members of the group to be engaged with the project, as enabling them to 'be silly about it', or as another said 'to do crazy things.' Funny, crazy and silly things are recognized as bridges to creative ideas and pressures to conform may simply force out the crazy. This role is often found in academic, scientific and research organizations.

Another role is called 'Fielder of the Bureaucracy', often found in large organizations, including, for example, a drug company. It consists in dealing with company documents, requests for information, returns, etc, and when they emanate from outside the research division, they can be about things which do not seem applicable to the project group, and as such they are seen as a tiresome irrelevance. The main job is to deal with the interruptions so that the team can get on with their (creative) tasks.

> **... dealing with the interruptions so that the team can get on**

Another role is called the 'Bridge'. One leader described how he had two styles; within his group he was as though in a circle with the other members of the group, sharing roles and activities; whereas his relationship to the rest of the organization was as a position on an hierarchical organization tree. In one he saw his main job as ensuring the free flow of discussion of cases (this was in an NHS Trust), and in the other, he had not only to represent the views of his group but also to act as a channel for directives coming down to the team. And he had to implement the policies and decisions taken by managers higher up the tree which were contained in these directives. 'If I agreed to something, can I carry the team with me, or do I go back and say that I can't? It all takes time.'

> **A spokesperson upwards and the implementer of organizational policies downwards**

The Bridge's job consists in being a Spokesperson upwards and the implementer of organizational policies in his or her own team; handling the constraints that are imposed from above, and ensuring freedoms in the team; handling the buck-passing that takes place in the organization above, while taking personal responsibility for his or her part in the team itself.

And another role is to act as the 'Lightning Conductor'. Pressures and tensions in creative groups can become intense, and they can give rise to the need for exceptions to rules and policies. In exercising their freedoms, members of project groups can easily bump into the boundaries set by the organization, yet in pursuit of their creative goal they need to be able to ignore those boundaries. Because creative groups are often charged with a great deal of emotional energy, what may seem small issues can become flash-points.

> **Small issues become flash-points**

For instance, someone working late finds that his papers have been sequestered by the cleaning contractor as part of the organization's clean-desks policy; in response to an urgent need, a specialist is flown out to Hong Kong in first class, in contravention of company policies. Each of these became a flash-point around which either those in the group or those in the rest of the organization rallied with emotional fervour. The Shielder had to assure one or the other party that the circumstances were exceptional and that there were good reasons for this exception. And for this purpose, he or she needed to have the trust and confidence of both sides. This role can be seen in organizations which are for the most part task-oriented, and which have clearly delineated policies and practices.

The effective leader needs to understand and to share the point of view of those who are influential elsewhere in the organization, and they in turn need to have confidence in him or her. 'I need to be able to know whether someone's interest in our work is genuine or mischievous, whether... he might need the same for another client... or wants to put a stop to it.' The organization's trust in this leader was based on the fact that he had qualified in and grown up in the firm, and that his roots were in it. His partners knew that he would not put at risk their (core) business, that he continued to subscribe to their objectives, and did not abrogate his responsibilities to them.

This same leader added: 'And it requires keeping people informed. I have a big network in the organization and I find myself in lots of different forums for lots of different purposes. All the time I am consciously marketing what is happening in our work. It helps when we get letters from clients, and I can say "Here is what we are doing" to lots of people in the firm. And the story gets passed on round, that we did a good/skilful job.'

SHIELDING INVOLVES TAKING RISKS ON BEHALF OF THE TEAM

In these situations, as shielder, the leader takes on some of the risk. Not only does he or she have a responsibility for the success of the project, but also for the impact of the work on the organization as a whole. As one leader said: 'If how you are viewed within the firm matters to you, then you would be nervous, but if what matters to you is your clients and those to whom you are responsible [your colleagues], then it is a different story, but you are of course open to the criticism of being disloyal to your Partners.'

The resulting pressures can be so great that the leader of workshops in musical improvisation was asked by a colleague whether he would rather not know what risks he was taking. In turn he suggested that what might be helping to remove some of the feeling of insecurity was the sense of mystery which he imparted to his work. A film producer commented that one of the advantages which young film directors benefited from was in not appreciating how great were the risks they were running.

Faced with these pressures, one group leader had evidently thought through his options, and he discussed the possible strategies which were open to him thus: 'I can quit; I can hit it on the head [tell them how it really is], but [if you did that] you'd have not to worry about your own job, or I can protect the team by ceasing to attend those meetings and spend more time with the team, or I can take the wheeler-dealer approach.' (He had adopted the last option.)

Leaders of creative groups do not find their position a comfortable one because their role as Shielder tends to compromise their position in their group. 'One's objective should surely be that of uniting people for a common purpose, not making them do something they do not necessarily want to do.' One leader added: 'I've been around long enough to deal with them [the responsibilities that get added from above to your existing ones]; some of them are uncomfortable and I don't like it; tasks imposed on me from above can undermine your leadership style.'

SHIELDING HELPS TO BUILD TEAMS

Boundaries work two ways: they keep pressures out, but they also keep something in: to provide an effective shield against unwanted pressures also helps to make the team more cohesive and to raise the team's morale.

Effective creative teams look inwards more than outwards for support: they tend to reject the 'help' of service departments, and spurn external training, as not meeting the (different) needs of the group, or as irrelevant, and they look for and find supporters inside the team.

This looking inwards also helps to reinforce the group's own distinctive culture. And by representing and supporting team members' points of view, what Peter Brook described as 'not betraying the essential bond of trust which is the basis for the actor and director's capacity to work together',[5] and by helping to find occasions for and helping to present their work, effective leaders also sustain group morale.

WHAT ARE THE CHARACTERISTICS OF EFFECTIVE SHIELDERS?

Effective Shielders need to have a mutual trust and confidence with their organization, and the ability to communicate well in it. They take over the risk, not only of the project, but also of its effect on the organization, and this is undermining, uncomfortable and stressful for them.

Those who are successful as Shielders tend to have two personalities, one for looking upwards (or outwards), and one for working in the team: one personality for being a leader in their team, and another personality for being a manager in the organization. As a leader in their team ('democratic', 'revolutionaries', 'protectors of the victimized'), in this personality they share the skills and characteristics of others in the team, just as they share the work.

And they have another personality for being a manager in the organization: 'trusted', 'having the same values and objectives as the rest of us', 'won't rock the boat'. In this personality, they are seen as someone in whom others elsewhere in the organization can have trust and confidence, especially as regards the impact of the work of the group on the rest of the organization.

WHAT DO EFFECTIVE SHIELDERS ACTUALLY DO?

Here are some of the things which effective Shielders do:
- They look for opportunities for group members to make presentations.
- They handle all the paperwork, so much of which asks questions from points of view which don't make sense to the creative group – HR competencies policies can be a case in point!
- They answer equivocal questions from the doubting Thomases elsewhere in the organization.
- They seek exceptions to rules; for pay, perks, facilities, conditions, because their staff do not match the rest of the organization or simply because they need it.
- They interpret organizational rules so that they are acceptable in their groups.
- They act as a steam vent.
- They turn a blind eye, as in skunk works.
- And they tell war stories about success.

To summarize, effective leaders need to 'shield' their groups from the organization, though shielding may also take place at higher levels in the organization. Creative groups have cultures which are different to the rest of the organization, and shielding is achieved by affirming these distinctions whilst maintaining the connections. Being a Shielder can entail playing a number of different roles, all of which involve taking risks on behalf of the team, but which also help to build the team. Shielders often have two distinct personalities, each appropriate for the two parties whom they have to satisfy.

NOTES

1. Amabile, T (1992) Social environments that kill creativity, in *Readings in Innovation*, eds SS Gryskiewicz and David A Hills, Center for Creative Leadership, Greensboro.
2. Bennis, W and Biederman, PW (1997) *Organizing Genius: The secrets of creative collaboration,* Nicholas Brealey, London.
3. Galbraith, J (1984) *Designing the Innovating Organisation.*
4. Shapero, A (1985) *Managing Professional People: Understanding creative performance*, Macmillan, Basingstoke.
5. Brook, P (1993) Thoughts on acting and theatre, in *There Are No Secrets*, Methuen Drama, London.

Dr MT: athletics manager

Dr MT a former Olympic track and field event manager, had been the team manager at the World Student Games in 1993, working in tandem with the team's coach. He was an Organizer, as much in relation to what happened around or away from the track/event as at it, so as to enable the athletes to achieve their best, making sure that everything ran like clockwork, thus removing pressures from the athletes. He was a Supporter, through his physical presence, his skilful feedback, and his personal relationships but established with some difficulty without being authoritarian or paternalistic. And he was an Evaluator in relation to the athletes' thinking about their aims, styles, preferences: he considered their potential.

He was an effective provider of feedback with sensitivity, honesty and integrity. 'He lets you have a chance to assess and critically analyse yourself first, then he plays his cards and says what he has to say.' 'He's not patronizing, he wouldn't shy away, but he wouldn't come up straight away.' 'He will say: "There is no point in torturing yourself".' 'He's not flippant, he knows how reactions affect individuals and how feedback is important.' 'If you didn't perform well he wouldn't lie to you, he knows you don't want to hear that.'

'He provided encouragement to help me get through my problems ('motherly' support as opposed to affirmation after success or 'fatherly' support).' 'He highlighted performance, wrote me a letter of assessment – what he felt, it meant a lot to me – the personal gesture was nice.'

He inspires confidence. He is a 'manager in whom I would have confidence that he would handle my problems well'. 'I had confidence in his ability to make things run smoothly.'

He organizes well, ensuring that information gets through to participants and he pre-plans and arranges things in advance. 'He was taking stock continually, and basing plans on circumstances in a rational and calm manner.' 'He has the situation in control; coaches were made well aware.' 'He was good at pre-planning/ organizing and arranging in advance.'

'He has a sound knowledge of team members based on previous experience of working with them' and he 'selects the management team'. 'He manages events to meet athletes' needs and styles,' and is 'out for the athletes and the sport'.

'He was giving support at all times, not just while training', and 'successfully devising routes to understanding how to support each individual athlete's aims, style, thinking, preferences, etc; providing support, and showing commitment for doing so'. 'He was always there, made out sheets, taking athletes to the track, asking for queries.' 'He was readily available for a chat/laugh/conversation', 'he doesn't distance himself from the team.' 'We were treated like we were important as individuals, representing the country'; he is 'not a... command-type figure, he is good at explaining what he is doing'.

He helps to empower individuals through a participative management style, but he also has the ability to force issues if needed, without having or using authority. 'As team manager, he organized through the coaches, well aware of what we should be doing without our being forced.' There was 'participative management within the management team' and 'participation as key motivating factor for team members'. The coach commented: 'He was giving authority/power', 'influencing without power (as consulting/getting support or advice/putting arguments forward)'.

'He was setting standards and providing expectations/positive thinking', 'helping top class athletes to top class performances' and 'removing blocks to individuals' better performance'. He was keen to explore what impact, if any, he could have personally in helping to motivate athletes.

'One is one's own most severe critic,' he added, 'so one is surprised when one finds virtues!' He sets high standards and is hard on himself.

It was obviously easy for MT to get it wrong: the athletes spoke about things that demotivated them, including the manager not knowing an athlete's name, or getting it wrong; being indecisive; lacking confidence; not ensuring that the logistic arrangements go smoothly (seen as the key role for the manager); or not acquiring sufficient funding for the event.

It would also have been easy to be interfering, for instance by offering feedback during an event rather than saving it up for post-games debriefing. This detracts from athletes 'keeping in the here-and-now state', something which is crucial for success. MT added that he had to bite his tongue a lot. He recalled one occasion when he wanted to provide an input which he felt would help one particular athlete's performance: he could offer it as a suggestion but not a recommendation; or alternatively he could use the coach, as someone who was closer to the athlete, as an intermediary, and let him decide whether to pass on the feedback at that time. 'The question of when feedback is given during an event is something which an athlete should have discussed with his coach before the games.'

He did not have the opportunity to get as close to the athletes as the coach did, and yet he still had a strong need to see that they did well and to do all within his power to ensure that that happens. As the manager, he had to take every opportunity to make personal contact and to build a rapport with the athletes, but sometimes the athletes did not want that; for example, they did not want the manager eating with them at the Games. One athlete pointed out that managers in general are perceived as 'school maamish', something reminiscent of his days when performing in youth teams. Nor did he always get feedback on how athletes were feeling and whether they were experiencing any problems, as the coach does, or as it transpired the physiotherapist does. Athletes open up to the physiotherapist when they are laid up on the couch, but expect that to be a confidential relationship; the physio can provide psychological as well as physical comfort.

200

Against the odds, as a manager, MT's influence went deeper than simply organizing things so that the athletes were provided with circumstances in which they could give of their best: he was 'devising routes to understand how to support each individual athlete's aims, style, thinking, preferences, etc; he was providing support, and showing commitment for doing so'.

CT: conductor and head of opera studies

At the Guildhall School of Music and Drama, CT led a rehearsal for the Opera Department's production of Mozart's *La Finta Giardiniera*, at which his expressed aims were to act as a focusing and galvanizing force to help individuals with a wide range of talents to work through specified difficulties. He aimed to get students to work together to realize their potential; to supply individuals with a direction which would enable them to function together with a common aim and objective; to create the conditions to solve particular problems that can occur in rehearsals; to help produce young professionals for the opera world and market-place through the process of rehearsal and performance; and to create possibilities for students to realize their talents and to perform at their best, by working with them to 'make music/opera' at the highest possible level.

He carefully communicates to the group the objectives of the work so that members know from the outset what is required and expected, and he keeps everyone informed. 'The Conductor's messages were clear and precise'; 'they were secure and unambiguous.' 'He keeps the information flowing.' He recognizes the importance of communication and briefing not only for the success of the production but also for student-learning. 'The relationship with the Director worked very well and we communicated well with each other.' 'The Conductor managed the dialogue well between himself and the other performers/managers, and was able to gather and retain attention.'

He is a good planner, meticulous about details, and very practical, for example in making sure rehearsals run to time. He sees order and structure as essential elements for the daily running of the opera school. 'The rehearsal was thoroughly planned in advance.' 'The Conductor gives more detailed indications.' 'The Conductor got through the work of the rehearsal; he was very time-disciplined'; 'it was well managed'. 'The rehearsal was a very practical event, the act comes out without you realizing it.'

His commitment to his students shows in the ways he matches pieces to students, and in the way he is always well versed in score and text. 'He chooses pieces more on the match to his students.' 'He came to the rehearsal well prepared and understood the text.' 'He went over sections in detail and put them back together again.'

He gives responsibility by degrees, depending on the nature of the project, and he finds a balance between giving out responsibility and being supportive to his students; 'he allowed me to be responsible at different levels'.

He understands what is needed to spur individuals into working harder and what is needed to develop their individual talents, 'by putting hurdles of the right height in front of the right people at the right time'. 'He looks for/sees evidence of improvement.'

'He fixes things that go wrong.' 'The project was a great learning experience.'

'I aim to give them overall objectives, provide opportunities, and light the blue touch-paper. It's all psychology, not music!'

He ensures progress at a steady rate and maintains momentum by careful management. 'Progress was made at the right rate.' 'The Conductor ensured continuity during rehearsal and kept the event flowing.'

He is analytical as well as being self-critical, and is constantly examining ways to improve the production. He highlights aspects of the performance to think about for the next rehearsal.

'Matching the comments you give to the needs of individuals is the biggest problem; it is a sort of game,' said CT. 'He has a good memory for predicting what areas might need attention at future rehearsals.' 'At the end of the rehearsal, he reflects upon how the rehearsal went, makes notes on where things could be improved and where necessary talks to individual players before the next rehearsal.'

'Different things develop at individual rehearsals: a long rehearsal may for instance develop the character being played.' 'It grew till you saw it as a whole at the end.' 'Exciting; lots of slow work over the previous four days bore real fruit'; 'the show must build on itself for improvement'. Different people saw different moments in the cycle of rehearsals as key incidents in the development of the production: the choice of the piece, everyone's first sight of the designs, the second stage and piano rehearsal, the first full dress-rehearsal with orchestra etc.

'Only when you have got it all organized can you show your artistry in the established (ensuing) performance.' 'You need to leave 5 per cent for inspiration of the moment.' 'The point of the exercise is to highlight individuality and harness it'; 'I am too heavy-handed: yet people can get lost with too much freedom. Taking the Director's instructions and running with it in you own way is best.' 'Some Producers introduce a great deal of uncertainty and take a lot of risks, and this can potentially produce an extraordinary performance'; and while 'risk and challenge create energy', it can also 'risk student confidence'.

'We are organized and reasonably gentle; maybe our efforts to achieve something that is smooth-running and with high morale contribute to a high quality performance, but they are never a sufficient condition for that.' 'Two different approaches may arrive at the same quality of performance.' 'My experimentation,' said CT, 'takes place in rehearsal by phrasing, interpretation, reflecting the intentions, ideas and emotions of the production; by speaking the text in rhythm or, as on one occasion, playing a piece in the dark so as to create the fear of people who can't "see where they're going"'. 'I do try and get a feel about what individuals might do or achieve; you can then hope that you have a basic level of presentation as a spring-board for a best performance on the night.' 'You are trying to give yourself,' said the Director, 'maximum chances of success. We did have something solid, we felt. Whether it was alright on the night or not would determine whether it was exceptional.' 'There is so much chance/ephemerality in success: how well it works on the night is so much at the behest of diverse, osmotic events; they take over.'

Professor FH: head of a child psychiatry clinic

FH had inherited a multi-disciplinary clinic in an NHS Mental Health Trust, and with it, a very distinctive culture. In the previous regime it was a place where individuals did what they liked without reference to other team members; where long-term, individual work was thought to be the best way of working; where long, detailed discussion was the focus of departmental meetings; where departmental parties were famous for their wonderful, home-cooked food; where rooms were completely devoid of decoration or personality, and deviation from this felt like a sin; but which had a strong sense of history and was itself a centre of excellence for child analytic knowledge and work. FH was seeking to change this by 'getting everyone to want to and agree to work within the same frame-work: developing team structures with a coherent philosophy, with clients being allocated on the basis of a thorough assessment from which a treatment plan could be clear, bringing together skills and ambitions that are subject to centrifugal forces'. ('If a case goes to someone in one particular discipline, the options are more limited,' he added.)

FH felt that the staff of the clinic were like adolescent children, wanting to go their own ways. 'I feel like someone treating a psychosomatic illness: you cannot discuss it with them as such, only in terms of the symptoms with which they present. But I need to test that from time to time by offering a coded message, to the effect that I know that it is psychosomatic, but I also know that they will not admit it; a message which may not be fully understood.' He added: 'This is not a strategy I favour; I feel obliged to use it because there is no genuine consensus about the basic aim of the clinic and structures to achieve them.'

'Similarly, my management messages need to be multi-layered and coded. I wish it were not so, but then I would be wishing away the causes of the problem from which the service draws strength: I would like my colleagues to be totally self-determined in the way they developed their own activities, but if they were, we could not achieve the better multi-disciplined team-work approach which I seek. If I am explicit in constraining them, I remove the very self-determination in them which I value and which they seek. So my messages must be coded and multi-layered.' He added: 'Again, the basic problem is that we do not agree about aims, objectives or the nature of the work of the clinic. The above strategies are used because ours may be regarded as (in some ways) a "dysfunctional group".'

In his best moments, he must have felt that he was making progress in the clinic; that the existing service was adequate; that he and his colleagues were at pains to get on with one another; that he organized things well; and that he succeeded in fostering experimentation and exploration in this field. In his worst moments, he clearly felt isolated, beleaguered, powerless, undermined and unsupported, giving on to a sense of despair.

FH at times adopted a directive approach. Some appeared to regard this as undesirable and therefore a weakness, but in the circumstances it might also be regarded as a strength. He sought (for instance at clinic meetings) to elicit different views from the whole team and to encourage participation, and he sought to encourage freedom for individual members of the team. He was surprised at how directive he was seen and thought an authoritarian style not uncommon among doctors.

Between him and certain members of the team, there were two fundamental differences: the first about power, as between different professions/disciplines, and the second about the proper objectives for the clinic.

The view had been expressed that psychiatrists should not have as much power as he exercised; indeed, FH said that it had even been proposed to management that psychiatrists should be barred from being clinically accountable for cases referred to the service. Loyalty and commitment were not always to the department, but to one's discipline, and at times this was seen as undermining.

Second, FH's view was that the clinic was a tertiary service (ie a specialist referral service) as well as a community secondary service, whereas there also existed the view that it should be a primary healthcare service (ie a community service).

In these circumstances, in order that decisions be made which were probably essential for the continuing running of the clinic, he had to take a number of these decisions himself. Others kept their heads down. And these disagreements seem to have given rise to some very unpleasant feelings, and even threats, as well as being potentially damaging to the service of the clinic.

There was general agreement that it was desirable to work to try and achieve a more cohesive team, and that perhaps they could find some 'issues we could all get interested in' and 'not feel threatened about', but ways of achieving that were suggested which seemed intended to pursue the different objectives which each side espoused. And, as one person commented, 'Issues regarding policy or strategy are often left unresolved.'

The group was seen as very supportive: it was held together by personal relationships, as it was by suppressing its difficulties and projecting them elsewhere. However, it was also seen as only partially open. 'There is a great deal of conflict avoidance around here.' 'Cautious'; 'playing safe'; 'practising getting to know one another'.

'FH solicited and supported the expression of different views.' 'He gives people an opportunity to voice their individual difficulties in new ways of working.' 'No one has to compromise their ideas by agreeing to someone else's plan.' Particularly in clinic meetings, he encouraged the exchange of ideas by adopting a more consensual style of leadership than was evident in other situations in the clinic. 'He asks what has been done since your last meeting.' 'He gets people to explore a particular case.' 'By keeping things open, he helps to bring about creative exchange.' 'He gives you new ideas from where you are at.'

He encouraged participation by team members. 'He gets people involved.'

'He encourages people to set the agenda'; and he encouraged experimentation. The staff talked about a culture that was 'exploratory', 'experimenting', and that 'built on existing approaches'.

He promoted the development of skills and knowledge in the team. Staff talked about 'doing innovative work that was good practice'; 'everyone here able to develop themselves and their potential'; and 'improving your ability to make differential diagnoses'.

However, despite all this, the members of the group did not see each other or the group and its activities in very similar terms: there was, nonetheless, fairly wide agreement on the fact that they were neither particularly successful nor creative.

PART VI

LEARNING HOW TO LEAD

16 *wearing learning spectacles*

SEEiNG EVERYTHiNG AS A LEARNiNG OPPORTUNiTY

How do effective leaders develop their skills and talents as leaders? What kinds of situations provide them with opportunities for doing so, and how do they approach and use those opportunities?

The conductor Sir Simon Rattle's father, who was in his spare time a jazz pianist, and his sister, who taught him to read scores and introduced him to 20th-century music, helped him, along with neighbours, when he was very young to give his Sunday afternoon concerts, which consisted of playing records with his 'live' added percussion. Totally driven by music, he learned several instruments, and 'could play the piano like a complete orchestra, could tell the singers what to do, and gave everyone confidence... in the nicest possible way, he took over'. An extrovert, he is an adept organizer of groups, performances and programmes. At 15, he conducted his first symphony at a charity concert, and continued to conduct the Merseyside Concert Orchestra once a week, becoming its appointed conductor before he left for the Royal Academy of Music. At 16, he went to the Royal Academy, where he raced 'round...with stars in his eyes', 'picking the brains of every professor in the building',[1] drawing honey from every musical flower he could find. In his third year at the Academy, against the odds, he won the John Player Conducting Competition and left the Academy because the prize consisted of a two-year stint with the Bournemouth Symphony Orchestra with its smaller Sinfonietta, which provided him with an essential opportunity to learn the repertory. He is always adventuring, slightly ahead of his experience and ability, and risking making bad music for the experience of trying and learning, his natural abilities as a conductor and musician continually developing and building.

SOURCES OF LEARNING

In many creative fields, there is little or no training for leadership, yet to become an effective leader of a creative group requires a completely new/different set of skills, which often have to be learned very fast.

I suggested (in Chapter 4) that in effective creative groups, everyone is from time to time a leader, and that one of the skills of leadership is that of making your contribution have its due weight. Successful leaders of creative groups are both experts in their own field as well as being effective leaders of their groups and, as such, their learning takes place in two different spheres. Moreover, their skills as learners are of special interest because, as we saw in Chapter 10, there is a very close relationship between learning and creativity.

> ### A rage to learn

Leaders of creative groups see every task, every project, every event as a learning opportunity (see Figure 16.1): they have what Howard Gardner has called 'a rage to learn'. One leader spoke about two tasks, in which he had been involved, as seminal experiences in his learning: one when he had been encouraged to develop his skills as a presenter and another when he had worked with a number of experts from various external fields on the pioneering development of 'activity-based costing'. Another leader spoke about how he had learned in a sales course, when he had given over the task of shooting a short film to a cameraman, how important it was for creative people to have what he called back-up services. The leader of another project group spoke about the way in which each successive project he undertook became an opportunity for learning in one way or another. 'I am a life-long learner,' he said. 'Every day is a learning experience. If I am not learning, I am not living!'

In a recent study of mine,[2] parents were seen as role-models in mentoring younger members, as supporters and encouragers, as making everything seem interesting and enjoyable, as open-minded, permissive and supportive, as *laissez-faire* ('I was never controlled at home'); mothers as calm and unflappable, and as approachable; a father as setting standards, being prepared to follow through and working with the positive; and parents as organizers and organized, and as both good teachers (mother a role model as a facilitator, and father dominant and a stronger influence).

Many talented people tell of how one particular teacher fired their imaginations for their subject, or of how he or she acted as a mentor or guide in their progress. Schools in the UK do not have as strong a tradition for synthesis and creativity as they do for analysis and deconstruction, and of those who become

6 = *very significant*
1 = *very insignificant*

Professor JP (See p 219)

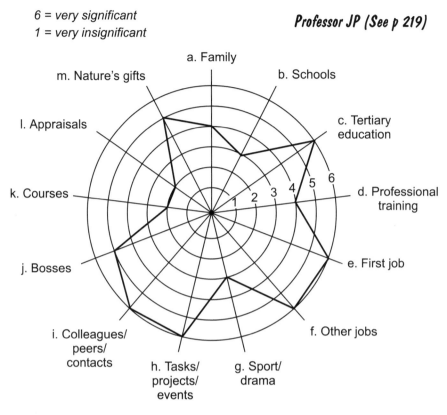

Figure 16.1 *Sources of learning*

leaders of successful creative groups, it is unsurprising to find as many who are negative about their schooling as are positive. For every one person who at school discovers their talent, finds help in developing it or in taking responsibility for their own learning, there is another who finds it a place in which subjects are taught in an intimidating style, where things are forced on you, or where there are blocks of one kind or another.

Tertiary education can of course also be the origin of one's present interest/passion, just as it may also be the place where you can make your own mark. Professional training may also be an important influence in learning, an encouragement to look into things and to take the initiative for one's own learning.

A study by Sosniak[3] of the learning of exceptionally talented children proposes three distinct phases of learning, to which these findings (above) can be compared. In the first, the child is immersed in the field, being provided with a wide variety of opportunities to experience and enjoy it. In the second phase, learning concentrates on detailed study and analysis of all aspects of the subject, including theory, practice, history etc. And in the third, the focus is upon particular issues, problems, controversies etc, and how they are handled and resolved or treated.

> **Sport and drama provide the main opportunities for learning about leadership at school or university**

My research also showed how learning about leadership at school or at university is something whose principal contexts are sport and drama. In other subjects, including science and technology, working in groups is rarely found in educational environments. It is therefore unsurprising that a high proportion of leaders (and perhaps leaders not only of creative groups) have been involved in sport, often in several sports, and often as captain, but also as coach/manager, and many have had experience of working in drama in their earlier lives.

After completion of formal education, and on entering the world of 'work', one's first job has an important influence upon one's learning, for instance in matching up one's skills to a practical task, as an apprenticeship, as an inspiration, but also, sometimes, as a shock! And each new job brings new interests, new lessons and new challenges especially in terms of dealing with people.

> **Bosses and colleagues as role models for learning about leadership**

Almost all leaders of creative groups find role models the most important influences in their learning, mainly their bosses, but also colleagues/peers/contacts, and occasionally, relations. They learn from their management/leadership style, they learn about the way they do things and the atmospheres they create. Most of this learning is derived from positive characteristics and experiences, though a considerable amount is also drawn from negative experiences. Successful leaders of creative groups seem to learn more from colleagues/peers/contacts etc, and they learn more from the positive than from the negative. From 'bad bosses', they sometimes learn most about interpersonal skills.

It seems extraordinary that this understanding, with its clear link to Kanigel's thesis that Nobel Prize winners commonly have other Nobel Prize winners as their mentors (see Chapter 10), has not resulted in a more conscious exploration of mentoring and its role in developing leadership in creative fields.

Training courses can help people to become more aware of their skills and talents as leaders, provided the content is appropriate and provided they are designed to help participants with the commonly perceived difficulty of implementing their learning. However, courses tend to be of inappropriate length: they do not match up with the times for which people can get away; they tend not to present material in the ways that participants find easiest to assimilate; they focus on knowledge rather than experience; they are often not about or relevant to the type of work in which participants are interested; and participants complain that they do not meet people on them whose work is similar enough to their own. They are also seen as too expensive! Overall, courses in management are not seen as a very valuable investment by those who work in creative fields, and the money is regarded as better spent on getting on with one's own thing!

Courses are naturally more likely to be a source of learning for those in larger organizations, where they tend to be offered in the form of a menu from which people can choose what they see as useful to them.

Appraisals contribute significantly to learning, provided they are seen as fair and realistic. Sometimes they are vitiated because they are given by a line or functional boss who does not know you so well, and sometimes insufficient time or care is devoted to them. Although the concept of appraisals is spreading beyond the corporate sector, some leaders (such as film directors) never receive an appraisal of what they do – of their 'performance' – as a director, and find it extremely difficult to get one.

However, not all skills and talents are learned (though most can be developed), and there are, of course, many personal qualities which are part of the equipment with which one is born, or which develop mainly in the earlier periods of life, such as temperament, sensitivity, competitiveness, sense of humour, learning styles, thinking styles and types of intelligence. One leader explained that he had always been a negotiator: 'I was always brilliant at swaps', and an organizer: 'aged 5, I was the organizer in the street gang!'

LEARNING BY DOING AND BY REFLECTING ON IT

Effective leaders of creative groups see management as being something that is experiential or evolutionary: you try something out, and if it does not work, you try something else. And it must surely be of some concern that many such leaders comment that one of their aims is to treat people as they would have wanted to be treated, and they are keen to spell out what that means.

Leadership of creative groups seems to be learned mainly by doing, by being on the job, more than it is by any other learning style. 'I put myself in new situations.' 'Life is a challenge... I throw myself into it and play for more than I can afford to lose.' And this learning-by-doing is accompanied by self-awareness'/

private reflection/learning retrospectively. This combination of learning styles puts the learning of leadership firmly into the Activist/Reflector quadrant of Honey and Mumford's analysis of learning styles[4] (see Figure 16.2).

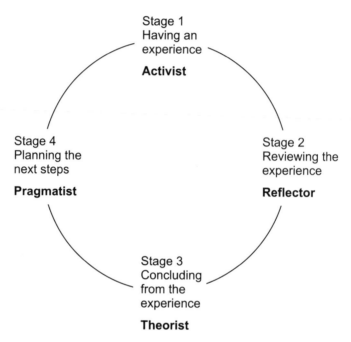

Figure 16.2 *Honey and Mumford's learning styles*

In their specialized fields, leaders of creative groups often have a strong ability to imagine (aural, visual or conceptual picturing and memory, skills on which neuro-linguistic programming focuses). Effective learners set up conversations, they talk, discuss, present arguments and seek explanations. While reading is a source of some learning, they are also good observers, listeners and watchers. And there are some who find 'models', pictures and diagrams useful adjuncts which help them to make sense of the world (see Figure 16.3).

Learning leadership is of course unlike learning a subject, a language or a machine; it is a performance skill; it is more like learning cookery or sex, it is something which you have to experiment with, reflect about, and then try again. One reflective leader (in academia) commented that learning about management was completely different from everything else he had to learn; there, he said, it is books first, whereas management is more like a life-skill, more like how to be a good father.

Effective leaders of creative groups see a part of their essence as being learners ('life-long learners'). One said, 'it is hard to distinguish learning from

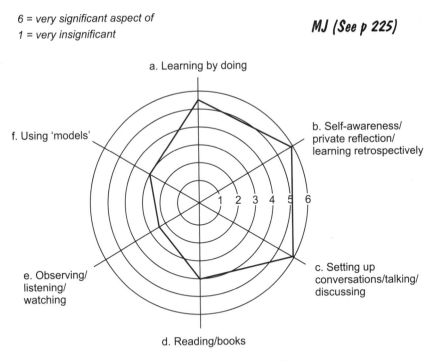

MJ (See p 225)

6 = *very significant aspect of*
1 = *very insignificant*

a. Learning by doing

f. Using 'models'

b. Self-awareness/
private reflection/
learning retrospectively

c. Setting up
conversations/talking/
discussing

d. Reading/books

e. Observing/
listening/
watching

Figure 16.3 *Learning styles*

creation'; and another spoke about how 'learning opportunities walk through my door in sufficient quantity nowadays'. They also see sources of learning as almost infinitely varied: among his sources of learning, one included having a goal, his squash coach, bringing up his children, and the way he himself was managed.

Learning leadership as a life skill

Most effective leaders see their learning as stimulated by challenges, targets and goals. Some see it as stimulated by pressure, or occasionally as blocked by the presence of pressure (see Figure 16.4). Sometimes a leader sees his learning as best stimulated by unstructured situations, sometimes by doing something totally different, occasionally by being able to see an immediate use for it.

Learning atmospheres are frequently seen as important, even 'crucial' for successful learning; one leader drew a distinction between the personal, the departmental and the organizational learning atmosphere. One organization was seen as being a supporter of personal development but less so of career development, another as not providing enough time for people to be able to develop new skills.

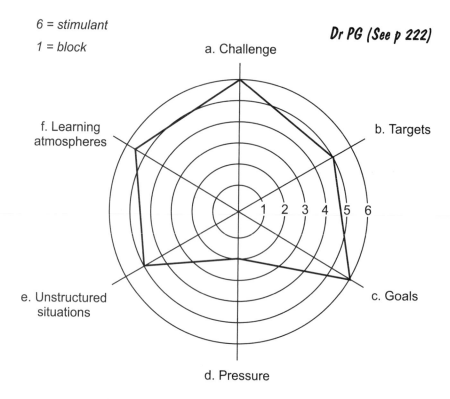

Figure 16.4 *Stimulants and blocks to learning*

WHAT ARE THE MOST URGENT LEARNING OBJECTIVES?

One common learning objective is about time management: the pressures on one's time are such that many managers/leaders need to do more of their management by means of fewer and more specific occasions. Some leaders feel they want to be able to express their opinions more, to be more explicit in what they say and do, and to become more concise, clearer, firmer and blunter, and to exercise their authority more overtly. And there are some who would like to become *less* blunt and subtler, and distinguish more between how they approach different individuals. Another common learning objective is to gain confidence and become more ambitious, to be braver and bolder, more radical and expansive. A fourth objective is political awareness, how the leader or his or her group influences and is influenced by the organization/world outside it, how that wider constituency is changing and how one's group fits in with it and its changes (see Figure 16.5).

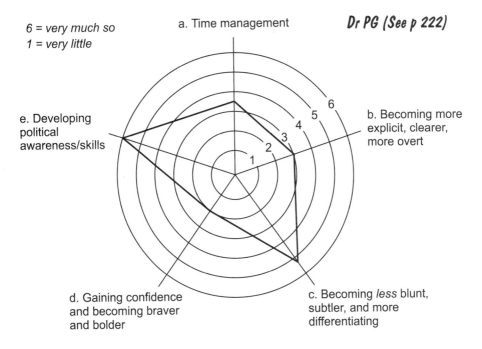

6 = very much so
1 = very little

a. Time management

Dr PG (See p 222)

e. Developing political awareness/skills

b. Becoming more explicit, clearer, more overt

d. Gaining confidence and becoming braver and bolder

c. Becoming *less* blunt, subtler, and more differentiating

Figure 16.5 *Learning objectives*

Another concern for such leaders is about imminent points in their careers when they will have to make a choice about whether their future lies in their own specialization or in management.

Finally, a number of leaders of creative groups are motivated by ways in which they have been treated in their early lives, sometimes vivid memories, which have had a traumatic impact upon their outlook and left them with a passionate determination to help or support others in a particular way. Someone who was not challenged by her parents sought to find the right opportunity to show the true quality of her talents; someone bullied at school was a passionate champion and empowerer of the victimized; someone who had suffered intense pain in early childhood with almost fatal effects sought to help us all to break our stereotypes, especially of people who have been damaged by life in some way.

To summarize, the most significant ways in which leaders of more creative and more successful groups said they did their learning were as follows:

- They indicated that their learning was based on role models, mainly but not solely bosses they had experienced, and from their negative characteristics as well as their positive.
- They indicated that their learning was also very much derived from their

own experiences – from their doing, including projects, tasks and events – as much as jobs they had had.

- They indicated that they did their learning mainly through self-awareness and by reflecting about their experience.

This is a picture not inconsistent with Schön's[5] depiction of the experiential learner as a 'reflective practitioner', but one in which the learning experiences are distinctively different from management in fields in which creativity is less important.

A striking aspect of a number of these leaders was their attitude to learning, as being of the essence of their work: they saw learning and creativity as very similar, if not different aspects of the same thing.

NOTES

1. Kenyon, N (1987) *Simon Rattle: The making of a conductor*, Faber and Faber, London.
2. Whatmore, J (1996) *Managing Creative Groups: what makes people good at it*, Roffey Park Management Institute, Sussex.
3. Sosniak, LA (1988) *Changing relationship between student and teacher in the development of talent*, Education and Society, **6** (1 and 2), pp 79–86.
4. Honey, P and Mumford, A (1992) *The Manual of Learning Styles*, Peter Honey.
5. Schön, DA (1995) *The Reflective Practitioner: How professionals think in action*, Arena, new edition.

Professor JP: a life-long learner, every day generating new learning experiences

Professor JP was the leader of a project to devise a multi-media package for enabling Fire Service Fire Controllers to learn how to control fires (see page 20). A life-long learner, with every day generating new learning experiences, he found himself with a succession of new interests, each providing unremitting fascination, and on a series of life-journeys with different people. 'I throw myself into the game; I play for more than I can afford to lose. Life is a challenge. I am a doer; and I will learn from it.'

'I first got into management,' he said, 'when I was 11 and became a prefect: there were so many injustices.

'And then when I first got a university job, I was appalled at the lack of management's willingness to make decisions, to take responsibility, to think out, to plan how things could be better. On one occasion, the authorities tried to get the Art Faculty, of which I was part, which worked a four-day week, to change to a five-day week, but without any increase in pay. I brought the Union and Clive Jenkins in. Ultimately we settled for a 20 per cent increase in pay instead of the 25 per cent we had asked for. But then I realized that the injustices are still there.

'And then I turned to research. The university didn't want me to do so, so it became a question of how to beat the system (my style of management is about turning the system to your advantage). Most architects are more concerned with the physical nature of the environment, but I was interested in the social, technical, managerial and anthropological nature of the environment. And as I learned, so I put into practice.

'One of the problems that came our way was why Housing Associations fail, and from that work with teams, we developed [the card game which enables teams to explore the roles which members play in teams, their Belbin roles] "Team Role Rummy".

'Then I became interested in the organic nature of teams. I began to explore the significance of events; for instance, how breaking bread together influenced the first Evangelists. After a time, momentum in teams can become unstoppable, but it takes time and hard work; the 'process' side needs working at. People aren't cussed, but they do need to have a tension; otherwise life becomes comfortable and easy. People enjoy being in my teams.

'And I am interested in the sociology of groups, so I began to look at their cultural values. If you can understand the culture from which people come, it is easier to understand them and to help you relate to them.

'I am on a series of journeys with different people.' He, as his team had done, talked of groups in metaphorical terms, as organisms, which interact, grow, change, split and decay.

'Management does give one a desire to control, but it is really all about adding value. By nature, I am a controller; if someone upsets me, I will revert to "controlling" my way out of the problem and I will tend to upset people by doing it in that way.

'One of the greatest influences upon me was a man I once met, an Admin Assistant, an ex-Rear Admiral, who had only one phrase: "I am Frank, and can I help you?" he would say. He had all of the university doing what he wanted! He would never say "Don't do it like that!" but rather: "I don't know whether I would have done it that way." Whenever I have a problem, I ask myself, "How would Frank have handled it?"

'Two people have been most influential in my life. The first one was the result of deciding to do a degree in Building. The Professor was a very small, old-fashioned prof, knowledgeable, open-minded: he convinced me to have confidence in myself. In the end, he had me give his final lectures at Manchester, while he sat in the audience and listened!

'The second was someone to whom I was introduced on a funny course which the building degree tapped into, called "Design Methodology". I spent a great deal of time arguing: he thought me a neo-fascist! He told me "You have spent 20 years as a scientist and mathematician, but you are not thinking. You do what you are good at, but you don't go beyond that: you must understand how people operate, how they manage." I spent four years thinking about that.

'I see everything in practical terms, and in terms of everyday examples.

'I am dynamic; I throw myself into the game; I play for more than I can afford to lose. Life is a challenge. I am a doer and I will learn from it.

'At university, I rarely went to a lecture: I can't listen for long, and my handwriting is so bad, but my labs were wonderful. So I worked with someone who read and wrote well: I did his experiments and he gave me his notes.

'When I do read, I have to read purposefully. Then I learn by reading and re-interpreting. At the moment, I am interested in autobiography and narratives about people who are in difficult circumstances, looking to understand the context into which people have got themselves.

'I am a life-long learner: every day is a learning experience. If I am not learning, I am not living! Macmillan had a note written up in his offices which said: "Cool, calm deliberation disentangles every knot." That is the antithesis of what I am!

'I am currently interested in the relationship between responsibility, capability and accountability: responsibility as the acceptance of a personal challenge, that one will engage one's capabilities to bring something about, and in that sense be responsible for how to do it, and for doing the necessary tasks. What is capability; how do you recognize when you have it; if you have it, how do you off-load things, and fulfil your responsibility? How do you ensure that you remain accountable during the process of taking responsibility? (I may have responsibility, but not the necessary empowerment. To take away responsibility sets up or takes back ownership of the problem to a different level.) And I am working these issues into a new research proposal.

'Currently I am interested in conflict. How does it arise? Do you just let it arise? And how do you handle it? If I have a bee in my bonnet, I'll set up a research project to handle it.

'Nowadays, learning challenges walk through the door: I have no trouble in finding them. What is frustrating is that so much time in organizations is spent in blaming; it is so natural, but it is not creative, that is no way to regenerate Great Britain. I am enjoying this portfolio of challenges, to have responsibilities I have never had before.

'I think I help others mainly by example. Academic staff say to me, "What can you do for me?" and I respond: "What do you do? Write me an A4 page on what you do." If they come back with that, that shows commitment and we will then see if we can put ourselves into a situation together, apply for a grant for something, or go to a conference together. Most people are in a double bind: either they have given up on their own self-development, or else they don't know how to work on it. If we don't get on or I can't help them, I will suggest how they might help themselves, or I'll say "I think I know ways of freeing you up." I recognized this pattern at my last university, but here, I am in a position to do something about it.

'I don't work with anyone in whom I don't see potential. At Oxbridge, you tend to get arrogant anarchists, but here there are many people who are incredibly capable, but they are lost so we must work together to achieve anything. It's all about recognizing potential skills and juxtaposing them with others (as Gregory Bateson said).

Dr PG: determination, curiosity and 'doings' as drivers of learning

Dr PG has taken a number of decisive decisions in the course of his education in order to ensure that his primary interest, first in science, later in chemistry, and then in colour chemistry, could flourish. Relaxed and gregarious on the outside, he has a steely interior and a tremendous will-to-win. As he has had to be more involved with people, he has found himself less tolerant and more rigorous with them; less patient and more forceful. Despite finding that he was needing to be more aware of organizational politics, he has still sometimes found himself too outspoken for comfort. He has an endless curiosity and enjoys motivating people by treating them fairly and with responsibility, and he hates injustice and privilege. He learns by doing, or seeing something done and by reading. He is a keen reader, writer and gardener.

A group leader for some seven or eight years, he now manages 12 to 15 scientists, working in groups on about a dozen projects. Before that, his interest was in 'the thrill of difficult [scientific and technological] targets and challenges, and of finding the simplest route for making money for the company'.

Until the age of 14, he was at a small primary school outside Wigan: 'we couldn't afford the 11+'. 'I always came top in all the tests, and those from lower down passed it.' 'Then I went on to a brand new secondary modern school where I got interested in science and there was a very good science teacher. My headmaster said I should go to the grammar school, and I did, for one day, but I found that they all knew one another and had done so since the age of 11, and the facilities for science were no good. So, from age 16 to 17, I went to Wigan Technical College three nights a week.

'At 19, I got a job at the company as a scientific assistant, the lowest possible grade, and at the same time, doing part-time day release plus three nights a week for my HNCs. Then I took the professional chemistry qualification ('GRIC'), but I felt maybe I was missing out on the university atmosphere. So I asked the company for a one-year release to do the final part, and perhaps a PhD afterwards. The company dithered, so I said "Sod it!" and went off and did it on my own. I got married that year and I got a first class, and an offer of a PhD at Salford University. But I also wanted a house and the house won! I re-applied to the company and got retaken on, four grades higher.

'While I am fairly relaxed and amiable, I have a steely interior: I am very competitive and have a tremendous will-to-win. I played a lot of rugby; I remember playing games as a 5- or 6-year-old, marbles and cards; I hated losing! I work hard and effectively and I expect that from others.

'I now have less time to work on the technical side, because I have to do more management; I don't like that, but you have to. And you become more firm in dealing with people, tougher, in subtle ways, as in telling them about their career prospects, or telling them when to change their approach; more forceful, less tolerant, less patient. I am not pleased with that: I *was* more understanding. I think it comes about from all the pressure, the responsibility for meeting deadlines, and more overseas trips last year.

'And I have become more aware of the politics. I am quite headstrong and outspoken. I recently told someone in marketing that he wasn't dealing with something properly, instead of going through the proper channels, and I have been reprimanded for that. I have learned to be more conscious of the politics just by being aware of what has happened in the past.

'I still spend twice as much time on the science as I do on management, that is what really interests me. I do enjoy writing (I have written two books and edited another) and I enjoy speaking at conferences. But I always enjoyed working with things more than I did working with people, and doing things in chemistry. I don't mind motivating people, but admin is just a chore, and 'initiatives' and things like safety, quality and audits take a lot of time.

'What have been the influences on my management style? I think the family is a good role model. If you treat people fairly and with responsibility, they'll do the same for you. That attitude comes from the family, from the aunts and uncles who brought me up, and from my schooling: the primary was a Methodist-type school where you either got a reward or a severe punishment.

'In 30 years, there are very few people who have got up my nose. Two of them were colleagues in technical research, and both of those were in the same group. One was particularly annoying: he had been spoon-fed all along; educated at Oxbridge, then did post-doc work; very bright, but so lazy; he gave the impression of being much better than he was, and that he didn't need to work hard. And his group leader, with the same background, condoned him. "The Dynamic Duo" they were called!

'I learn best by doing something or seeing something done or by reading. I read at an early age and enjoyed science fiction. I loved guns and Westerns. And I love horror films and science fiction films (as a teenager, there was nothing like a film on a Friday night, followed by fish, chips and peas), all escapism! I don't read tough books if I can help it, but then, of course, if you want something badly enough, you'll do it.

'And I liked writing, the physical pleasure in writing beautifully and in colouring in; I remember at the age of 12, colouring in pictures which compared atoms with the solar system. At the age of 14 I did technical drawing, yet I hated it and failed the exam!

'And I had an allotment, and got interested in gardening. I have an inquisitive mind: I am interested in why things are different and in what they are made of, and that has always been the slant from aged 14 onwards.

'I am trying to become more relaxed, less stressed; to be more like I used to be, less hard, less steely, less abrupt, and more caring, more tolerant, and more understanding in dealing with people.

'I don't mind doing appraisals, it's an important part of the job: salaries depend on it so you must do it fairly. We get a lot of training in that; first, I get together all of the five people whom I appraise, to discuss it and to get a fair ranking; I am comfortable with the system now. Some people always think they are better than they are, and sometimes a lot better. I don't let them get away with it: I tell them in a nice way that they have to be realistic. I am realistic and I assess them against their key objectives.

'My role in developing others consists in: getting the right people onto a project; making sure they have the right environment to do well in; being aware of any training needs they have (e.g. presentational skills); and helping them to attend relevant conferences, being fair on that. People are encouraged to develop to their full potential: that is company policy, by enabling them to go on day release etc, and one or two on full-time MSc and PhD release, and by moving people to the right job.

'And I always have coffee in the labs, both morning and afternoon and so take an interest in others at the lower level; I give suggestions, and they fall about laughing; I chat generally and keep up a rapport. Some of the other Group Heads don't do all that. You have to be careful for that not to be seen as interference. I do that by saying: "Have you thought about..." so it comes as their idea, trying to lead people to the idea and only being assertive if I have a strong view.

'My big ambition is to write a good science fiction novel!'

MJ: learning as understanding self through past, present and future

Bullied at school, which went unrecognized by his parents and by the authorities, MJ subsequently refused obstinately to follow the directions which his evident talents suggested. New directions were at various times in his life suggested by mentors who saw new potential in him. He oscillates between 'challenging' and 'conforming', between being on the inside and being on the outside. His preferred learning style is one of discussing a subject with experts, allied with some reading. He has an insatiable appetite for learning about self, which he addresses by putting himself into new situations, and which expresses itself in terms of interest in understanding what stimulates people. In order to satisfy his need to challenge, to 'do the craziest things', he needs first to have a solid base, home, income, beliefs, values, and to develop firm relationships and satisfy his sense of community.

'I went to Public School at 13 and loathed it. They were the five most miserable years of my life. There was a great deal of physical bullying. I have a profound dislike of the establishment there and what they allowed to happen. My parents didn't seem to understand why I was so miserable. So I tried to upset the establishment, if I could without breaking the rules. I said that I wouldn't take 'O' levels; they said Divinity was important: I said I wouldn't do it. I won the Latin Prize at 15 and then gave up Latin. I won a place at Oxford and then said I wouldn't take it up. I got three 'A's in Science and then chose to read Economics at Bristol. I wouldn't become a prefect. I have a real anger at what is done in the name of the establishment without it being challenged.

'At Bristol University, I had a ball! They were the best days of my life. I was of course physically bigger then, and I ended up i/c boats. I played all sports, I was a member of the Student Union and finally I was given my degree – because I was ill – a good trick!

'Another strong influence in my life was a Vicar in whose digs I lodged. He was very caring, very liberal, 'my other family'. He had a strong influence on my Christian beliefs. I'm not an artist, but he caused an awakening in me of beliefs about human beings, love for music, a general spiritual awakening.

'My first three years in the firm were alright. I had been able to pass exams: I was not bright, but I had a photographic memory. I was a blue-eyed boy; I was told that I was likely to get a partnership after ten years, but I said I wouldn't stay. I chose instead to go and work as an accountant in a cement company: that's a conversation-stopper at drinks parties!

'I was brought up in suburban Surrey, where everyone commuted. My grandfather was a bank manager, and my father was a chartered accountant and the finance director of an insurance company. It was expected that my choice of career would be in the professions or in the City. To be an engineer or to go into manufacturing was "not on the screen". On one audit of a steel works, I loved watching the steel rolling; I saw that as the creation of real wealth, real things and I love the idea of touching real things.

'After the cement company, I returned to the firm, to the consultancy side for three years. It was like an on-the-job MBA and after that I thought I would do a line job. And I qualified as a cost and management accountant.

'The things that stand out for me in this firm over the last 25 years have been: first a two-week induction course. You had to make a presentation and I simply told the training manager that I thought I had made the wrong decision! "Did you do acting?" he asked. Later on, he asked me to run a session of a finance course for non-financial people, which went fine, and I did more and more of that. So I can now talk about anything though I know nothing about it! He built up my courage, as soon as I realized that I was not floundering.

'Then I spent five years in the Middle East and in East Africa. That was character-building; surviving, sleeping on the floor in the Yemen, being fired at, flying high enough in a Piper to get over the SAM missiles. We were on our own: there was no support from Head Office, and no constraints.

'One of my more memorable tasks was to build up activity-based costing. I like exploring new ideas and challenging accepted wisdom, and I enjoyed meeting academics – from Harvard, Cranfield, Templeton, and from Europe – who had their feet on the ground and were free thinkers; they caused my mind to work again. It was nice to have intellectual space: most of the time, our minds are being used only on client-problems.

'I like being a millionaire or a tramp: control the work or opt out, that is my style. I am very conventional, though bits of my life have been unconventional. I oscillate between challenging and conforming, between being on the inside and the outside; I like challenging from the inside, but I oscillate between the poles. And when I have been challenging, I find it fun, but then I keep asking myself: "Am I going too far?", because I dislike conflict. I ban the word "hate" in my house because challenge can cause discomfort, but it can also turn into conflict or aggression. So I may back down, because I have been upset in my life.

'Learning style? Haven't done much lately. I read a lot, though reading alone is less successful for me. I am not so good at learning in the abstract; I'd rather be talking about a topic, for instance on a research project, where I might be with academics.

'Learning about self? I learn most through putting myself into new situations. I am not frightened at learning about myself; indeed I am quite good at it. I am a shocker for wanting to understand myself: I always want more. While others might say that I was self-confident, I don't think of myself in that way. To be confident you have to go on aiming to understand yourself: your new understandings of today have lost their value tomorrow; they have a shelf-life. It is a continuous journey; otherwise it becomes boring.

'Supporting self-learning? I like motivating interest and inquisitiveness in children, encouraging self-exploration, and finding ways in which they can understand for themselves. I think you learn from thinking about your objectives. I shan't have many staff for whom I shall be responsible in Amsterdam, but there is one person, who is a PhD, and who eats the task of writing up methodologies. I shall want to get her brain working. I'll try and stimulate her by throwing out wild ideas; I don't really know how I will do it.

'I reckon I have an intuitive ability for stimulating people, just as I think most of my skills are intuitive, though my presentational skills were taught me, partly through my acting at school, and partly by the man who got me into that training work here. And I have done quite a lot of courses and lecturing with other people who taught/coached each other. That appeals to my best learning style, just as consultancy does.

'You need a solid base, a home, income, beliefs, values, then you can do the craziest of things. Otherwise you have nothing to fall back on. I like developing relationships, like getting known at a restaurant. And a sense of community is important too, to come back to. I treat my family and my group in the firm in the same way in this respect. For me those are the firm bases which give me the opportunity to oscillate between conformity and challenge. 'I have very much enjoyed my job; I have been fulfilled in my life.'

17 sow into well-prepared soil, then provide water, heat and light

'ENABLERS' AND 'DISABLERS'

'It's easier to put out fires than it is to light them.'

Leaders need a variety of different skills and talents for the different tasks, the different projects and the different performances which they tackle. Common to their task is a search for 'keys' with which to 'unlock' the problem and the creativity in the members of their teams.

This book has aimed to provide frameworks for analysing what kind of 'keys' you need, as well as what sort of person you are as leader, and what sorts of process skills you and your team members have. Armed with these frameworks, you can paint your own picture of your issues, and of the kind of actions which you might take as leader. In this chapter, I review some of the most common 'enablers' and 'disablers' of creative groups.

Cultivation and fertilization of the soil are essential for growing flowers, they are the 'enablers'; but seeds will not germinate nor plants grow without water, heat and light, and each at the right moment; drought, cold and darkness are the 'disablers'. Only if the right nutrients are already in the soil, the enablers are in place, can drought, cold and darkness have any effect as disablers.

Creative groups can be seen as fragile eco-systems, which can easily become progressively disabled; but which, if they get the right support at the right time, can also produce amazing results. The factors which 'disable' project groups are not simply the opposite of those which make groups successful: there is an asymmetry between them. Moreover while causes are hard to assign, if a creative group fails in its creativity, the reasons are usually several rather than single. (A team can spot and fix one problem, but several problems present a much more difficult situation.)

This asymmetry is illustrated in Teresa Amabile's work on the social psychology of creativity.[1] Her frameworks for understanding positive and negative factors include social-psychological factors that are negative and positive to creativity.

Social-psychological factors that are negative to creativity include:

- constraints over choice;
- reward, when it is the incentive;
- motivation, where it is extrinsic;
- evaluation, expected external evaluation, or prior evaluation;
- peer pressure to conform;
- surveillance where the task is easily observable;
- stress and pressure;
- fear of failure;
- preoccupation with order and tradition;
- failure to see one's own strengths and those of others;
- over-reliance on ineffective algorithms;
- reluctance to assert one's own ideas.

Social-psychological factors that are positive to creativity include:

- choice over tasks and methods;
- reward as recognition;
- motivation (intrinsic);
- modelling of individuals or from an earlier 'generation';
- stimulation, cognitive and perceptual, from physical environments;
- play and fantasy oriented activities and the freedom to exercise them;
- job security and generous support;
- climate/culture that [expects] the use of creativity heuristics;
- climate conducive to new ideas;
- organizational structure flexible enough to bend to innovation;
- established process for [taking forward] new ideas;
- support from the highest level of management.

SOME COMMON 'DISABLERS'

In many creative disciplines, common 'disablers' include:

- *Group members having different objectives for the group, or the group's objectives unclear or not agreed.* More successful creative groups have the ability to pursue several objectives at the same time; and less successful groups are either less able to do that or have objectives which are mutually incompatible, or objectives about which they either do not come to agree or else actively disagree.

- *Leaders having less interest in the personal development of people who work for them.* Less successful creative groups sometimes have leaders who are either not encouraged to be responsible for and/or are not significantly interested in the personal development of people within their team.
- *Little discussion/interaction between members of the group.* The leader of one group commented that although he was at the hub of the communication network in his project group, he did not have enough time for each of the people who worked on the project. Although he encouraged them to get together more often, the lay-out of the office made that difficult.
- *Leader having too high a workload to have enough time for team members.* Some leaders, for one reason or another, do not have enough time for their groups or for the members of their teams, but leaders of successful creative groups give enough time to their teams so that their particular contributions are effective ones.
- *Leader not a 'people' person.* Leaders of less successful groups are often those who have less empathy and understanding for people, whereas those who lead more successful groups, particularly those in which there is a great deal of explicit tension and risk, tend to be more interested in people.
- *Little sense of the group as a team.* The members of one group saw their project more as a collection of individual performances than as the performance of the group as a whole and one peer spoke of a group as 'a bunch of individuals who sometimes come together'.
- *Leader not skilful in 'process'.* Leaders of more successful creative groups have more interest in and are more skilful at 'process', as the way things are done.
- *Leader having only partial responsibility for group activities.* One leader was not responsible for the selection of team members and another felt that her team was blamed for things over which she and they had no control.
- *Bosses, by acting as generators of ideas, appropriating the essence of creative jobs.* One leader was very conscious that although providing ideas to another group would be helpful, idea-generation is perhaps the most important function of a creative group, and he should keep his own ideas in a pot for a rainy day!

ORGANIZATIONAL 'DISABLERS'

While effective leaders succeed in shielding their groups from the disabling effects of their organizations, it is where they need help or support from the rest of the organization that they are more likely to fail their groups: influencing the organization is more difficult than shielding against it. Common ways in which leaders fail to exert necessary influences on their organizations include:

- *Cycle time for approval of projects too long.* Groups sometimes comment on the difficulties which result from having to wait for long for a decision about a proposal; people become disinterested and it is difficult to pick projects up again later.
- *Compartmentalization of jobs.* Sometimes, for those who do certain jobs, their work, and indeed their entire approach to their job, are constrained both by established attitudes to the job and by the definition of the job.
- *Physical space inappropriate for creative groups.* Physical spaces can be obstructive: whereas they need to facilitate the key characteristics of effective groups, most notably that inconsequential interaction which can give rise to unexpected connections, sometimes they can obstruct interaction, discussion or debate.
- *Inadequate personal/organizational support for the leader.* Leaders can feel unsupported: just as leaders of creative groups are great providers of support, they themselves also need support and unless the organization recognizes and provides for this need, the absence of support can disable the group.
- *Leader and group powerless to get what they need.* One group felt that it was being 'used' by management; another that it was powerless to achieve its objectives without the necessary support from elsewhere in the organization.

Two disastrous project groups[2] illustrate some of the most serious 'disablers'. There were sharp disagreements among the members of two groups: in one case about the objectives of the group, in terms of the brief for the project; in the other case, the disagreements were about the very mission of the unit, as well as about the appropriate structure for achieving it. Both groups also worked simultaneously for two separate paymasters.

They displayed a lack of openness and did not discuss the real issues. In one case, the leader – a psychiatrist – was acutely aware of this, and treated the group as a 'dysfunctional' group, and in the other, there seemed to be a lack of consciousness about the fact that they were not addressing the real issues.

It was therefore not surprising that in both cases, members of the groups had different views about the process needs of the project: they had different views about which team-roles they regarded as important for the success of the project; and they had different views about the contributions of group members in the various team-roles. They saw their groups as not having the right members for the job, and they felt that the contributions of team members in certain key roles were less than adequate for the project, notably that of Innovator (or Ideas Generator) and that of Team builder.

The leaders of both groups felt 'unsupported'; they felt that the organizations of which they were part did not provide them with the degree of support they needed. One of these two leaders had an autocratic style, which was not seen as appropriate by members of the group. The other had a manipulative style of leadership, in relation, not to the elicitation of individual performances, as a coach does, but to the process of the group.

SOME COMMON 'ENABLERS'

If the above are some of the reasons why creative groups become disabled, what can make them work well?

Leadership as a moment-to-moment quality

The title of 'leader' is unhelpful for those whose job it is to lead creative groups. Leadership is commonly seen as a moment-to-moment quality: whoever is able to make a contribution is the leader for the moment. Where someone is *appointed* as the leader, he or she may bring influences which are likely to interfere with the creative processes.

Members take the leadership when they have an answer, an approach, a contribution which no one else in the group has, and which they should therefore make available. Deciding to take on the leadership therefore depends upon how well each person knows the other members of the group, how well someone senses that their contribution might advance the group's thinking, or stimulate, support or provoke someone else to make a significant contribution.

Leadership as pitching in one's penny's worth

The paradox of leadership consists in the fact that organizations give responsibility to individuals (or sometimes to two or more leaders where they operate some form of matrix management structure), yet the very existence of that responsibility is less than helpful in the role that they play in relation to other members of the team. While they seek to influence the group in whatever way they believe will improve its chances of success (because in the end their progress depends on the success of their projects), they are valued within the team for their contribution in enabling individuals to achieve their objectives.

Leaders of creative groups as Visionaries

Leaders of more successful project groups are usually Visionaries, Ideas Generators or Ideas Prompters. Many of them possess a powerful ability to imagine (either aurally, visually or conceptually), and they use this ability both to picture and to recall images. Visionaries have associative minds and memories, and they have an ability to spot gaps and make connections which others might not be able to do.

> **Visionaries as people who are able to see unusual connections**

Conventional wisdom has it that we currently need more Visionaries, more people who can influence the future because they have an appreciation of the potential that exists in their area of knowledge, and of how the forces at work are likely to affect the development of that potential. But it is less clear what Visionaries are, what they do or how they come to be such.

The Department of Trade and Industry set up its Technology Foresight Panels in an attempt to make use of the visionary skills of those who are presumed to understand more about the future in their fields of activity. The aim is to influence the thrust of research and development effort in this country along more relevant and coherent lines. In its turn, the report of the Panels has called for improved market knowledge and vision.

It might therefore be useful to explore what makes someone a successful Visionary, what are the skills and talents of successful Visionaries, how they use them effectively, and how they come to have them in the first place.

Leaders emerging in their own creative fields

It has often been suggested that people are appointed to head creative groups because they are the best in their field rather than because they have the qualities necessary to make them good leaders. However, if they are not among the best in their field, they are unlikely to make successful leaders. Unless they have a wide and deep understanding of their field, they are unlikely to be able to identify key questions in the field, or to generate ideas about their solution.

Leaders as people who have a good overview in their own field

In addition, they also need to have a number of other characteristics and abilities as leaders. Some of these are likely to be innate (and selection techniques need to ensure that these are identified), and many will be able to be developed (with appropriate training/development approaches).

Matching up the leader, the team and the task

Successful leaders and teams are usually very well matched to each other, just as they are to the task which they undertake. Not only do they need to be matched in terms of their technical skills (and different technical perspectives can often usefully complement one another), but they also need to be matched in process terms. The most common way in which process has been examined is in terms of team-roles in groups.

Successful teams are well matched in all sorts of ways

Different kinds of creative projects need team-role players of different kinds. Successful teams need to include at least one person who is skilful at playing each of the team-roles which is necessary for success in that project, and each team-role has a number of different aspects, each of which can be usefully adopted by a different team member.

Another way in which process can be looked at is in terms of support. For a team to be successful, each team member must receive the kind of support that they need and this may differ at different stages of the project.

Effective project group leaders take clear responsibility for the selection of their teams and they take trouble in making their selection. In doing so, they use criteria which relate to process as well as criteria that relate to task and they use a wide variety of process criteria.

Democratic, manipulative and autocratic leaders

Most leaders of successful and creative groups use a democratic style. In certain circumstances, a manipulative style may be more successful (eg to elicit a specific performance) and in certain circumstances, an autocratic style may be more successful (eg to get people to work together, or when the leader has a powerful vision). But an autocratic style does not much help people to learn.

Creativity and risk

In creative endeavours, experimentation is of the essence; failure rates are high and reputations are always on the line. Creative people feel insecure, exposed, even naked.

> **Protecting people from their feelings of insecurity**

Effective leaders provide a cushion for failure and they protect people from their feelings of insecurity. Sometimes they will even allow those involved to remain unaware of how great are the risks they are running.

Organizations which are risk-averse and are oriented to 'delivery' often have cultures which do not acknowledge people's success, nor do they provide a cushion for failure or protection from feelings of insecurity.

Leaders as supporters

One creative director from the advertising world has suggested that the single most important characteristic of effective leaders of creative groups is their ability to provide support. They are particularly skilful at this and at ensuring that members of their team provide support for one another. Moreover, the riskier the project, the greater the need and the opportunity for creativity, and the greater the need for support. And, of course, the creative directors themselves need support from their bosses.

> **Effective leaders as architects of 'support'**

Each individual needs particular kinds of support just as they have particular ways in which they are good at giving support. To be creative and successful, individuals need to receive their preferred styles of support, and for a team to be creative and successful, everyone who plays a key role in the team needs to receive their kind of support.

Project leaders give considerable thought to the question of how to give support: it is important to get the time and place right, and to ensure that it is done in the way that suits each individual best.

Leaders as Shielders

Some organizations have characteristics which act as 'disablers' of creative groups. Sometimes groups are shielded from these pressures at a higher level, at departmental or divisional level, but frequently leaders of creative project groups have to act as shielders of their groups against the disabling influences of power, control, bureaucracy or hierarchy.

> **Leaders as Shielders against 'disablers'**

Effective leaders are also Shielders of their groups in another sense: they provide a membrane around the group so that the group will have the necessary time and space for them to be creative; they shield the group from influences which could disable the sensitive creative process.

Paradox and fluidity in leadership

It is sometimes suggested that fluid role players are not normally successful team players, yet many of the leaders of more successful and creative groups are very fluid in their contributions in a variety of ways.

> **Leaders as 'fixers' who just lend a hand when they can**

Leaders of creative projects live with ambiguity (with persistent problems); they play a variety of team-roles; they represent their project groups to the organization, as well as contributing to the work of their groups and alongside all of that they usually continue to carry out their own special projects and activities.

They have to set challenges, yet help people to succeed; to provide rigorous feedback yet give support against feelings of insecurity; to think in process terms despite the fact that the language of discourse is very much in task terms.

The effective leader needs to be able to pursue contrasting objectives simultaneously, and from one moment to another to argue from the same facts to different ends, a skill described by the head of one research laboratory as being able 'to be a chameleon but with integrity'.

It is therefore perhaps unsurprising that one view of the effective leader of a creative group is that he or she simply fits in and provides whatever is necessary wherever it is necessary, a 'fixer', whose main role is to be a provider of whatever is needed, or as one senior manager described the job, 'just giving a hand where you can!'

Learning by experience, by doing and by reflecting on it

Most effective leaders learn mainly from other managers or leaders whom they have worked with; their learning style is one of 'learning-by-doing' combined with 'private reflection', very like Schön's depiction of the experiential learner as a Reflective Practitioner.[3]

Avid but discreet learners

ARE LEADERS OF CREATIVE GROUPS BORN OR MADE?

Leaders of creative groups have rarely had any significant training for their job, yet it requires a whole new set of skills which have to be learnt very quickly. Successful leaders of such groups are both born and made; they need to have a number of characteristics which are likely to be innate, and many which, as inveterate learners, they then develop.

Many skills are natural, but many that can be developed

Kenneth Rea's report for the Calouste-Gulbenkian Foundation on Directors in the Performing Arts[4] suggested that while there were great difficulties about helping such people to practise (does anyone want to be practised upon?), nonetheless much could be done to develop their skills, including especially the necessary craft skills. People who work in creative fields are usually highly self-motivated, and see the development of their talents as itself an experimental and creative task.

CRITICAL EXPERIENCES TURNED INTO DRIVING FORCES

While leaders often see schools and universities as having shaped their thoughts and ideas (often they have been captains of sports or involved in the performing arts), the way some have been treated early in their lives has had a traumatic impact, and has left them with a passionate determination to help and support others.

ADVENTURE AND PERSONAL DEVELOPMENT

The development of talent and of potential is something which is very closely associated with successful creative output (learning and creativity are very closely associated).

Successful and creative project groups sometimes see their group as on a life journey together: at the death of one project, they will move on to the birth of another, which will be the next step in their own life journey.

> **Leaders, like all creative people, as on a life journey**

Does 'a group of people all developing together' provide a good cooking pot for creativity? And do escapades, both physical and mental, provide those opportunities for 'doing it differently' that are associated with experimentation and creative output?

ARTICULATING THOUGHTS AND FEELINGS

Especially in those groups or organizations which are traditionally or culturally very task-oriented, articulating their thoughts and feelings is something to which members of project groups are often unaccustomed, but without reviewing process, without exploring their successes and failures, they are unlikely to develop their skills as a creative group.

> **Learning by talking about it**

On one occasion, one team member commented that 'until I produced that stream of words, I was not aware of why I could not get on with that man', and on another, an actress simply said, 'I never knew I thought all those thoughts!' There are, of course, times when one needs to be 'in the moment', just as there are times that are right for reviewing and team members need to be able to slip into the right mode at the right time.

Leaders of creative groups from different creative disciplines are often surprised at how similar their problems are, and they find it valuable to compare and contrast them.

POSTSCRIPT

If creativity is usually the outcome of passionate people working with intense enthusiasm and dedication on things that are of intrinsic interest to them, then leadership is a deft and discreet activity of securing provision of whatever is missing in order that sparks fly, that reactions take place and the dough rises: it may be different things in different situations and at different moments.

I will be pleased if this book has at least offered some useful ways of looking at what such leadership may be in different situations ('frameworks'), so as to enable aspects of leading creative groups to be articulated, discussed and developed, in other words, if it proves to be useful!

NOTES

1. Amabile, TM (1983) *The Social Psychology of Creativity*, Springer-Verlag, New York.
2. Whatmore, J (1996) *Managing Creative Groups: What makes people good at it*, Roffey Park Management Institute, Sussex.
3. Schön, DA (1995) *The Reflective Practitioner: How professionals think in action*, Arena, new edition, London.
4. Rea, K (1989) *A Better Direction: A national enquiry into the training of Directors for theatre, film and television*, Calouste-Gulbenkian Foundation, London.

Index